THE TEETH AND CLAWS
OF THE BUDDHA

THE TEETH AND CLAWS OF THE BUDDHA

Monastic Warriors
and *Sōhei*
in Japanese History

MIKAEL S. ADOLPHSON

University of Hawai'i Press
Honolulu

© 2007 University of Hawai'i Press
All rights reserved
Printed in the United States of America
12 11 10 09 08 07   6 5 4 3 2 1

Library of Congress Cataloging-in-Publication Data
Adolphson, Mikael S.
The teeth and claws of the Buddha :
monastic warriors and sohei in Japanese history /
Mikael S. Adolphson.
p. cm.
Includes bibliographical references and index.
ISBN-13: 978-0-8248-3064-9 (hardcover : alk. paper)
ISBN-13: 978-0-8248-3123-3 (pbk. : alk. paper)
1. Buddhist monks as soldiers—Japan—History.
2. Buddhism—Japan—History—To 1185.
3. Buddhism—Japan—History—1185–1600.
4. Japan—History, Military—Religious aspects.
I. Title. II. Title: Monastic warriors and sohei in Japanese history.
BQ680.M65A36 2007
306.2′70952—dc22
2006025432

University of Hawai'i Press books are printed on
acid-free paper and meet the guidelines for permanence
and durability of the Council on Library Resources.

Designed by Kaelin Chappell Broaddus

For Silvia,
Mauricio, and Alexander

CONTENTS

MAPS AND FIGURES

ACKNOWLEDGMENTS

This study is an extension of and complement to my first book, *The Gates of Power*, which dealt primarily with the political, judicial, and ideological powers of religious institutions. I therefore remain indebted to the same colleagues and friends who encouraged me during my years at Stanford as a graduate student and the early years of my life as a teacher. I would be remiss, however, if I did not again express my gratitude to my mentor, Jeffrey P. Mass, whose unwavering support made all the difference in a young scholar's life. His premature passing in 2001 has left a void of scholarship, academic passion, and sagely advice that many still miss.

For this manuscript, I have been fortunate to receive continued guidance and support from many colleagues. Above all, I benefited from the expertise and advice of Karl Friday to interpret and contextualize many terms on weaponry and warfare. Thomas Conlan's works and knowledge were also instrumental in my endeavors to understand how the monastic forces fought. In short, without their works, the Heian and Kamakura worlds of violence and battles would have been considerably more difficult to grasp. I should also like to thank the participants for their insightful questions and comments at talks I was privileged to give at the University of Pennsylvania, Stanford University, Aoyama Gakuin, International Christian University in Tokyo, University of Oregon, at the annual meetings of the Association of Asian Studies in 1998 and 2003, and at the meeting of the European Association of Japanese Studies in 2005. For their support and interest during those occasions, I am especially indebted to G. Cameron Hurst III, Asai Kazuhiro, Ken Robinson, Andrew Goble, Mark Unno, Brian Ruppert, Roy Ron, and Paul Varley. I should furthermore like to express my profound gratitude to Hurst and William Wayne Farris for their careful reading of and suggestions to an earlier version of the manuscript.

At Harvard I have benefited from the support of colleagues in several departments, but would like to express my thanks in particular to the members of the Department of East Asian Languages and Civilizations. Harold Bolitho and Andrew Gordon have been particularly supportive during the last several years of this project, and Sun Joo Kim kindly assisted me with the Korean material. I am also indebted to Melissa McCormick and Yukio Lippit for their advice and suggestions concerning many of the works of art that appear in this book. I have additionally been helped by a generation of young scholars with various sections and would like to extend my thanks to Marjan Boogert, Jeffrey Moser, and Jungwon Kim. Ivan Grail deserves special mention for his careful reading and helpful comments. I should also like to acknowledge the staff at the Harvard-Yenching Library, as well as Gustavo Espada and Susan Kashiwa at my department, for their kind assistance whenever I needed help with various aspects associated with research. With the encouragement of such colleagues and friends, it has been a joy to complete this project, and I owe each and every one my gratitude.

I have many Japanese scholars to thank for their interest and advice but will limit my acknowledgments to those I have pestered the most. Kondō Shigekazu has unselfishly spent hours, days, and even weeks discussing the reading and translation of important sources, as well as the general character of monastic forces in premodern Japan. I am grateful not only for the opportunities I have had to benefit from his expertise but also for the passion we share for the field and for engaging scholars both in and outside of Japan in the writing of Japanese history. Hotate Michihisa and Tajima Tadashi at the Historiographical Institute have likewise been supportive, and I continue to enjoy their friendship. Other colleagues from whom I have benefited include Motoki Yasuo, Kinugawa Satoshi, Nedachi Kensuke, and Mikawa Kei. Finally, I would like to offer my grateful thanks to the institutes and temples from which I have been privileged to obtain photos and permission to reprint them in this volume. I am especially indebted to Matsuōji Kazuhiro at Kitano Tenmangū, Mekata Zenji at Ishiyamadera, Aida Satoko of TNM Archives, and Mr. Ichiya Junzō, the executive director of the Sōjutsu School of the Hōzōinryū.

Few scholars can complete their research projects without some financial support, and I am no exception. I am deeply indebted to the Japan Foundation for offering me the opportunity to work full time on the monastic forces during a wonderful year in Tokyo. I have now accrued a substantial debt of gratitude to the foundation for its support on two occasions, but I hope that it will continue to be engaged in various academic projects that will promote a deeper understanding of Japan's premodern past and the construction of it. The Edwin O. Reischauer Institute of Japanese Studies at Harvard has allowed me, through its generous support, to take additional trips to Japan, and to secure photos and permissions. It is in large thanks to its economic assistance and the personal support of its staff, former director Andrew Gordon and current director Susan Pharr, that I have been able to complete this project in a timely fashion.

TERMINOLOGY AND TRANSLATION

Owing to the character of previous scholarship on "monk-warriors" (*sōhei*), nomenclature is one important aspect of this work. I have attempted to be consistent in my translations of the many terms associated with the monastic complexes, but it is ultimately impossible to find exact equivalents in English for the many variations that are used in historical sources. One reason is that such terms referred to different types of groups or people depending on the era. Thus, *hosshi* (master of the law) might at one point refer to an ordained monk of some status, but in later sources the same term denotes warriors who had taken Buddhist vows but in all other aspects lived as they had done before and might therefore best be described as lay monks. Another reason, as I argue in chapter 3, is the sheer variety of terms that might denote one and the same group; these complications suggest that terms were often used without much precision. In fact, nobles discussing the activities of menial workers, shrine servants, or lower-ranking clerics were rarely well informed about who comprised these groups, and therefore used a range of terms meaningful for the discussants but not particularly revealing. Thus, in translating these terms, I have looked for words that can reflect the diverse nature of these groups' social and occupational status.

Japanese names are given with the surname first, followed by the given name. In the case of large noble families, I have inserted the genitive *no* after the surname, as was common in the pre-1600 era. For dates in citations, I have followed the commonly accepted practice in academe of listing the year according to the Gregorian calendar with the lunar month and day. The Japanese era names are consistently listed in the notes for those interested in finding the source citations. Chinese characters are included in the bibliography for all historical sources used and for all authors of secondary works. For those interested in further studying figures and events mentioned in this study, the index contains Chinese characters for all names and terms listed. Readers wishing to explore *sōhei* images, sources, and translations further are encouraged to visit www.teethandclaws.net, where comments and questions can be posted as well.

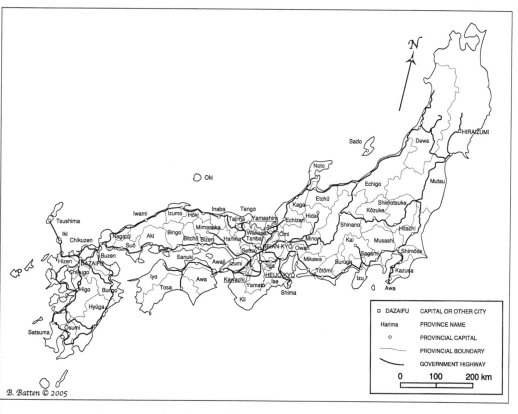

MAP 1. Provinces and Highways of Premodern Japan.
Printed with permission from Bruce Batten.

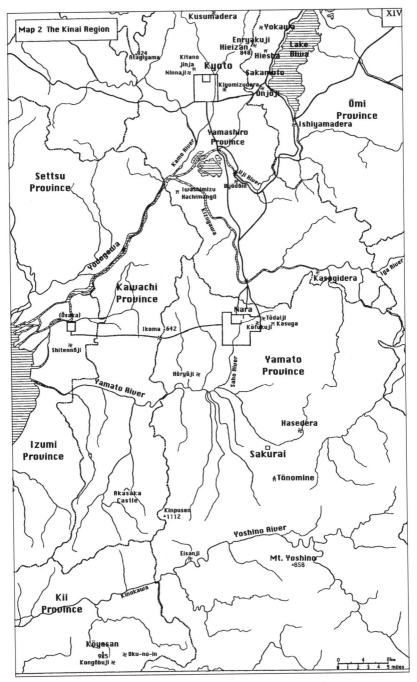

MAP 2. Central Japan. Adapted from volume 4 of *Niho no rekishi: Ritsuryō kokka* (Tokyo: Shōgakkan, 1974).

ONE

Discourses on Religious Violence and Armed Clerics

To most modern scholars and observers, violence involving religious centers and ideologies is deeply disturbing. Such sentiments only increased following the events of 9/11, when religious beliefs became inexorably associated with terror acts. In fact, one scholar concluded, in conjunction with a conference on religion and violence in 2004, that "the modern period [is] particularly prone to religious violence in part because religion is a powerful resource to mobilize individuals and groups to do violence (whether physical or ideological violence) against modern states and political ideologies."[1] In contrast to the common assumption that religions played a more prominent role in premodern societies, this is indeed a refreshing perspective. Nevertheless, one cannot help but wonder if a distinction between secular and religious violence can be sustained in a historical analysis. After all, many wars have been fought and conquests made in the name of religious ideals, whether in the modern or premodern eras. More importantly, one must ask why conflicts justified by religious rhetoric are perceived differently from those motivated by other beliefs. For instance, to what extent are the putative secular ideals of Western societies (i.e., democracy and freedom) substantially different from religious ones in times of war? Is it useful to talk about "religious wars" as a separate category, or "religious warriors" as a particular type of soldier? Are there, in other words, wars that are not ideologically justified, whether we perceive the rhetoric as religious or not?

The promise of rewards in the afterlife may obviously have inspired many commanders and soldiers, but, by the same token, some of the most aggressive and ambitious conquerors in history appear to have had little use for religious rhetoric. What sets religious discourses apart from secular ones, it appears, is the discrepancy between religious precepts promoting peace and prohibiting the use of arms and the violent activities of many monastics, which has induced those who subscribe to the modern, and predominantly Western, notion of separate political and religious spheres to be critical of such forces. However, such criticism seems especially misplaced when applied to premodern societies, where the socio-political and ideological frameworks are different from those of our own, and where religions and religious institutions frequently occupied a more prominent place in state ceremonies and everyday life. For example, Europe's Thirty-Year War (1618–1648), the military orders and crusaders of the Middle Ages, and the Moors of Spain invoke images of warriors eager to fight because of their religious beliefs. Of course, as has often been claimed, religions may simply have served as a smokescreen for personal ambitions and secular desires, or to use Karl Marx's words, as "an opium of the people."[2] More significantly, however, the treatment of religious warriors may differ widely depending on the observer's perspective, ranging from the idolization of crusading knights to the vilification of fighters from "outsider religions." It seems, then, that blanket statements regarding religious rhetoric in violence and war deserve further scrutiny in order for us to better understand how religions affect the way wars and battles were fought in the past, our present day diplomacy and politics, and our reconstructions of the past. We need, in other words, to contextualize religious violence and consider it, not only from an ideological perspective, but also from a social and political vantage point. It is my hope that this study may contribute to such a correction by focusing on armed religious forces and on two images that have come to represent religious warriors in premodern Japan: the *sōhei*, or "monk-warrior," a decidedly negative figure, and the mythical monk-warrior Benkei (?–1185), who has become the lone hero of this category because of his loyalty to the legendary and tragic warrior Minamoto no Yoshitsune (1159–1189).

The *sōhei* have come to represent not only the secular power of temples in the premodern era but also the decline of the government from the late Heian age (794–1185). Indeed, a handful temples, most notably Enryakuji on Mt. Hiei just northeast of Kyoto, Onjōji in Ōtsu on the shore of Lake Biwa, Kōfukuji and Tōdaiji in Nara, Kōyasan and Negoroji in Kii Province south of the capital (see Map 2), remained powerful presences from the twelfth to the sixteenth centuries, when they were eventually subdued by the warlords of the Sengoku age (1467–1573). Yet whereas our understanding of the warrior class has progressed in the last two decades, little effort has been made to examine just who the fighting servants of Buddha actually were, and why they remain such a visible part of Japanese culture even today. One of my own experiences may illustrate their continued currency.

When I first visited Kyoto in the summer of 1986, I was disappointed to find several of the best-known temples closed to visitors. Bewildered, I returned to my school outside Osaka, where I studied until I transferred to Kyoto University later that fall. It was only several years later that I found out what lay behind the unexpected temple closings. In 1985 the mayor of Kyoto wanted to raise revenues by assessing a tourist tax of ¥50 per adult and ¥30 per child on forty of Kyoto's most popular cultural attractions. Of these, thirty-six were temples, whose monks and abbots responded that as tax-exempt institutions, their temples should not be subject to such impositions. Mayor Nishiyama was, however, determined to carry out his plan, and when negotiations broke down, several of the best-known temples, including Kiyomizudera and Ginkakuji, closed their gates in a time-proven method of protest.[3] The mayor eventually won out, and tourists wishing to enjoy the cultural treasures of Kyoto thereafter encountered admission fees up to twice as high as those the previous year.[4]

Although I vividly remember this first experience in Kyoto, I did not reflect on it much until years later when I read the press coverage of the protest. One might expect most journalists to be critical of new taxes on local tourist attractions, but it was in fact the protesting monks who were maligned for their actions. The temples' resistance recalled images of rampaging monks of the past—one headline read, "Monk-Warriors [sōhei] Riot against the Old Capital's New Tax," while another stated "The Riots of Monk-Warriors Have Not Yet Ended." One of the articles further claimed that "monk-warriors no longer exist but when one looks at the dispute over the 'old capital tax,' one realizes that Kyoto is a historical city still tied to its medieval heritage."[5] The photos accompanying these articles are even more telling, for they show, despite the strident headlines and texts referring to sōhei, rather peaceful-looking monks announcing their objections to the new tax.

These journalists may not enjoy the status of Japanese scholars, but little appears to separate the views of these two groups on premodern monastic warriors and religious violence. Where the military exploits and martial prowess of secular warriors are seen as valuable topics worthy of scholarly inquiry, monastic forces have been all but ignored, and where they have been treated, they have frequently been looked down upon.[6] Consider, for example, that militarily powerful monasteries such as Enryakuji and Kōyasan both outlasted the combined Kamakura (1185–1333) and Muromachi (1336–

1573) shogunates, yet not a single study has looked at either of these complexes in their military capacity.

In Western academe, the neglect of monastic forces in important wars and transitions is nothing short of stunning. Not one scholar dealing with the Genpei War of 1180–1185 or the Hōgen Incident (1155–1156) leading up to it has mentioned the important role the forces of temples and shrines played. The authoritative *Cambridge History of Japan: Volume 3, Medieval Japan,* for example, does not contain a single reference to the armed forces of the temples.[7] This is remarkable considering that the plotters in the failed coup of 1156 were surprised and beaten by forces loyal to Emperor Go-Shirakawa (1127–1192, ruled 1155–1158) because they were waiting for reinforcements under the leadership of the monk-commander Shinjitsu (1086–?) of Kōfukuji. Moreover, when the forces of Kiso Yoshinaka (1154–1184) approached Kyoto to unseat the Taira in 1183, Yoshinaka's first order of business before entering the capital was to secure the support of the monastic complex of Enryakuji.[8]

In volume 2 of *The Cambridge History,* which treats Heian Japan, Stanley Weinstein does in fact address the issue of religious factionalism in the tenth century, noting briefly violent clashes between temples or sections within the major monastic complexes. He is, however, laudably cautious about referring to the combating parties as monk-warriors and even more perceptively notes the difference between monastic protests and armed confrontations involving clerics.[9] Nevertheless, the editors of *The Cambridge History* have in their index inexplicably but diligently applied the term *sōhei* to all references to armed confrontations or temple protests throughout the volume, even when their authors deliberately avoid making such references. Moreover, while numerous studies have been devoted to war chronicles such as the *Heike monogatari (The Tale of the Heike),* analyses of monastic warriors in such works are all but nonexistent. For example, "The Battle of the Bridge" chapter of the *Heike monogatari* features a worker-monk, who has barely been noted:[10]

> "You must have heard of me long ago. See me now with your own eyes! Everyone at Miidera [Onjōji] knows me! I am the worker-monk Jōmyō Meishū [Jōmyō Myōshu][11] from Tsutsui, a warrior worth a thousand men. If any here consider themselves my equals, let them come forward. I'll meet them!" He let fly a fast and furious barrage from his twenty-four-arrow quiver, which killed twelve men instantly and wounded eleven others. Then, with one arrow left, he sent the bow clattering away, untied and discarded

the quiver, cast off his fur boots, and ran nimbly along a bridge beam in his bare feet. Others had feared to attempt the crossing: Jōmyō acted as though it were Ichijō or Nijō Avenue. He mowed down five enemies with his spear and was engaging a sixth when the blade snapped in the middle. He abandoned the weapon and fought with his sword. Hard-pressed by the enemy host, he slashed in every direction, using the zigzag, interlacing, crosswise, dragon-fly reverse, and waterwheel maneuvers. After cutting down eight men on the spot, he struck the helmet top of a ninth so hard that the blade snapped on the hilt rivet, slipped loose, and splashed into the river. Then he fought on desperately with a dirk as his sole resource.[12]

The general neglect of such accounts is in part grounded in the modern notion that religion and politics are and should be distinctively separate entities and that any influence on political and military matters of the state by religious institutions therefore is inappropriate and unworthy of academic scrutiny.[13] But there is more to this problem than mere modern political ideology. There is in fact a long history of distortion and prejudice against monastic warriors that dates to the fourteenth century, gaining particular momentum from the eighteenth century and on. Intimately related to the rise and rule of the warrior class, this bias has conditioned and forged the image that later scholars have come to rely on. Specifically, the few serious studies that have focused on the *sōhei* as military figures have failed to recognize the difference between these constructs and the historical figures on which they were based. To further complicate matters, one monk-warrior, the aforementioned Benkei, has, in contrast to all other images and interpretations, been heralded as one of the greatest and most unselfish heroes in Japanese culture. According to later accounts, Benkei was a giant of a monk, who after having ravaged the Kyoto area as a rogue duelist, became the loyal servant of Minamoto no Yoshitsune (1159–1189), whose exploits in the Genpei War and tragic fate thereafter have captured the imagination of generations of scholars and Japanese readers. In fact, an NHK *Taiga dorama* series launched in 2005 focuses on Yoshitsune, reflecting the tremendous popularity of both this tragic hero and his loyal monk companion.

It seems obvious, then, that a study on Japan's monastic warriors is warranted, not only for their importance in Japanese history, but also because of a need to situate monastic warfare and violence, as well as images thereof, in their historical context. This study will address two sets of issues requiring slightly different approaches to present a more balanced view of monastic warriors in Japan's history. First, my historical inquiry will explore the figures that can best be described as monastic warriors in the late Heian and Kamakura eras, periods with which the *sōhei* image is most commonly connected. Who were those men, fighting in the name of temples and the Buddha? What was their relationship to members of the warrior class? And what were their distinguishing features? Second, there is the historiographical question of how and why monastic warriors became stereotyped as *sōhei*. How did monk robes and cowls, the long glaive (sometimes called a halberd) known as *naginata*,[14] and clogs become the widely recognized attributes of the *sōhei* generally and the figure of Benkei as well? Can we find specific characters or groups within the monasteries that correspond to these images? When and why did such images come to represent monastic warriors?

Given that this study ranges over several historical eras and deals with two different themes—one constructive, the other deconstructive—I have attempted to organize it so the chapters can be read more or less independently, with the exception of chapters 3 and 4, which are best read together and in order. Accordingly, for those interested in the modern historiographical context of this study and the interpretations against which I am arguing, the survey below should prove helpful. Other readers may want to proceed to chapter 2, which provides a chronographic analysis of religious violence in Japan from its introduction in the sixth century to the fourteenth century, tracing it also to China. It argues that armed confrontations and incidents were part of the societies into which the Buddhist schools were introduced and thus were never disassociated from them; the emergence of monastic warriors in organized bands must be seen in conjunction with the general militarization of society rather than the decline of Buddhism or certain monasteries. The next chapter deals with monks who were actually involved in armed battles and skirmishes in the Heian and Kamakura eras. These clerics came from a range of places and classes in society, and most were involved in mid-level administration and menial duties within the monastic complexes, but none seem to match the *sōhei* stereotype. They were drawn into the factional struggles of the capital by their noble monk-commanders, who are the focus of chapter 4. In contrast to the warriors and armed menial workers who rarely left records of their own and therefore remain anonymous, a range of documents, diary entries, and temple records make it possible to reconstruct substantial parts of the monk-commanders' lives. The episodes recounted in this chapter flesh out the issues that prompted armed conflicts both between monasteries and between factional groups within them. Finally, chapter 5 focuses on the construction of the *sōhei* and Benkei images, which developed along different trajectories from the fourteenth century. The anonymous monk-warrior representation can be traced to late Kamakura picture scrolls, where it appears to be only one among many images of monastic forces. The image of Benkei, in contrast, has its origins in literary and theatrical works but came to borrow several characteristics from the visual arts as stylized images became more common. It is when the warrior class came to dominate politics and culture from the Muromachi age (1336–1572) that we detect an increasing preference for the monk-warrior image; this seems to reflect a desire to separate the "pure warrior" (whom we refer to as "samurai" in the West) from men fighting for religious institutions. By the Tokugawa age (1600–1868) the monk-warrior image had become firmly entrenched in Japanese culture, and when the term *sōhei* was first used for this figure in the early eighteenth century, it set a precedent that would be followed by scholars into the modern age.[15]

A Modern Historiography of Monastic Forces in Pre-Tokugawa Japan

Although monastic warriors play only the smallest role in studies of the warrior class, they have not gone unnoticed. Following the Meiji Restoration of 1868, one of the first to note the presence of *sōhei* in Japanese history was Shigeno Yasutsugu (1827–1910), who stated that monk-warriors first emerged in Japan under the leadership of Tendai head abbot Ryōgen (912–985), but he went no further in explaining exactly how or why.[16] Several textbooks in the Meiji era (1868–1912) similarly blamed Ryōgen for putting Heian Buddhism on the wrong path, tending toward what intellectuals at that time regarded as exercising undue influence on politics. Some of these works even included dramatic illustrations of fearsome monk-warriors to underscore these clerics' unique character.[17] In his *Nihon bukkyō shiyō* (A History of Japanese Buddhism, 1901), Sakaino Tetsu (also known as Sakaino Kōyō, 1871–1933) displayed his dislike for monastic forces in a chapter entitled "The Infestation of the Monk-Warriors" (Sōhei no bakko), where he claimed that this category of cleric had arisen from the influx of warrior-retainers accompanying Heian-era nobles into the monasteries; yet in the end he singled out temples such as Kōfukuji and Enryakuji for criticism for their failure to control their clergies.[18] A few years later, the military section of the 1906 encyclopedia *Koji ruien* contained almost thirty pages on the *sōhei*. Without offering any criteria, it simply labeled *sōhei* as "clerical warriors" *(hosshi musha)*, asserting and reinforcing the notion of their distinct character.[19]

By the 1920s a debate emerged concerning the origins of the *sōhei*, beginning with Takasu Baikei (1880–1948), who criticized the Buddhist establishment for allowing this group to emerge within its communities. Like so many before him, he put much of the blame on Ryōgen, under whose tenure struggles had erupted within the Tendai School, between the Enryakuji and Onjōji (Miidera) factions. In Takasu's view, it was the monks' desire for worldly possessions, caused by an increasing number of nobles' sons and warrior families taking Buddhist vows, that led to militarization.[20] Shortly thereafter Takeoka Katsuya (1893–1958) published an article in which he claimed the *sōhei* could be traced back as early as in the Nara age (710–784). He nevertheless concluded that it was not until the *insei* period (1086–1185), when the monk-warrior became one of the pillars of medieval society, that the *sōhei* reached its mature form.[21] Ōya Tokujō's (1882–1950) chapter "Sōhei ron" (An Essay on Monk-Warriors) in his *Nihon bukkyō shi no kenkyū* (A Study of the History of Japanese Buddhism) published in 1928–1929, offered yet another perspective on the *sōhei*. Ōya distinguished between individual monks who armed themselves and the groups of armed monks that he claimed constituted the *sōhei*. He concluded that it was commoners taking Buddhist vows without state sanction to evade paying taxes that caused not only the breakdown of the Buddhist hierarchies, but also brought arms into the monasteries. Ōya dated the emergence of the *sōhei* to the first half of the Heian age, pointing to the lack of governmental response to an increasingly unstable situation in the provinces, which in turn precipitated the sudden increase of armed-servants-turned-monks. Rather than looking to individual armed monks, Ōya concluded that the marker of the *sōhei* phenomenon was the emergence of organized forces within monastic complexes in the mid-to-late Heian age, a development that could be more precisely dated to the tenth century.[22] Both Takeoka and Ōya located the impetus for militarization within the monastic complexes themselves, and Ōya even labeled Heian society as one based on "mistaken beliefs," which seems more to reflect his modern expectations of religion's role in society than its actual historical role.[23] The emergence of *sōhei* was, according to this view, an upshot of the "secularization" of Buddhism.

These early treatments notwithstanding, it was Tsuji Zennosuke (1877–1955) who became the guiding light for generations of scholars in Japan with his *Nihon bukkyō shi no kenkyū*, first published in 1931.[24] Tsuji's study presented an assumption that the emergence of the *sōhei* signaled a turning point for Buddhism in Japan, and, like many of his successors, Tsuji was committed to finding an explanation for that emergence within the monasteries themselves. He found what he called the decline of the monastic bureaucracy already evident in the eighth century, when factional struggles of the imperial court spilled over into the religious world. He blamed in particular the failures of the ordination system, since ordinary people and nobles could claim status as monks for a variety of reasons, whether to escape taxes, punishments, or simply to make a career.[25]

In earlier scholarship, then, the emergence of the *sōhei* was synonymous with a perceived decline of Buddhism, and the dating of its origin became for many scholars an important means to discover how, why, and above all, just when religious institutions went wrong. Indeed, the *sōhei* debate in published monographs and articles centered almost entirely on these issues and can accordingly be classified by the period scholars have pointed to for the emergence of this group—the Nara period, the tenth century, the late Heian age (the *insei* era, 1086–1185), or the Kamakura period. In the first category, we find only a small cohort of scholars, including Tsuji Zennosuke, who saw the origins of the *sōhei* in the pre-Heian period, when a few isolated violent incidents occurred. Specifically, he pointed to the breakdown of the ordination system and to sporadic evidence of religious violence that can be found in later sources. Unfortunately, no sources indicate any direct relation between the increase of privately "ordained" monks and the few incidents of violence that we find in the seventh and eighth centuries. Tsuji noted a reference to monks and novices in the war against Emi no Oshikatsu (Fujiwara no Nakamaro, 706–764) in the 760s (see chapter 2) in Ōmi Province, close to the capital area.[26] He concluded that it was these figures who foreshadowed the emergence of organized armed monastics and found in them the origins of the *sōhei*.[27]

Another important member of this group was Hioki Shōichi (1904–1960), one of the best-known *sōhei* scholars and the first one to devote an entire work to monastic warriors in his main opus, *Nihon sōhei kenkyū* (A Study of Japan's Monk-Warriors), published in 1934. Like Tsuji, he focused on the use of weapons among monks and asserted that monk-warriors represented a response to the decline of the bureaucratic state and its administrative and penal codes *(ritsuryō);* he also added that the need for private protection grew with the increasing number of estates coming under direct control of temples in the Heian era, which allowed the *sōhei* to assume a more important place in Japanese society.[28] Hioki saw continuity in developments from the Nara to the Heian age, but he also pointed to armed confrontations between Enryakuji and Onjōji—the first major fight taking place in 1081—as the earliest appearance of warriors bands within the temples. These warriors were not primarily monks but rather local managers of temple estates who, of their own accord, put on monk's robes to fight for their master-temple.[29]

In contrast to Tsuji and Hioki, scholars of the second category followed Ōya by arguing that the tenth century was the crucial juncture for the *sōhei*'s emergence. Ignoring the early and isolated incidents caused by violent individuals, these scholars defined the *sōhei*, as Katsuno Ryūshin (1899–1969) put it in his 1955 work *Sōhei*, as "groups of monks with arms." Katsuno pointed to two sources in particular—an edict of twenty-six articles authored by Ryōgen in 970 and the 914 memorandum submitted to the court by Miyoshi Kiyoyuki (both are treated in chapter 2).[30] Contesting the position of previous scholars, moreover, Katsuno asserted that armed monastics were not in fact monks but rather servants of the temple who regularly performed various menial tasks while holding novice status within their monastic communities.[31] Other scholars, such as Murayama Shūichi (b. 1914) and Hirabayashi Moritoku (b. 1933), have agreed with Ōya and Katsuno, pointing to other events in the tenth century that indicate the emergence of monk-warriors. The former saw Ryōgen's takeover of Gionsha and the forcible separation of Onjōji from Enryakuji as evidence that the abbot must have resorted to using armed monks, despite his prohibitions against them.[32] Hirabayashi cites a brawl between Kōfukuji and Tōdaiji in 968, when armed men from both complexes faced off over a small piece of land in Nara, in support of his interpretation.[33]

Hiraoka Jōkai (b. 1923), who has written extensively on Buddhist institutions, belongs to a third cohort that views the late Heian age as the starting point of the *sōhei*. Like Hioki, he views the lower-level menial workers as the class that spurred the arming of the clergy, but he has also noted that the process continued into the Kamakura age, when the various categories of residents within the monasteries—scholar-monks, worker-monks, cart carriers, hamlet residents, and shrine servants—came together to form armed bands.[34] Unlike Katsuno, Hiraoka sees the organization of armed monastic forces coming to fruition in the late Heian age under the leadership of noble monks who dominated ranking monk offices from the late eleventh century. The onus was thus placed on aristocrats rather than commoners, since the noble abbots' leadership over the various workers, shrine servants, and residents of temple estates made it possible for them to gather and direct armed forces from within their communities.[35]

Ōshima Yukio (b. 1937) has concurred with this notion, concluding that the tenth century set in motion developments that became the foundation for the emergence of monastic forces. Specifically, the spread of private estates gave rise to more competition in which the use of military force became essential, as, in his view, members of the lower echelons of the clergy primarily involved in menial work started using tools and arms already available to them. The tenth century marked a change from the peaceful resolution of disputes between temples to increased reliance on violence. By the late twelfth century, the occasional skirmishes had been replaced by large-scale confrontations, which Ōshima believes signaled the transition into an age of *sōhei* violence.[36] The main difference between the Nara and the two Heian interpretations here lies in how they gauge the acts of individuals versus those of the group. In Tsuji's view, the emergence of violence involving individual monks is sufficient to signal the beginning of the *sōhei* phenomenon; but to Hiraoka, Ōya, Katsuno, and Ōshima it is the collective use of force and endorsement of that use by the temple communities that marks the *sōhei*'s emergence.

A fourth interpretation was developed by Hirata Toshiharu (1911–1996), who located the first *sōhei* in the late Kamakura age. His view hinges on yet another interpretation of just what constituted the *sōhei*, which he defined as ordained monks who arm themselves as a group.[37] Hirata focused on the activities of the group as a defining characteristic, and, writing in the early 1960s, he compared the clergy movements *(daishu undō)* to political movements *(seiji undō)* and the democratic movements *(minshū shugi undō)* of his own period.[38] Instead of seeing instances of religious violence in the late Heian as defining a new stage of development within the monastic centers, he saw them as reflections of the general political developments in which secular warriors, not monks, became involved in temple disputes. Those carrying arms within the temples—monastic workers and warriors serving as administrators on the private estates *(shōen)*—should, according to Hirata, be characterized as merely precursors to the *sōhei*, which he defined more strictly as *monks* who also trained as warriors.[39] For Hirata, two developments in the late Kamakura age set it apart from religious violence in the Heian. First, he asserted that the use of weapons had become widespread among the clergy beginning in the late thirteenth and fourteenth centuries. Second, force of arms had become more common for resolving conflicts within all major monasteries and among monks. In short, the de facto transformation of monks into professional warriors is what signaled the emergence of the *sōhei* in late medieval society.[40]

Another helpful way to categorize *sōhei* studies, as suggested by Kinugawa Satoshi, is to look at how scholars have interpreted the causes behind the emergence of monastic forces. The first interpretation, represented by

Ōya and many of the early scholars, argues that the decline of the imperial
bureaucratic state was the immediate factor behind unsanctioned ordina-
tions of commoners, who entered the monastic complexes without the ac-
knowledgement of the state. The second explanation looks to the other end
of the social spectrum, namely to the influx of nobles who, owing to their
pedigrees, contacts in the imperial court, and financial resources, came to
dominate all ranking monk offices beginning in the late Heian. Regarding
this second group, moreover, Kinugawa pointed to three scenarios. One,
as suggested by Sakaino, was that the *sōhei* were warrior-retainers of noble
monks who accompanied their masters into the monasteries. Another scenario involved the noble monks bringing with them the factional disputes
of the imperial court, which meant armed personnel were critical to sustain
these struggles—a phenomenon that Tsuji in particular had pointed out.
The final scenario showed militarization to be a result of class conflict between the noble monks and the lower ranks within the monasteries. Taking a
Marxist view, scholars represented by Tamamuro Taijō (1902–1966) pointed
to the conflicting interests of commoners, who had entered the monasteries to form bands based on loyalty, and of nobles' sons, who took Buddhist
vows for financial reasons.[41] Kinugawa's third explanation viewed the private estates that emerged in the mid-Heian as the foundation of the monastic forces. According to this view, first presented by Hosokawa Kameichi
(1905–1962) in 1931, temples and nobles alike employed warriors to safe-
guard the assets of these private estates, where the warriors also served as administrators.[42] Ōshima, who argues for the origins of the *sōhei* in the tenth
century, also pointed to competition for estates, emphasizing the causal relationship between that competition and increasing disputes between various
temples, and between temples and local landlords.[43] Hirata similarly concluded that as warfare became more prevalent and force of arms was deemed
critical to securing property and boundaries, military might became accepted within monasteries just as it was in society and politics in general. By
the thirteenth and fourteenth centuries, monasteries used arms to not only
protect their assets but also to resist the warrior aristocracy and its growing
influence. The monasteries had, in other words, become militarized.[44]

In the final analysis, the problem with all these interpretations is not
only the different criteria used for explaining militarization of the temples,
but more importantly, these scholars' desire to determine a single category
of historical actor that corresponds to the phenomenon of the *sōhei*. First,
as should be obvious from the preceding survey, modern classifications of
secular and religious violence do not readily apply to the complexity of the
monastic communities in premodern Japan. For instance, the numerous at-

tempts to label one group as monks and others as purely secular servants do not adequately account for the range of clerics within the temple complexes. Second, since the term *sōhei* was itself an invention of later observers, any attempt to match it to much earlier historical figures is bound to be problematic. Kuroda Toshio (1926–1993), one of the most influential historians of the postwar era, was less wedded to modern notions about the role of religion than any of his predecessors. The emergence of armed monks was not simply a curiosity but an integral part of a major transition that marked the end of the ancient era *(kodai)* and the beginning of the middle ages. This transition was a drawn-out process lasting from the late tenth to the twelfth centuries, which involved steady growth in the number of monks and the emergence of independent monastic centers. Kuroda refused to see armed clerics as a group separate from their social and political contexts, claiming instead that "someone who uses arms when necessary, even a monk, must be considered a warrior *[bushi]*." Thus pointing to their similarities, Kuroda stated that armed monks and warriors were twins born from the same social developments.[45]

This was not an entirely new view, since a few scholars before Kuroda had in fact pointed to members of the warrior class, often referred to as "secular warriors" *(zokuhei),* as constituting the bulk of the monastic forces. Already in the 1920s Takeoka Katsuya saw the emergence of the *sōhei* as parallel to the rise of the warrior class during the *insei* era, 1086–1185, and Hirata emphatically argued that the *sōhei* of the Heian age were actually secular warriors.[46] Nevertheless, what sets Kuroda apart from his predecessors and colleagues was his refusal to refer to monk-warriors as *sōhei,* pointing out for the first time that this term did not appear in Japanese sources until 1715, when it was used in a Confucian work. Accordingly, he concluded, it would be inappropriate to use the term for such warriors in the medieval age. Hirata had expressed similar sentiments when he acknowledged the term's inappropriateness for the armed clergy of that time, but he simply replaced *sōhei* with *akusō* (evil monks), who, in his view, were the historical equivalent.[47]

Kuroda's observations represented a watershed for the field of history and for the application of a more stringent source criticism. And indeed, recent scholarship offers a more nuanced understanding by recognizing the limitations of queries directed at identifying the *sōhei.* Mikawa Kei, for example, acknowledges the challenges associated with the term in his recent work on Go-Shirakawa, noting that "because it is problematic to use a term with a negative image to discuss history objectively, [the term *sōhei*] is rarely used recently in the academic world."[48] Going a step further, Kinugawa

Satoshi concludes that Kuroda's *Jisha seiryoku: Mō hitotsu no chūsei shakai* (The Secular Power of Temples and Shrines: Another Medieval Society, 1980) essentially discouraged further research on monastic warriors, so convincingly did it demonstrate *sōhei* to be a construct that reflected a particular consciousness within the warrior class of the Tokugawa age.[49]

Kinugawa's claims notwithstanding, a few studies have in fact dealt with monastic forces in the last two and a half decades since Kuroda's study. What is remarkable, however, is that even though today's scholars are by and large aware of the anachronism and the mischaracterization it entails, they have been unable to disassociate the image of the *sōhei* from the monastic forces they claim to examine. For example, Takeuchi Rizō (1907–1997), one of the most eminent scholars and editors of source compilations at the University of Tokyo, indiscriminately used the term in a survey history reprinted in 1980.[50] Similarly, Tsunoda Bun'ei refers to the general clergy *(daishu)* as *sōhei* in a work from 1977.[51] More recent works show the same tendency, and one must therefore conclude that despite Kuroda's fame among historians, his ideas regarding the *sōhei* may not have gained the general acceptance one might expect. It is difficult to assess why, but one possible explanation might lie in the tendency and desire of Japanese scholars to focus on the unique features of their own history. Hiraoka Jōkai, for instance, considered the *sōhei* unique to Japanese society, a kind of medieval religious equivalent of "the Japanese people theory" *(Nihonjin ron)*, which asserts the uniqueness of Japanese character in explaining a number of cultural traits. Hiraoka's version might best be called "the monk-warrior theory" *(sōhei ron)*.[52]

In the end, however, the identification debate has yet to subside because the term has taken on a life of its own and is easily recognized by Japanese readers and historians. For example, Seita Yoshihide mentions monk-warriors several times in his 1995 work on the legal structures of medieval temples without acknowledging its obvious anachronism and the problems associated with the term. Furthermore, he identifies the *sōhei* as monastic workers *(dōshu)* but provides no explanation of when they were armed, where they came from, or where they received their training.[53] Watanabe Morimichi in a fairly recent work entitled *Sōhei seisuiki* (A Record of the Rise and Fall of Monk-Warriors, 1984) also adheres to the traditional view, using literary and artistic sources without any measure of critical analysis. In his opinion, the *sōhei* emerged first in Nara because of a need to protect the treasures and the structures of the monastic complexes, whereas at Enryakuji, it was internal strife over the head abbotship that caused monks to arm themselves. These armed temple residents were not primarily monks, however, but workers and servants, who worked in administration and armed themselves to be able to protect the temple properties and to perform their duties.[54] Finally, the most recent work, a 2003 republication of Hioki's work, with additional details and explanation of source quotations prepared by his son, suggests that little progress has been made in the past fifty years. To mention just one error on the very opening page, the author offers a quote from the battle scene with Jōmyō Myōshu as "Onjōji's *sōhei*, Jōmyō Myōshu of Tsutsui."[55] That the term *sōhei* does not appear in the literary text he quotes does not seem to bother him, and so the *sōhei* image is perpetuated even in this very recent publication.

Few scholars outside Japan have addressed armed conflicts involving religious institutions, but when they have, they have added little to the Japanese discussion except further unreflective support for the *sōhei* stereotype. The most extensive treatment to date is G. Rénondeau's "Histoire des Moines Guerriers du Japon," published about half a century ago.[56] Largely unknown among American researchers, this work is, as the title suggests, merely a narrative of violent religious incidents. In fact, Rénondeau's work is void of original research and analysis of historical sources, and merely follows the work of Japanese researchers. The case is no different for the few references we have in English-language works. George Sansom, convinced that religious institutions had no business affecting politics, heavily criticized Buddhist temples in the pre-1600 era for not providing the moral leadership he expected of them. While claiming that the "monastic armies were a remarkable feature of mediaeval life in Japan," he concludes that armed men were primarily recruited by temples to protect their estates, and that the "unscrupulous use" of divine threats preying on the fears of nobles in the capital only reflected the weakness of the court and the failure of the religious community to live up to its moral duties.[57] Neil McMullin also noted the problems associated with the *sōhei* image, citing Kuroda's revealing studies in a footnote. Nevertheless, he continued to use the term throughout his study on Buddhism and the state in the sixteenth century, and it is perhaps not surprising that his remarks therefore appear to have gone unnoticed by other scholars.[58] George Perkins, for example, in his translation of *Masu kagami* (The Clear View Mirror), insists on equating the Japanese term for clergy *(daishu)* with *sōhei,* a fundamental mistake that reflects not only a poor understanding of monastic organizations but also a grave error in interpreting the historical circumstances and role of religious institutions therein.[59] Since translations of premodern literary works have tended to take a similar approach, he is, however, in good company: these include Helen McCullough's translation of the *Heike monogatari* and William R. Wilson's work on the *Hōgen monogatari*.[60]

The prevalence of this view of the *sōhei* can be further supported if one includes unpublished works. One particularly troublesome account is provided by the anthropologist Wayne van Horn, who claims that the medieval religious orders in Japan and Europe (specifically the Teutonic Knights and the Hospitallers) "have more than a superficial resemblance to one another and may provide an important key to understanding the evolution of feudal societies into premodern states."[61] While a comparison of the knightly European monastic orders and monastic armies in Japan may certainly be illuminating and useful, this paper's faults include a dangerous degree of circular reasoning: It begins with the assumption that both Japan and Europe have a feudal stage in common, and then proceeds to delineate this societal configuration by comparing religious military orders, which have already been defined as one of the characteristics of feudal societies. Only one recent study, a master's thesis, attempts to summarize the state of the field, but like all other works in English, it relies largely on secondary works and cannot approach the depth possible only through primary research.[62]

This consistent focus on the stereotype of the *sōhei* has undoubtedly constrained the studies of religious institutions and their armed forces. The endless quest to identify the group or groups that constituted *sōhei* in the premodern age has led to useless attempts to reconcile the image with what can be found in the sources. While these studies have uncovered ample material that concerns clashes and confrontations involving monastic warriors, they lack explanatory power because the definition of the *sōhei*, which depends on the scholar's own preferences, must dictate which temple warriors and commanders are or are not included. This obsession can lead to mind-boggling constructs, as in Hirata Toshiharu's work, where he describes the monks involved in a clash as "monk-warrior-like evil monks" *(sōheiteki akusō)* or refers to their emergence as "the *sōhei*-fication of evil monks" *(akusō no sōheika)*.[63] Needless to say, the use of anachronistic terms—which impart no precise meaning and misrepresent crucial aspects of the past—to sustain a paradigm that interprets or judges a past society through the lens of modern ideas should be unacceptable to all historians.

A second and equally serious flaw in the majority of Japanese studies on monk-warriors is the tendency to rely on later pictorial sources as accurate descriptions of the events they portray. Lacking a social analysis of the art works themselves—who they were created by, and for whom—many Japanese scholars have simply treated them as reliable illustrations.

As I show in chapter 5, however, those representations cannot be taken at face value. Perhaps the most misleading use of these sources has involved their depictions of the "forceful protests" (gōso) staged by temples to voice their displeasure with decisions made at the imperial court. Several of the early scholars mentioned above devoted considerable attention to the gōso without questioning the claims later inserted by artists and other observers. For example, Tsuji asserted that as competition between various schools became more intense in the Heian age, military means were used in appeals. He then proceeds to describe the protests and appeals of the clergies, shrine servants, and monk-warriors of the temples and shrines. As a result, the participation of monk-warriors in the demonstrations now appears to be an "unquestioned fact," even though there is no indication in contemporary sources that armed monks actually took part in such protests.[64]

The most striking example of confusion around monk-warrior involvement in temple protests can be found in Katsuno's Sōhei, where he devotes a good two-thirds of his account to protests rather than to armed conflicts. His extensive treatment of the Kōfukuji protests, amounting to forty pages in his short book, stands out as being particularly misplaced, for while he calls these events "monk-warrior protests," he never explains the exact relationship between the occasion of the protests and the sōhei.[65] Astoundingly, Katsuno failed to note that the participants in these protests were generally unarmed, which casts no little doubt on his working premise. Elsewhere Kageyama Haruki (1916–1985), whose works focused mainly on Enryakuji, treated the armed clerics and protests as all but indistinguishable in his article entitled "The History of the Sōhei and the Gōso."[66] And Hirata's major study, Sōhei to bushi—which implies an important connection between the monk-warriors and the warrior class in general—is more than half devoted to matters unrelated to armed conflict, and his comparison of the protests and clergy to the popular rights movements of the postwar era never arrives at an explanation of sōhei involvement in such activities.[67]

As I argued in The Gates of Power, these demonstrations were not intended to become violent, nor were the protesters prepared to engage in armed confrontations. Rather, the main thrust of the protests was the invocation of local deities, the kami, which often exerted enough pressure on nobles in Kyoto to interrupt governmental activities or even to induce a judgment in favor of the protesting temple. In point of fact, the contrast between the level of violence in these protests and battles involving monastic forces is nothing short of striking, as is many historians' failure to note it. It is only in this light that one can understand George Sansom's apparent confusion as he claims that the "military capacity of these monastic armies was not very great" yet repeatedly insists on their importance.[68] It never occurred to Sansom, despite the written record, that the clerics involved in protests were in fact not well armed and therefore could easily be bested by court warriors. But in times of strife, monastic fighters were as sought after by feuding factions as other warriors.

Japanese scholars, falling prey to the habit of recycling images and quotes from other works, seem to accept the image of "*sōhei* protests" even today. Just to mention a few examples, Seita Toshihide claims in a recent book that those who were armed during the protests, whether dressed in monk attire or not, as shown in picture scrolls, were *sōhei*.[69] The eminent historian Gomi Fumihiko explicitly asserts that later picture scrolls accurately depict armed monks as participants in the *gōso*.[70] Japanese scholars of a later generation have unfortunately not progressed much beyond these constructs. Mikawa Kei, for example, simply repeats what previous scholars have stated, reaching the identical conclusion when he claims that the *gōso* and the *sōhei* were essentially inseparable. Kinugawa similarly claims that those who participated in the protests wore armor and swords even though he acknowledges that pressure was exerted mainly by the invocation of local deities.[71] Ōshima, who sees most of the *sōhei* emerging from the lower echelons of the monasteries, claims that the protests were yet another opportunity for these classes to make their voices heard, and he therefore assumes that they were also armed on those occasions.[72] In point of fact, Ōshima is correct in identifying the protesters, but one is hard pressed to find any evidence of armed warriors or monk-warriors. Finally, Watanabe inexplicably uses the *Heike monogatari* account of a demonstration that took place in 1177 as an example of activity by military forces.[73]

Watanabe's use of a literary account, which ironically does not indicate that the protesters were armed, typifies the lack of source criticism in studies of the temple protests. This observation must sound absurd to most Western scholars who have worked in Japan, since the field of *komonjogaku*—the field of diplomatics (in its original sense, "the study of historical documents")—is central to history departments in Japan. However, despite an almost unmatched commitment to source criticism and the use of original and contemporary documents, an astonishing number of unreliable and/or embellished literary and artistic sources have remained the foundation for interpretations of the "secularization" of religious institutions. Hirata, for example, relies heavily on the anecdotal *Konjaku monogatari,* believed to have been written in the twelfth century, to demonstrate changes that supposedly took place in the monastic communities.[74] Given these tendencies, it is not difficult to imagine where the articles linking the monastic tax protests in Kyoto with the *sōhei* drew their inspiration.

Another problem is the tendency to interpret monastic militarization, whether it took place in the Nara period or in the Kamakura age, as a result of a decline of Buddhism itself. Overlooking social and political developments in society in general, many scholars have instead chosen to look for its origins within the monasteries. Even Hirata, with his emphasis on the Kamakura age, begins his treatment with a substantial description of the status and role of Buddhism from the pre-Nara age.[75] And his use of terms such as "secularization of the temples" and "decline of the ordination system" reveals his preconceived notions that Buddhism in Japan at one point or another enjoyed a pure phase without any political involvement or influence and that the "medieval age" was, due to its lack of central control, a step back from the preceding age.[76]

One way of understanding Japanese scholars' attempts to discredit armed monastic forces is to point to the implicit modern bias of the scholarship, according to which religion and politics must not be mixed. However, this bias extended to other less visible areas as well. In terms of approaches to the field of history, the works of Japanese scholars reveal a heavy emphasis on institutional history, in which religious violence is characterized, narrated, and analyzed in terms of monasteries. Thus, for example, violence between the Tendai siblings and neighbors, Enryakuji and Onjōji, or between the Tendai branch Tōnomine and Kōfukuji in Yamato Province, is seen as a result of the decline of those institutions, or as competition over religious leadership or land. While such narratives provide a context for the specific conflict in question, they do not consider why violence was used in the first place. It is commonly assumed that degenerate religious institutions resorted to armed solutions by default. However, from the perspective of world history, a number of cases come to mind where religious institutions did not arm themselves in similar contexts.

Explanations focusing only on the origins of individual armed conflicts without reference to other non-religious developments are not helpful in the larger context, nor is a quantification of the number of battles involving certain institutions. The social setting is frequently left out, which is even more surprising if one considers that most historical analyses of the last half century or so have taken a Marxist approach. However, such analyses have been framed by the most conservative and restrictive perspectives of that school, remaining bogged down in class struggle. The clergy is seen as one easily defined and constrained class thus hampering a socially grounded explanation of the emergence of warriors within the monasteries. The goal of this study therefore is to explore and analyze, above all, the contexts in which religious institutions and their supporters, whether monks, menial workers, secular warriors, or any other group, used arms as a means to resolve conflicts. Although the historical terminology in the sources will be carefully considered in characterizing these religious forces, it is not my intention to allow specific terms to limit the scope of this study. In addition, by surveying cases of violence over a span of several centuries, from the earliest recorded instances in the sixth century to those in the fourteenth, and by also touching upon armed religious forces in China and Korea, I hope to situate religious violence in the East Asian Buddhist world within its proper milieu. Finally, by tracing the emergence and use of the images that became Benkei and the stereotypical *sōhei*, I hope to offer an explanation of their rise and continued prominence in contemporary Japan.

TWO

The Contexts of
Monastic Violence and Warfare

History has repeatedly shown that religious precepts and actual practices do not always correspond. One might even argue that religious beliefs have as often been used to condone violence as to condemn it. In that light, Buddhism in Japan seems no different from Christianity in Europe or South America or Islam in Minor Asia, neither do Japanese monastic warriors appear any different from European Crusaders or Spanish Moors. Although most Buddhist centers in premodern Japan did in fact maintain armed forces at one time or another, one must be careful not to impose on all denominations the views and practices of a few. The historian's task is not to pass judgment on such communities, but rather to explain exactly how and why violence was used by clerics, how it was perceived and justified, and whether it is appropriate to categorize it apart from other forms of violence.

Among the Buddhist scriptures, the *Bonmōkyō* (Ch. *Fanwang jing; Sutra of Brahma's Net*), a Chinese text from the early fifth century revered for its commandments concerning monastic discipline, specifically prohibits monks from carrying arms: "A disciple of the Buddha should not possess swords, spears, bows, arrows, pikes, axes or any other fighting devices. Even if one's father or mother were slain, one should not retaliate."[1] Given the wars and uncertainty of the post-Han era when the text was authored, these proscriptions must be considered as much a product of circumstances as the expression of a religious ideal. In fact, there are indications that temples maintained arms not long after Buddhism gained a foothold in China, when the Northern Wei ruler, Tai Wudi, attacked Chang'an in 446 to put down a rebellion led by one Gai Wu. When Tai Wudi entered the capital, he is said to have been enraged to find stacks of "bows, arrows, spears and

FIGURE 1. Shitennō deity,
eighth century, Tōdaiji.
Courtesy of Tōdaiji, Nara.

shields" in one of the Buddhist temples. Assuming that these stashes were
part of the rebellion against him, Tai Wudi ordered the burning of Buddha
images and the execution of the city's monks.[2] It remains unclear whether
the temple in question actually participated actively in the rebellion or
just stored weapons for other reasons, and given Tai Wudi's antipathy toward Buddhism, it is not unlikely that the discovery was used as a pretext
to eliminate temples in the capital. Nevertheless, there is enough evidence
to suggest that weapons were not uncommon in Chinese monasteries. The
well-known Shaolin monastery, for instance, located just east of Luoyang,
is recorded to have been militarily active in the early seventh century. It first
armed itself, according to legend, when it was attacked by bandits, but it
also came to play an important role in the pacification of Henan Province
in the early years of the Tang dynasty (618–907). A general of the defeated
Sui dynasty (589–618), Wang Shichong (?–621), had dug in at Luoyang;
there Li Shimin (599–649, r. 626–649), son of the first Tang emperor, bat-
tled Wang for over a year beginning in 620. A stele at the Shaolin monastery
states that monks aided Li in the fight against Wang, defeating his forces
at a strategically located mountain where the monastery had proprietary

FIGURE 2. Fudō Myōō,
Daikakuji, late Heian period.
Courtesy of Daikakuji,
Kyoto.

interests. Led by the monks, the Shaolin forces even captured crucial Wang
allies and relatives, which earned them rewards and was later commemo-
rated in the celebratory stele.[3]

There was naturally no criticism against the military involvement of the
temples at that juncture, undoubtedly because they could be useful to military and political leaders during unstable times. And the temples could justify resorting to arms, despite the precepts, since there was also a discourse
about deities defending the faith with the help of weapons against evil, as evidenced by several armed deities in the Buddhist pantheon. These images also
reached Japan from the inception of Buddhism, as indicated by statues of the
Four Deva Kings (Shitennō) and Fudō Myōō, who are frequently depicted
with spears and swords in Japanese temples (see figures 1, opposite, and 2).

Moreover, since Buddhism was constructed as a protector of the state
in Japan, violence could be justified in defending not only the faith itself but
also the court and the ruling family. The Northern Wei dynasty in China
had used Buddhism in such a manner, and Buddhist protection was an important part of the legitimizing rhetoric of the Koryŏ dynasty (918–1392)
on the Korean peninsula. In this discursive environment, the use of arms by

monasteries, whether in the interest of Buddhism itself or in the name of the state, was never far away. Indeed, shortly after its introduction in Japan, the Soga family—the principal promoters of Buddhism in the late sixth century—were embroiled in bitter fighting with other clans who wished to preserve the primacy of the native beliefs. While the two faiths served more as banners for those favoring a centralized style of government (the Soga) and those preferring more local independence, the adoption of Buddhism in Japan was steeped in blood from the outset, with the clash between clans ending at the famous defeat of the Mononobe in 589.

The brand of Buddhism introduced into Japan carried traditions not only from India but above all from China and Korea. Basing its early legal codes and stipulations on those of the Tang, the Japanese court included twenty-seven articles about the behavior expected of clerics in its *Sōni ryō* (Regulations for Monks and Nuns) of 718. This code specifically prohibits monks and nuns from killing, stealing, keeping and reading military manuals, forming rambunctious bands, and receiving donations of serfs, oxen, horses, or weapons.[4] Buddhism was thus never disassociated from the general political environment from or into which it was introduced, and Japan's experience was no exception. While certainly devout believers might have followed the precepts to the glyph, there were also those who saw Buddhism more as a professional career than as a spiritual calling. One entry in the early eighth-century chronicle, the *Nihon shoki*, relates that a monk struck his paternal grandfather with an axe in 624, which raised great concern and anger among the nobles. They decided to expel or punish all Buddhist adherents in Japan, but an eloquent memorial by a highly respected monk from Paekche apparently saved the day for Buddhism, which thus survived in Japan, where it would continue to grow and eventually prosper.[5]

Considering the didactic purposes of the *Nihon shoki* as well as its later compilation date, one must be cautious in accepting such accounts at face value. Given the obstacles the court and its supporters faced in implementing many of its reforms across the country in the seventh and eighth centuries, it is only reasonable to conclude that the early years of Buddhism in Japan would have left accounts of unruly monks. In the eighth century, mandatory military service was one of the heaviest burdens for farming families, since it removed able-bodied men from the family fields. Since monks were exempt, some locals evaded service by taking Buddhist vows on their own, ignoring the sanctioned ordination platforms controlled by the imperial court. It need hardly be pointed out that such clerics were unlikely to follow the religious precepts very closely. Even the imperial court indirectly acknowledged the utility of cleric participation in armed conflicts, for young novices were part of the government army that defeated Emi no Oshikatsu (706–764) in Ōmi Province when he rebelled in 764.[6] Although some scholars have taken this entry to mean that these were actually fighters and so precursors of the "monk-warriors," the record does not state that they carried weapons.[7] It is just as conceivable that they served in other capacities, such as performing ceremonies to ensure victory for the imperial army.

Most scholars today agree that monasteries adopted the use of arms to resolve conflicts during the Heian age, but beyond that it is difficult to find any consensus. The most significant problems lie in the scattered evidence of violence throughout the entire age and the difficulty of determining precisely which forces can be seen as part of the institutional and social make-up of temples.[8] In short, it is a question of separating isolated cases of local and individual violence from a general trend, or—to use terms from the world of business—differentiating between "invention" and "implementation." The scant recorded instances indicate that monastic violence in the early Heian tended to be highly localized, rarely involving more than a few rogue clerics.

For instance, in 850 the Gangōji monk Myōsen was appointed to the Office of Monastic Affairs (sōgō), but a number of monks of Tōdaiji and Kōfukuji in Nara opposed the appointment. They perceived Myōsen to be less worthy of this honor than other more experienced monks at their own institutions and because he lived in a separate cloister outside Gangōji, the temple for which he served as abbot. Myōsen was subsequently attacked and ensnared by about sixty strongmen (kyōrikisha) and menial workers (zōshikinin) who carried arms, but they seem to have retreated without harming him.[9] The source of this event, a hagiography of Myōsen, does not reveal how his attackers were associated with Tōdaiji and Kōfukuji, and we must, moreover, be cautious in trusting this legend, for such texts naturally tend to exaggerate obstacles the monk may have encountered. Still, other sources corroborate the existence of armed followers within monastic complexes at the time. A slightly later incident in the Nihon sandai jitsuroku features two monk novices, named Kyōhō and Zenpuku, who led more than forty "rowdy monks" (ransō) in Tanba Province; there they wreaked havoc, killing a Fujiwara servant and torching residences. The court investigated the matter and found the monks guilty. They were sentenced to death by decapitation, although in the end they were spared and sent into exile.[10]

The term ransō is of some importance. It appears with increasing frequency in the ninth century, as does the term akusō (evil monks), which first emerges in the Ruijū kokushi, an encyclopedic work believed to have

been compiled and completed by Sugawara no Michizane (845–903) in
892.[11] Both terms indicate clerics who engaged in a wide range of activities beyond those normally expected of men who had taken Buddhist vows.
Their rowdy or evil acts were, in other words, not limited to military activity. Of course, "evil" in this context depends entirely on the circumstances
and perspective of the observer. In the view of nobles, monks who wreaked
havoc inside the monasteries and disturbed the idealized peace of Heian-
kyō in central Japan could be described as troublemakers; other monks,
who helped maintain the integrity of the imperial state even with force of
arms, might be seen as heroes. In many cases, however, these figures have
been nearly forgotten precisely because of their monk status. One such case
involves Jōza Menkin of the provincial temple (kokubunji) on the island of
Tsushima, who successfully led a number of warriors in defense of the island
against some forty-five ships of attacking pirates from Silla in 894.[12] More
than a century later, in 1013, officials of the governmental branch in Kyushu,
the Dazaifu, sent a report to the capital praising the monk Jōkaku for his
battles against pirates on the island of Iki. These examples suggest the importance of circumstance in the court's attitudes toward clerical violence.[13]

Local bandits, pirates, and other armed men were not uncommon in
the countryside in the ninth century, and it should come as no surprise
that rowdy behavior also occurred inside some of the monastic complexes.
Secular and monastic violence simply cannot be separated from one another, and their causes also appear strikingly similar. In fact, early monastic violence, by and large, lacked direct connections to either the monastic
institutions or to Buddhism generally. But in contrast to the isolated incidents of the early Heian period, monastic violence took on a new character beginning in the mid-tenth century, when it involved large factions or
groups within monastic complexes, as well as warriors recruited from outside the monasteries.

The Unsettling Tenth Century and Its Aftermath

If lawless and violent monks were nothing new to Buddhism, even at the
time of its introduction to Japan, then it follows that using the accounts
above as "evidence" of Buddhism's decline, as many scholars have done, is
pointless. What their studies suggest, in fact, is a general escalation of the
difficulties the capital elites faced in controlling the provinces. These problems reached a critical juncture in the early part of the tenth century—

described in a recent collaborative work as "something of a quiet revolution"—when the imperial court, facing challenges in the countryside, made important adjustments to bolster its supremacy.[14] Regional challenges to the central court are readily apparent in records of Fujiwara no Sumitomo's piracy in the Inland Sea and the Taira no Masakado uprising in the Kantō in the 930s. Less known, though equally important, locals who wore monk robes also engaged in such lawlessness. In 914 Miyoshi Kiyoyuki, a ranking noble, submitted a twelve-article report to the imperial court concerning the situation in the provinces. One of the articles specifically addresses the various evil deeds performed by people in cleric's garb, contending that self-ordained monks in the countryside were committing rebellious and malicious acts. Kiyoyuki also complained that land-holding farmers were evading labor service, as well as product and land taxes by cutting their own hair and putting on monk robes without being properly ordained. As if to further prove that these provincials were not proper monks, he continues:

> They all keep wives and children in their houses, and they put smelly meats in their mouths. In appearance, they resemble novices but their hearts are like hunters [who kill for a living], not to mention more extreme persons who gather to make up gangs of thieves and secretly mint coins on their own. They do not fear Heaven's admonitions and do not look twice at the Buddhist monastic rules.[15]

The capital elites thus faced serious challenges in various parts of the realm even before the Sumitomo and Masakado incidents, although it should be noted that there is no extant original of this oft-cited memorandum. Rather, it is quoted in a collection of poems and statements known as the *Honchō monzui,* compiled in the late 1030s or early 1040s by Fujiwara no Akihira (989–1066).[16] Nevertheless, the memorandum is generally believed to be credible, and because it is not the only record we have of troubles involving monks in the tenth century, it likely fairly represents an increasing concern with clerical violence. Other examples include a riot by the menial workers of Tōdaiji in 935, calmed only by the dispatch of an imperial police captain *(kebiishi).*[17] The 959 conflict between Gion's Kanjin'in and Kiyomizudera, a branch of Kōfukuji, resulted in skirmishes that again forced the imperial court to dispatch imperial police captains to arrest the violators.[18] And in 968 supporters of Tōdaiji and Kōfukuji fought over a small piece of land—little more than one *tan*—in Nara, which resulted in some casualties.[19]

If violence involving members of Japan's religious communities became more common and intense in the early tenth century, how do we explain it? An increased general tendency toward violence in this period is beyond doubt, yet this does not in itself explain the increase in monastic violence. Monasteries and churches in northern Europe, for example, did not arm themselves during the wars of the seventeenth century, but remained in essence defenseless despite the tradition of knightly monastic orders, some of which still survived. As noted in my introduction, some Japanese scholars have pointed to the defense of private estates as the direct cause of monastic militarization, but this is problematic because those estates were not so very common in the tenth century. Kinugawa Satoshi has offered an interesting variation on the defense scenario, suggesting that monastic violence in these early stages was a response to the attacks and thievery many Buddhist complexes suffered in the mid-Heian age. This explanation is bolstered by accompanying rhetoric that justified violence to protect Buddhist property and the Law. And there indeed seems to have been a need for self-defense, with the increase of local lawlessness. More importantly, official temples *(kanji)* seem to have presented special targets for attack. One temple was burned during disturbances involving captured *emishi* (unsettled people from the north) in 875, and there is evidence that bands of evildoers in Suruga Province "surrounded provincial network temples, stole various objects and killed residents" in 940.[20]

Although Kinugawa's conclusions sound similar to old views that monastic militarization was caused by the decline of Buddhism, he locates the initial impetus outside the sphere of religion itself, a point that deserves credit. Buddhist institutions and monks in premodern Japan did not exist in a vacuum, and they were heavily dependent upon and involved in the social politics of their time. But other issues need to be addressed as well. As already indicated here, several early incidents do not tally with Kinugawa's analysis, since the record shows individual monks and clerics using arms long before the incidents he notes, with no indication that they were engaged in defensive measures. Ultimately, too many cases simply do not fit his theory, and Kinugawa, despite his perceptive observations, seems locked into the notion of a single causal explanation that ignores the complexity indicated by the historical sources.

Mid-Heian Japan was a society where military power would come to play a more important role both locally and centrally. Local violence indicated the inability of the court to control the provinces by promulgation of laws and edicts, which prompted the central elites to try and co-opt the emerging authority of warriors in the countryside, in hopes of ensuring that they served within the system rather than outside it. The deliberate relaxation of the state's direct control of the provinces was done by necessity, lest the armed administrators and provincial strongmen challenge the rule of the Kyoto elites outright. Centrally, factionalism had become more pronounced in court politics as elites in the capital area moved away from a political and social system that relied exclusively on a bureaucratic framework. While adjustments made allowed for more direct and effective ties between the emerging local powers and individual noble houses, they also ushered in a new element of violence.

It is in this context that nobles and temples created and came to rely on their own networks of resources and supporters in the disproportionately intensified cultural and socio-political competition in central Japan. The ideological milieu did not generally contest monasteries having armed forces, and perhaps even mitigated in favor of it. One of the court's main ideological concepts from the tenth century held that the Imperial Law and Buddhism were intimately connected and that their fates were intertwined. The codependence of these spheres—usually referred to as *ōbō buppō sōi*, the mutual dependence of the Imperial and Buddhist Laws—in fact justified monastic violence not only in times of prosperity, but above all in times of perceived decline, since Buddhism was seen as protector of the imperial state. By the late tenth and eleventh centuries, ideas of Buddhism's decline (*mappō*, the end of the law) had spread among noble elites, and the violence associated with monasteries could be seen either as a sign of that decline, for which there was not much one could do, or as the final line of defense against continued decline.

The most persuasive records reflecting the surge of monastic violence and factionalism concern the Tendai abbot Ryōgen (912–985).[21] Ryōgen was a talented and well-connected monk, who appears to have made quite a name for himself in religious debates held in the capital. In 937 he was awarded a prestigious function in Kōfukuji's Yuima ceremony, despite having been trained in a different school. We learn from an eleventh-century chronicle that a number of "evil monks from Nara" *(nanto akusō)* wearing head cowls and carrying staffs tried to stop Ryōgen from participating as he approached Nara.[22] Although we do not know exactly what occurred during the confrontation, which did not seem to involve swords, glaives, or any other weapons, the description of the hooded monks provides some important clues to who the assailants were. Their cowls, known as *katō*, were pieces of cloth, sometimes ripped from the monk's robes, worn wrapped around the head to conceal the identity of the wearer. These eventually became a key attribute in representations of *sōhei*, but this was not the case in the

Heian age, as is shown in another source related to Ryōgen. In the seventh month of 970, during his tenure as head abbot of the Tendai sect, Ryōgen issued a set of twenty-six articles meant to regulate the behavior of his monks. Among these articles, two in effect confirm the presence of rowdy monks in this period. One of them prohibits hooded monks, such as those Ryōgen encountered three decades earlier, from appearing at Enryakuji. It proclaims that clerics in head cowls had interrupted lectures and ceremonies on Mt. Hiei, scaring away those attending with their swords and staffs *(tōjō)*.[23] To stop such behavior, Ryōgen warned that anyone wearing a hood over his head would be understood to be a troublemaker and could not attend such ceremonies; if any monks disobeyed this order, they were to be reported and punished.[24]

The appearance of armed clerics in cowls who were not averse to using their gear, despite Buddhist regulations, can thus be confirmed from the mid-tenth century. Perhaps it is not surprising, then, that cowls in particular have come to mark such monks and denote their questionable activities. Later sources, especially picture scrolls, often depict monastic warriors in such cowls, but their use was not exclusive to armed monks or for specifically rebellious activities, as demonstrated by Ryōgen's own regulations. These cowls were first and foremost used to conceal the identity of clerics and other people who wished to attend ceremonies and sneak into places from which they were normally excluded. For example, young nobles and women could attend exclusive Buddhist rituals by wearing such hoods. And monk-teachers could whisper answers to their disciples during difficult examinations, while acolytes could get sneak previews of ceremonial procedures by wrapping a piece of cloth around their heads.[25] Head cowls could thus be used in a variety of situations, despite their later exclusive association in the arts (treated in detail in chapter 5) with armed monks.

In another article, Ryōgen directly addressed the issue of weapons on Mt. Hiei. He proclaimed that those who have taken Buddhist vows should concern themselves only with the sutras, and the bearing of military equipment should be reserved for secular warriors. Revealingly, Ryōgen also noted:

> I have heard that monks now assemble bands in large gatherings, forgetting the merits [of Buddha's Way] and embracing anger. They carry swords hidden in the folds [of their robes] going in and out of monk dwellings, while others have bows and arrows attached to their bodies, freely going back and forth into the sacred grounds. To kill and cause injury to other people at will is no different from

[being] butchers, and to embrace the behavior of violence is to behave like drunken elephants. This is a great shame for the entire
sect, and a peril for the three Buddhist treasures.[26]

Ryōgen accordingly ordered that the prohibition of arms on Mt. Hiei be
strictly enforced, and that swords and staffs, bows and arrows be forever
banned and discarded from its precincts. To enforce such a proclamation,
he encouraged righteous and courageous men to report and arrest anyone
violating it, while invoking the punishing powers of the deities who protect
the Law of the Buddha.[27] Thus we know that armed people frequented Mt.
Hiei during Ryōgen's tenure, but it is not clear even from these articles who
they were. Some ordained monks appear to have carried swords, but it is
less clear who the members of their bands were, especially those armed with
bows and arrows. It seems apparent that these bands may have included
men of more secular vocations.

Despite these regulations, Ryōgen has been characterized as an aggressive and militant monk. His tenure as head abbot on Mt. Hiei was without doubt successful, since he managed to restore temple halls and residences that had fallen into disrepair. He also established strong ties with the
Fujiwara Regent's line, receiving land donations and accepting nobles as his
disciples. He might be best known, however, for driving a fatal wedge between the Ennin and Enchin factions at Enryakuji and for expanding the
temple's prestige and possessions by converting smaller temples and shrines,
including the prestigious Gionsha, into branch temples; all these activities
resulted in an intensification of factional conflicts.[28] The Gion takeover is
particularly famous because of the account given in the *Konjaku monogatari,*
which offers a detailed narrative. As the dispute over a maple tree bordering the precincts of Gion and Rengeji, which was affiliated with Enryakuji,
escalated into armed confrontation, Rōzan, the abbot of Gion, prepared an
army by assembling and employing the followers of a renowned Taira warrior. Ryōgen had his own resources, however. He hired one monk known
as the number-one man in the art of fighting *(bugei daiichi no mono),* and
brought on another monk, the younger brother of Taira no Muneyori, master of the Taira troops. When the fighting started Muneyori, rather than
firing on his brother, left the area and allowed Gion to become a branch of
Enryakuji.[29]

Enticing as this story is, it cannot be taken at face value. As Neil
McMullin astutely points out, Rōzan had in fact died five years before its
events supposedly took place.[30] In addition, the few contemporary sources
we have do not support this account. It is more likely that this "takeover"

occurred the same way many other branches were created in this same period—through donations or mutual interests of protection and support between the patron institution and the branch.[31] But later observers, seeing in Ryōgen's leadership the roots of an aggressive and belligerent cleric culture, criticized his success. By challenging monks of the rival Enchin-line faction, which eventually led to their departure from Mt. Hiei for the nearby Onjōji, Ryōgen earned a reputation for militarizing the clergy among chroniclers in the fourteenth century and historians of the Tokugawa era, even though in his twenty-six articles he tried to address and contain that trend, already clearly under way.[32]

One cannot deny that the separation of the two factions resulted in an intensification of violence between them, but this must be seen as a sign of the times rather than as the direct result of the actions of one individual. Ryōgen consistently favored monks of his own lineage, but the specific event that led to the split occurred in 980, when he omitted important monks from the Enchin faction while inviting others from Nara. He gave further insult by offering the best seats to members of his own cohort at a ceremony held in memory of Saichō, the founder of Enryakuji, at the Konpon Chūdō, the central building on Mt. Hiei. Later the following year, the imperial court appointed the abbot of Onjōji, Yokei (918–991), to be abbot of Hosshōji in Kyoto. Hosshōji was a relatively young temple, founded in 925 by the Fujiwara chieftain and the Tendai head abbot Son'i. It had quickly become an important Tendai institution, earning it the status of certified temple *(jōgakuji)* and imperially vowed temple *(goganji)* in the 930s, while it also served as the most important temple for the regent's line of the Fujiwara in Kyoto. In addition, by Ryōgen's time it had already become something of a tradition that Tendai head abbots be appointed from among those who had served as abbots of Hosshōji. Given these circumstances, it is not difficult to imagine the concerns over Yokei's appointment among the Ennin followers. When the court did not revoke the appointment despite complaints from the Ennin faction, twenty-two ranking monks were reported to have led some 160 followers to the Fujiwara chieftain's mansion to protest. Under such intense pressure, the court gave in, but this incident turned out to be only the beginning of more fierce rivalry between the two factions.[33]

On the heels of these developments, many members of Ryōgen's faction were determined to prevent the rival lineage from posing a similar threat in the future, and the rumors flew that they would attack and destroy buildings belonging to the Enchin faction on Mt. Hiei. This caused Yokei and many of his followers to take refuge at Onjōji. With some three hundred monks remaining on Mt. Hiei to guard the buildings and treasures of the Enchin lineage, Yokei proceeded to place his disciples at important temples in and around Kyoto. Rumors persisted and the court issued an edict in 982 stating that members of the Enchin line should station guards at their buildings to protect them from possible attacks.[34] This edict, quoted in the *Fusō ryakki*, is especially noteworthy because it demonstrates the court's own double standard vis-à-vis monastic violence—condoning it at times, condemning at other times. In 988, three years after Ryōgen's death, the court turned around and prohibited ranking monks from having armed followers. It specifically noted that monks who had twenty or thirty followers indulged in wanton displays of status, going about with an entourage, weapons, and fancy clothes. Accordingly, the edict stipulated the number of followers allowed for various monastic ranks, according grand master monks *(sōjō)* six monk-followers and ten pages, down to regular monks, who were allowed two novices and four pages.[35]

The imperial court was not, in other words, principally against armed clerics, especially when they might serve the court's purposes. It did, however, attempt to limit and control their activities, as it did other violence, albeit not always successfully. Moreover, one can hardly claim that the court exhausted every means to avoid potential conflicts, since it again appointed Yokei Tendai head abbot *(zasu)* in 989. As could be expected, monks of the opposing faction reacted immediately, descending the western slopes of Mt. Hiei to stop the imperial messenger, a certain Minamoto no Yoshitō, from delivering the edict. There is no record of weapons used in this confrontation, but the courtiers were understandably concerned and so dispatched another messenger under imperial guard escort, to make the appointment official on Mt. Hiei. Still fearing resistance, Yokei brought "skillful warriors" *(seihei)* for protection when he was due to perform a ceremony on Mt. Hiei, but the service was interrupted by his agitated opponents, who "during the dark night let arrows fly as the Yokei monks gathered."[36] To the delight of his opponents, Yokei was forced to resign after only three months. Four years later, members of the Enchin faction burned a temple associated with Ennin on the western slopes of Mt. Hiei, resulting in a furious retaliation in which forty Enchin buildings were burned. The Enchin monks subsequently left the mountain, which resulted in the physical separation of the factions into the "Mountain Gate Lineage" *(sanmon monto)* and the "Temple Gate Lineage" *(jimon monto).*[37]

The tensions surrounding Yokei and the abbotships of several important temples in the Kyoto area reflect the significance of factionalism in the increase of monastic violence in the capital region at that time. First, it is clear that both Ryōgen and Yokei were equally ambitious to establish their respective lineage's control of Tendai. But Ryōgen's success, in the eyes of later observers, suggested that he may have been more prone to violence. Second, as Paul Groner has pointed out, competition for sectarian leadership was not only a question of religious lineages but also directly related to factionalism in the capital. In fact, both the Fujiwara Regent's line and the imperial family were mired in severe factional struggles, and the events at court had a tremendous impact on the two abbots, who were, of course, lined up on opposing sides. Noble patronage, factionalism, and sectarian competition were intricately intertwined.[38] Third, this intensified factionalism led to an increased tendency to involve warriors and resort to violence in Kyoto. The Anna Incident of 969, in which the Fujiwara chieftain eliminated competitors at the imperial court with the help of his main warrior retainer, Minamoto no Mitsunaka (912–997), known in later sources as "the teeth and claws of the Fujiwara," occurred only one year prior to the promulgation of Ryōgen's articles and is thus a prime example of this trend.[39] By the tenth century, violence or the threat of violence was commonly used to resolve disputes and factional competition that could not easily be settled through legal measures, as was the case with the Tendai factionalism in Ryōgen's time. From that perspective, perhaps it would be more appropriate to view Ryōgen's leadership as successful in *deterring* violence on Mt. Hiei, even if that deterrence only lasted during his own lifetime.

By the early eleventh century factional tensions regularly turned into armed confrontations. In 1013 a preceptor *(risshi)* from Enryakuji's Dannon'in named Kaiju led about forty followers armed with bows and arrows and long and short swords into the grounds of another compound on Mt. Hiei, destroying sutras and Buddhist statues as well as an entire temple hall. Kaiju did this in pursuit of another ranking monk, the master *(ajari)* Henkyū, who he claimed was performing curses against him.[40] The difference between this incident and those that had taken place in the ninth and early tenth century is remarkable. Heightened competition between cloisters in the eleventh century led to one ranking monk leading fellows in full armor. Although it is unclear exactly who his followers were, the contemporary diary that recounts this incident does not indicate that they were monks, which suggests they may have been menial workers and disciples or even warrior-retainers brought in from outside the monastery.

It goes without saying that tensions between the clergy of Onjōji and Enryakuji continued, and in 1035 when Enryakuji clerics *(hosshi)* went to attend the Mio Myōjin Festival at Onjōji, they got into a brawl with ser-

vants of one of the ranking monks. Various people from the neighbor-
hood of the temple joined the fray, and the Enryakuji clerics were outnumbered, resulting in one casualty. Even though the Onjōji abbot arrested
the servants, rumors circulated in the capital that Enryakuji was preparing an attack on Onjōji, and that the latter was preparing to defend itself
with the help of a band of warriors *(gunpyō* or *gunpei)*.[41] Four years later
the Enryakuji clergy objected to the court's attempts to appoint the Onjōji
abbot, Myōson, Tendai head abbot. Contemporary records are not extant,
but the late twelfth-century *Fusō ryakki,* states that more than three thousand monks descended Mt. Hiei in 1039, a figure that is meaningful inas-
much as it represents a large group of monks, not an exact number.[42] Facing
the protesters, the Fujiwara chieftain, Yorimichi, responded by closing the
gates to his mansion and calling for government warriors to protect the
area, which left the protesters with no option but to camp outside. They
were eventually forced to retreat following a skirmish in which a few of the
clerics were hit by arrows, while others were arrested the next day for their
rowdy behavior.[43]

A gradual increase of clerical violence is thus evident from the historical record, but to what extent does this fact indicate the incorporation of
religious forces into the institutional framework—some might call it the
"militarization"—of the temples? First, as noted earlier, violence by clerics
was nothing new, although there is evidence of more frequent occurrences
during the tenth and early eleventh centuries. Second, the sources make it
abundantly clear that the armed monastics were either lower ranking clerics or warriors from the various estates and branches, but there is no indication that they resembled the coherent groups of *sōhei* referred to in later
sources. As I will show in the next chapter, any other reading of the record
is ahistorical and unsupported by empirical evidence. What is most salient
here, however, is the increased tendency from the tenth century on to settle conflicts with force of arms, a trend that was not limited to religious institutions, as demonstrated by the aforementioned Anna Incident of 969.
Perhaps developments in this age can best be described as a "partial militarization," in which some families and individuals selectively used armed men
to support their interests in factional struggles. But the growing presence
of warriors in the provinces—the crucial precondition for developments of
the mid- and late-Heian—combined with increased competition for land
revenues and instability within the religious hierarchy during the resur-
gence of the imperial family in the *insei* age (1086–1185), soon led to a more
complete change in favor of military pressure to effect conflict resolution.

Monastic Forces in the *Insei* and Kamakura Eras

Isolated incidents and minor skirmishes involving armed clerics were replaced by outright attacks by the late eleventh century. In the 1156 Hōgen Disturbance, the losing faction went so far as to recruit a force led by a Kōfukuji monk, marking the first appearance of monastic forces in a strictly political dispute (see chapter 4). This transformation was gradual but inexorable as competition for land and religious status among the leading monasteries intensified and became increasingly violent. The late eleventh century, and the year 1081 in particular, stands out as a kind of watershed in this process.

A combined force of armed monks and secular retainers from Enryakuji attacked and burned down parts of Onjōji, and this action launched a series of destructive acts that fueled running disputes between the two Tendai centers. This first confrontation can be traced to the fourth month of 1081, when service people in the city of Ōtsu, situated between the shoreline of Lake Biwa and the eastern slopes of Mt. Hiei (see Map 2, Hieizan), objected to new taxes imposed by Enryakuji to fund the annual Hie Festival. Exploiting the animosity between the two Tendai centers, the festival organizers invited Onjōji monks, who brought "several hundred warriors" *(sūhyaku no tsuwamono)* with them to back the Ōtsu service people in their resistance, in the end causing the entire festival to be cancelled.[44] A second attempt to hold the festival the following month was similarly stopped by the Onjōji clergy, prompting Enryakuji denizens to put on armor and lead local warriors in the first recorded attack on its Tendai sibling. The Onjōji supporters appear to have planned retaliation, but a court-dispatched imperial police captain managed to prevent further fighting. The court attempted to mete out justice by ordering both temples to hand over those responsible for the conflict, but neither of the monasteries complied. Shortly thereafter, Onjōji monks ascended Mt. Hiei leading several warriors in an attempt to retaliate. But while little damage was done to Enryakuji, the resulting counter-attack was devastating, and few buildings were left standing inside the Onjōji complex. The court did little to punish these actions, although a record from the tenth month reports that some of Onjōji's armed supporters from a local village had been arrested.[45]

On another front, forces from Kōfukuji attacked Tōnomine, a branch temple of Enryakuji in Yamato Province, in the third month of 1081 in what would be the first of many burnings.[46] According to the *Tōnomine engi,* a later chronicle, Enju, the director *(kengyō)* of Tōnomine, had sent out one of his disciples, a monk and administrator of provincial origins named

Genchi, to perform an extraordinary inspection of an estate. Apparently, Genchi was drunk when he returned, and he was accused of having shot a dog, which had spooked a bullock. A Kōfukuji administrator named Enkai, however, claimed that Genchi had in fact shot the bullock, an act taken quite seriously by the villagers. The Tōnomine abbot became enraged when he learned about the accusations, and summoned Enkai for questioning. Enkai was eventually pardoned and let go, but when he returned to Kōfukuji, he complained that the Tōnomine clergy had harassed him. The monastic workers of Kōfukuji took umbrage at this and set off to burn dwellings within Tōnomine's domain. The Tōnomine clergy planned to retaliate, but after debates about the pros and cons of escalation, decided to approach the Fujiwara chieftain, who soon issued an order to stop the unruliness, and matters appear to have calmed down forthwith.[47]

Thus, on two occasions in the late spring of 1081 forces that included monastery personnel as well warriors attacked another temple in a premeditated assault. In the following decades a dramatic increase in armed conflicts between temples, and between temples and members of the emerging class of warrior-land managers, set a pattern of violent engagement that persisted to the end of the Kamakura age. Several Japanese scholars have produced extensive lists of the hundreds of confrontations recorded in the various sources, and the interested reader should certainly consult those works.[48] But it is questionable whether lists can relay political and social conditions, or explain anything beyond the increased frequency of conflicts as recorded in available sources. In fact, the exercise of listing armed conflicts that involved monasteries and monastics as a separate category is doomed to misrepresent the nature of those events. It prejudges their specific character based simply on their association with religious entities, and as a result, little or no attention is paid to the actual nature of the conflicts, much less to the men who actually participated in them.

Battle preparations were of a different kind and magnitude than the "forceful protests" in which temples used judicial and ideological rhetoric to exert pressure on the imperial court. Monastic warfare involved no sacred palanquins, and the fighting was no different from that involving the secular elites. Moreover, monastics were fighting for the same reasons as secular elites, and anyone looking for larger religious motivations will be disappointed. Clergy, too, were consumed with the factional struggles that maintained or contested supremacy of a lineage, such as the conflicts between Enryakuji and Onjōji. Other conflicts arose from competition for resources and land, and often originated in local conditions, as in the Tōnomine and Kōfukuji incident in 1081. By examining these two categories of dispute, I hope to re-incorporate "religious violence" into the fuller sociopolitical and cultural context of late Heian and Kamakura Japan.

Succession Disputes and Factional Supremacy

Instability at the Kyoto court from the twelfth century resulted from succession disputes, and the use of warriors in these conflicts allowed the Minamoto and Taira to reach the pinnacle of the warrior hierarchy and enabled them to eventually challenge the court's supremacy. Throughout the *insei* and Kamakura ages, factionalism was the order of the day; it permeated politics and social relations on all levels of authority, including those of the temples. In the religious arena, competition between Onjōji and Enryakuji over leadership of the Tendai sect or alternatively over the Onjōji's independence is undoubtedly the best-known drama, and following the events of 1081 battles between the Tendai siblings became quite common. During the twelfth century alone, there were six separate occasions of attacks, battles, and arson—occurring in 1121, 1123, 1140, 1142, 1146, and 1163. In the thirteenth century, confrontations are recorded for 1214–1215, when hundreds of buildings were destroyed despite newly erected barricades, and for 1247, 1264, and 1280, with a few attacks also reported for the early fourteenth century.

Although less frequent, confrontations between Kōfukuji and Enryakuji could turn out just as violent and bloody. Perhaps no incident in the twelfth century proves this more than the dispute over the appointment of an abbot for Kiyomizudera, Kōfukuji's branch in the eastern hills of Kyoto. In 1113 the court appointed Ensei, a monk with Enryakuji affiliations, which caused the Kōfukuji clergy to stage a protest at the Fujiwara chieftain's mansion and resulted in the appointment of another monk.[49] Hundreds of Enryakuji followers, who had observed in silence until that point, suddenly descended to the capital to attack Kiyomizudera. They justified their attack by claiming that monks from Kōfukuji had stolen property from Gion during the protest a week earlier. At any rate, Enryakuji's attack resulted in devastating destruction at Kiyomizudera, causing Kōfukuji to demand severe punishment of the perpetrators and of temple leaders, but the court seemed unable to make a decision.[50]

With the court paralyzed, Enryakuji and Kōfukuji seemed determined to settle the matter themselves and each temple prepared for armed confrontation. On the thirtieth day of the fourth month of 1113, monks from the two monasteries set out for the capital where they expected to clash. The Kōfukuji forces, which included supporters from other branches and estates in Yamato, approached the capital from the south, arriving first at Uji, where the Fujiwara chieftain's residential compound was located (Map 2). The imperial court, for its part, had dispatched warriors led by the imperial police captain Taira no Masamori to stop the Yamato forces, which resulted in a brief battle significant enough to be memorialized in a later picture scroll (see chapter 5). More than forty Kōfukuji warriors were killed, with only two fatalities on the government side, indicating that the court's forces were superior on this occasion. Since the court ultimately stopped the Kōfukuji forces, Enryakuji's supporters never engaged them and returned peacefully to Mt. Hiei after hearing news of the battle.[51]

Another important factional rivalry was that between Kōyasan, or more specifically its main section, Kongōbuji, and Negoroji, located just down the Ategawa River not far from Kōyasan. Negoroji was founded by Kakuban (1095–1143) as a branch of his own cloister, the Daidenbōin, which he had established on Mt. Kōya in 1132. He was a popular monk at the imperial court, and with the backing of Retired Emperor Toba (1103–1156; ruled 1105–1123), he secured substantial funding through several important estates donated to his cloister. Kakuban gained control of Kongōbuji in 1134 despite internal resistance, earning him the animosity of other groups and lineages on Mt. Kōya. The opposition he faced eventually overwhelmed him, and he felt compelled to resign. But his influence continued to be so great that his opponents on Mt. Kōya attacked his cloister in 1140, forcing him to leave the mountain with hundreds of his disciples and settle at Negoroji.[52] Tensions remained, however, because of the relative proximity of the complexes and because of the religious competition the Kakuban lineage presented. In addition, the considerable income from the Daidenbōin estates invited competing claims. A quarrel in 1162 over the procedures of a Daidenbōin ceremony led both the Kongōbuji clergy and the Kakuban side to bring in armed supporters.[53] Another confrontation took place five years later over the same issue, with armed followers again jumping in on both sides. This incident resulted in the exile of some of the ringleaders, but competition flared up once again in 1175, when Kongōbuji residential retainers attacked and burned Daidenbōin buildings. The court determined that the Kongōbuji side had been the aggressor, and two monks were exiled for their role in the fighting.[54] Matters remained calm for a while, but in 1241 the Daidenbōin clergy recruited villagers of another branch cloister for an attack on the Kongōbuji clergy. The retaliation was furious and destructive, as heavily armed followers, many from the Oku-no-in, the largest and most powerful of the sections on the mountain, torched the Daidenbōin in the seventh month of 1242. Despite attempts by the abbot to quell the disturbance, fighting continued for months and the dispute remained unresolved even though more than thirty monks were ordered into exile in the first month of 1244.[55] The rivalry continued into the next several decades, until 1288, when a large number of monks from the Daidenbōin left the mountain to establish a separate branch of the Shingon sect (Shingi Shingon) at Negoroji. Like Onjōji, this sibling establishment became a competitor, both politically and religiously, with the main temple.

As suggested by the Kakuban confrontations, many of the succession conflicts involved factions within one and the same monastic complex. On Mt. Hiei the Saitō and Tōtō sections, two of the three main sections within Enryakuji, often disputed over control of the monastery. When a large number of monks attacked the dwellings of head abbot Ryōshin, he responded by burning part of the Saitō section in 1093. Eleven years later, the clergy again attacked its own leader, this time driving head abbot Keichō off Mt. Hiei.[56] Further, when nobles established cloisters (monzeki) with their own assets, the cloisters instead became the preferred means of identifying lineages. As a result, fights commonly erupted between them, such as the clashes between the Enryakuji cloisters Shōren'in and Nashimoto. At Kōfukuji, the two disputing factions were the noble cloisters Ichijōin and Daijōin, founded in the late tenth and eleventh centuries respectively. They came under the patronage of competing lineages within the Fujiwara in their efforts to control both the clan temple and the clan itself. Many of these confrontations date to the fourteenth century, but two early incidents occurred in 1293 and 1295, when clerics from the two cloisters squared off during the Wakanomiya Festival at Kasuga.[57] The conflicts were largely caused by competition for important offices, especially abbotships, a problem that had spread to most monastic communities by the thirteenth century. In 1237, for example, following the death of the incumbent abbot at Shitennōji, the head administrator (jōza) Kakujun brought over two hundred followers with him to the temple to support his "candidacy." He was met by an opposing band, however, and in the battle that ensued, Kakujun and more than ninety of his retainers were reportedly killed, and several buildings within the monastery were burned.[58]

Other internal conflicts pitted diverse social groups against one another, as when lower-ranking members of the monastic communities opposed and confronted the privileged noble leaders, who would monopolize all ranking titles from the insei age onward. For example, in 1177, the newly appointed abbot at Tōdaiji, Binkaku, apparently had problems assuming his post, since he was only able to enter the main temple precinct with the help of his armed supporters who destroyed several monk residences in the process.[59] But, it was above all the clashes at Enryakuji and Kōfukuji that stand out most, both for their ferocity and frequency. On Mt. Hiei, tensions between the scholar-monks *(gakushō)* and the monastic workers (treated in more detail in chapter 3) erupted into full-blown conflict late in the twelfth century, beginning with a dispute over land in 1175.[60] The imperial court, undoubtedly sensing the tensions and interested in protecting their monk-robed noble relatives, issued an edict in the seventh month of 1178 prohibiting "illegal activities" and fighting on Mt. Hiei. This edict had little effect on the menial monks, however, whose military strength apparently gave them the upper hand in the conflict and caused ranking monks to petition the court for assistance. Court warriors did help the scholar-monks to turn the tables, and with court backing they were emboldened to take more aggressive measures to subdue the monastic workers in the eleventh month.[61]

The confrontation temporarily subsided but flared up again in the middle of 1179, causing Retired Emperor Go-Shirakawa (1127–1192; ruled 1155–1158) to order government warriors to attack the workers and cut off all main passages to the mountain. But failing to isolate the monastic workers from their supporters and resources on nearby estates, the ranking monks launched a desperate attack that only resulted in their own devastating defeat.[62] The ensuing division within Enryakuji had a profound effect on the Genpei War, since it became impossible for Taira no Kiyomori (1118–1181), who was counting on its support through his close connection with the head abbot Myōun (1115–1183), to secure it as a reliable ally. Other skirmishes between the two groups occurred over the course of the thirteenth century, but none was as protracted and all-encompassing as the one in 1179. Nevertheless, those clashes were similar in that ranking monks of noble descent often found themselves at a military disadvantage and were forced to call on the imperial court for help. In 1203–1204, for example, warriors of the prominent warrior family in nearby Ōtsu, the Sasaki, were called in to attack the monastic workers, who, in turn, rioted in Ōtsu harbor two years later.[63]

At Kōfukuji internal disputes became common toward the second half of the thirteenth century, somewhat later than those on Mt. Hiei. There the lower echelons of the Buddhist clergy as well as shrine members began to oppose the scholar-monks *(gakuryō)* who held ranking positions within the temple administration. In time the monastic workers who mainly performed menial and administrative tasks eventually wrested control of the Kōfukuji's decision-making process by dominating temple meetings. Enjitsu, son of the prominent courtier Kujō Michiie (1193–1252), offers an illuminating example. Enjitsu was appointed head abbot in 1235 at the tender age of twenty-three, a clear reflection of the monopoly noble families had gained over such positions, which they controlled for their own purposes. In fact, Enjitsu's younger brother had also embarked on a monastic career, becoming head abbot of Enryakuji in 1238.[64] During Enjitsu's second stint as abbot of Kōfukuji, he alienated large numbers of the lower-ranking clergy, when, in 1264, he failed to support a petition submitted to the imperial court by the clergy about the mismanagement of one of the temple's estates. Evidently, Enjitsu chose to support his blood relatives over his monastery, since the accused warrior-managers were retainers of the Fujiwara chieftain, Nijō Yoshizane (1216–1270), Enjitsu's older brother.[65] With their own head abbot unwilling to support their appeals, the clergy soon directed their anger against him. When the Hōjō regent, whose retainer was one of the managers extorting extraordinary taxes at one of the Kōfukuji estates, died in the eighth month of 1264 at the age of thirty-five, the clergy claimed divine retribution and filed petitions to have Enjitsu and his followers punished and removed. The bakufu confirmed the estates' tax-exempt status, and the court sentenced Enjitsu to exile on the island of Awa.[66] An attempt to regain control of Kōfukuji two years later failed, and Enjitsu was eventually forced to give up on his ambitions. The failure of the noble abbot, the Fujiwara chieftain, and the bakufu to control Kōfukuji's clergy are supremely evident in this incident. The lower-ranking clergy's numbers and access to arms had come to outweigh the social status and the judicial powers of the political authorities.

Conflicts over Land

Armed confrontations over land commonly manifested themselves in one of two ways—as border conflicts between monasteries or as conflicts over estates between local warrior-administrators and the temple proprietors. Of the first kind, the battles between Kōfukuji and Tōnomine are among the best known and the most telling. Aside from the 1081 attack already recounted above, Kōfukuji followers burned structures in the Tōnomine complex again in 1108, 1173, and in 1227–1228, when hundreds of buildings were burned to the ground.[67] That proprietary claims lurked behind each of these confrontations is easy to understand. In 1173, for example, Tōnomine followers objected to new Kōfukuji tollgates raised in Yamato Province, which that temple had long sought to control. Tōnomine members voiced their objections by destroying one of the gates in the fifth month, which resulted in the violent and extensive retaliation by a Kōfukuji force. New clashes occurred in 1284 and 1312, after which Tōnomine-Kōfukuji confrontations declined substantially.[68] In part, this must be attributed to the weakening of Kōfukuji's presence in Yamato, but changing political and military circumstances must also be taken into account. The fourteenth century struggles between the Hōjō and Go-Daigo supporters, and later between followers of the Southern and Northern Courts, made immediate defense against and attacks on local warriors a more pressing need for the monasteries of central Japan.

Kōfukuji was also engaged in long-standing conflicts with Iwashimizu Hachimangū. Like Tōnomine, Iwashimizu had land holdings in Yamato Province, and a dispute over land rights between two adjacent estates, Takigi and Ōsumi, emerged in the fifth month of 1235 when residents of Takigi, belonging to Iwashimizu, attacked and killed farmers in Ōsumi, which was a possession of Kōfukuji. Kōfukuji followers retaliated by burning some sixty homesteads and killing several Iwashimizu supporters in Takigi. The court attempted to placate Iwashimizu by granting it additional estates to avert further problems and a protest in the capital.[69] Nevertheless, later that year, when the new abbot of Iwashimizu dispatched messengers to survey the borders between the two estates, a brawl with a number of Kasuga followers ensued. Since some of the Kasuga people were killed, Kōfukuji began preparing for a protest but was stopped by the bakufu, which used a combination of rewards and threats to calm the clergy. In the end, the bakufu felt compelled to take the unprecedented measure of appointing a military governor (*shugo*) for Yamato and several land stewards (*jitō*) for some of the Kōfukuji estates; these were eventually withdrawn and Kōfukuji's privileged status in Yamato was restored shortly thereafter.[70]

Shrines also became embroiled in violent conflicts, but fewer records remain for the many shrines in Japan, so they are rarely as well documented as those involving temples. But since most shrines were associated with one temple or another, they provided them assistance in various forms. The most prominent group associated with the shrines were the *jinnin* (literally "people of the gods," or "shrine people"), but they are notoriously difficult to track. They were not afforded monastic status, living instead among regular residents in market places or in villages and cities close to the shrines, and therefore rarely appear by name in temple records. In either case, we know that a number of violent conflicts involving shrines were no less significant than those involving temples. For example, in 1094 skirmishes occurred between members of the Kuramadera clergy and the Kamo shrine members. Unfortunately, we do not know in detail what the conflict was about, but given the proximity of the two religious centers it may have been a dispute over land.[71] Twelve years later, the administrator of Kamo Shrine, Sukesue, argued with members of the Enryakuji clergy over territory presumably belonging to the shrine in the Shirakawa section of Kyoto. When he had the monks residing there driven out, Enryakuji followers responded by attacking Sukesue's dwelling. But he was apparently not intimidated and even detained some of his attackers. Retired Emperor Go-Shirakawa, angered over Sukesue's taking matters into his own hands, removed the shrine head from his office and exiled leaders on both sides.[72]

Kinpusen was yet another powerful temple south of Kyoto and frequently a thorn in Kōfukuji's side until it was converted into a Kōfukuji branch late in the twelfth century. Until that time, Kinpusen had held its own in armed confrontations. Records of an extended armed conflict between the two in 1145 relate how the lay monk Morotō donated to Kōfukuji a proprietary share of a dry field in Uchi District that he claimed was his ancestral possession. But then Morotō changed his mind and turned the land over to Kinpusen because he thought Kōfukuji's share of the yield was too high, which of course indicates that the donation was in fact a scheme to secure Morotō's own income from an estate to which he had dubious claims. The Kōfukuji clergy subsequently became upset and attempted to apprehend Morotō, but he escaped to Kinpusen, which led to the initial skirmishes. Kōfukuji cut off the food supply by besieging and thus isolating Kinpusen. Unable to endure these conditions, Morotō then escaped to Uchi, and the Kinpusen clergy promptly pursued him to try and force his return in the fourth month of the following year: "The Kinpusen clergy led over five hundred warriors (gunpei) to Uchi District in Yamato Province to detain the lay monk Morotō. At that juncture, the district administrator Fujiwara no Yorikane dispatched warriors to defend the area. There were too many casualties to count."[73] Unfortunately, the records do not indicate how this conflict ended, but the involvement of warriors and the clergies of two temples in land disputes demonstrates not only the intense competition for resources, but also the social and spatial proximity of warriors and many members of the clergy.

Kōfukuji eventually subdued Kinpusen in the late twelfth century, but Kinpusen continued to be a strong presence south of the capital. In 1208 Kinpusen seems to have taken over the role of attacking Tōnomine in lieu of Kōfukuji, perhaps even acting on the latter's behalf, when its supporters destroyed one of the main shrine buildings, several monk residences, a number of statues, and other valuable objects. The Fujiwara chieftain dispatched imperial police captains, who reported that the fires on the Tōnomine ridge could be seen from afar. Captains were also sent to Kōfukuji, which indicates that the court suspected that the temple might have encouraged the attacks.[74]

Some of Kinpusen's estates bordered those of Kōyasan, which claimed that a substantial area around Mt. Kōya was part of the original land donated to the founder Kūkai in Kii Province. Repeated problems sprang up between the two in the early thirteenth century. In 1219, for example, Retired Emperor Go-Toba (1180–1239; ruled 1183–1198) was forced to issue an edict that ordered a stop to intrusions by the Kinpusen clergy.[75] Four years later "evil bands from Yoshino" (Yoshino *akutō*), perhaps under Kinpusen orders, again moved into Kōyasan property. Kōyasan now directed a complaint to the bakufu, which, in the absence of an assertive court in the aftermath of the Jōkyū War, issued an edict condemning Kinpusen's actions.[76] Apparently these measures were insufficient, for in the eighth month of 1225, the bakufu dispatched warriors to stop Kinpusen followers from attacking and setting Kōyasan property afire.[77]

Disputes involving local warriors and temple managers were also common, and although many of those that are known to us did not result in large-scale battles during the Kamakura period, armed confrontations were by no means unusual. The conflicts between Enryakuji and the Sasaki family, land stewards of Sasaki Estate, which was designated to provide provisions for the monks on Mt. Hiei, are perhaps most instructive. In 1191 when shrine officials from Hiesha were dispatched to collect unpaid dues, they became embroiled in a violent confrontation with the steward's son. Some Hiesha personnel were injured or killed, and a protest was lodged that eventually resulted in Yoritomo himself exiling both father and son, and confiscating some of the Sasaki family's titles. The Sasaki were, however, important supporters of the Kamakura Bakufu, and Yoritomo soon pardoned the culprits, even promoting the Sasaki chieftain to be military governor (*shugo*) of Ōmi, which only exacerbated the intense competition between the temple and the warrior family.[78] A 1235 conflict over fees associated with Hiesha shrine members escalated into a brawl with local warrior officials in which one shrine member was killed.[79]

Other conflicts of similar character occurred during the Kamakura period, but overall, records of confrontations between religious institutions are more numerous than those of temple- or shrine-warrior conflict. One can imagine several reasons for this, but a key factor was the bakufu's determination to contain the local warrior class, a policy that encouraged noble and religious proprietors to petition the warrior government for redress rather than confronting the local warriors directly. It is also important to keep in mind that while courtiers noted battles between monasteries with some frequency in their diaries—and these are by far the most informative records concerning such events—we know about local confrontations between the managerial warriors and clerics because they were brought as law suits before the bakufu. In these suits the culprits were more often than not warriors, but as is well known, the bakufu preferred non-violent solutions and rarely punished violators beyond admonishing them, extracting promises of appropriate behavior, or in the rare case, dismissing them from their posts. Edicts became the principal method of controlling aggression, whether by warriors or monastics, and this brings us to efforts made by the secular authorities to contain monastic violence.

Court-Bakufu Responses and Monastic Armies in Secular Conflicts

The imperial court and the bakufu frequently condemned armed conflicts involving monasteries and clerics, as is evident in the many edicts that prohibited the use of arms by members of a monastic community. One edict issued in 1114 banned weapons on Mt. Hiei after the clergy had showed its disapproval of an appointment by attacking several monk residences inside the monastic complex.[80] In 1151 the court issued a similar prohibition for Kōfukuji in response to an internal brawl that resulted in the destruction of the home of the head of Kasuga, Kōfukuji's main shrine affiliate.[81] A more general prohibition was issued in the intercalary ninth month of 1156, shortly after the Hōgen Incident, in which the monk-commander Shinjitsu of Kōfukuji (see also chapter 4) might have played a major role on the Fujiwara side had not Emperor Go-Shirakawa's forces preempted the coup. While it does not directly mention arms, this edict reveals an increased concern with violent behavior by clerics, stating that "temples have called together large groups of clergy members, who willfully claim to uphold the authority [of the temple], interrupt and obstruct provincial administrators, frequently run wild in the hamlets and villages, and even attack and harass the provincial headquarters."[82]

Since the Hōgen Incident marks the first mobilization of monastic forces by nobles to assist directly in a factional conflict in Kyoto, one can only describe this edict as ironic. Still, it is a point of fact that the various court factions time and again sought support of the monasteries in their struggles. Indeed, nobles scrambled for monastic allies during both the Genpei War of 1180–1185 and the half-decade or so preceding it. Taira no Kiyomori's attempt to forge an alliance with Enryakuji only to be thwarted by the divided Tendai center's inability to commit is one obvious example.[83] And in the fifth month of 1180, when Prince Mochihito (1151–1180), the disgruntled son of Go-Shirakawa, called for a general uprising against the usurper Kiyomori, he had hopes of gaining the support of both provincial warriors and temples.[84] Although Onjōji responded affirmatively, Kōfukuji and Enryakuji wavered, even if individual monks within both of those monasteries were more than willing to join the uprising. Among the Enryakuji monks, a certain Chinkei advocated, unsuccessfully, for the entire clergy to support Onjōji. He nonetheless brought his own men to assist the monks of Onjōji, and somehow managed to escape punishment late in 1180, when Taira forces struck back by destroying Onjōji as well as Tōdaiji and Kōfukuji in Nara. The Taira retaliation itself provides compelling evidence of the importance of monastic forces in the war.[85]

The contributions of temple forces during the Genpei War should certainly not be underestimated, and it is no exaggeration to conclude that the monastic resistance the Taira encountered in the Kinai was one of the major reasons they failed to hold off the Minamoto there in 1183. Chinkei and his companions resurfaced opportunistically in the sixth month of that year, when the forces of Kiso Yoshinaka (1154–1184) approached the capital in an attempt to dislodge the Taira. Since the Taira leader had failed to gain the support or even a promise of neutrality from Enryakuji, Yoshinaka was able to safely enter the capital on the twenty-third day of the seventh month as Go-Shirakawa and many of his noble supporters fled to Mt. Hiei. No battle ensued because the Taira decided to withdraw westward to regroup, and when Go-Shirakawa triumphantly returned to Kyoto on the twenty-seventh, he was accompanied by Chinkei in warrior attire along with several Minamoto supporters.[86]

According to the *Genpei seisuiki,* many monks actively sided with the Minamoto, and Yoshinaka seems to have relied to a large extent on the support of many temples in central Japan.[87] Kakumyō of Kōfukuji, for example, originally worked as a scribe at the Kangakuin, the Fujiwara administrative headquarters in Kyoto, before taking Buddhist vows and moving to Nara. Already at the time of the call to arms against the Taira in 1180, he is said to have played a central role when Onjōji invited Kōfukuji to join the uprising against Kiyomori. Kakumyō was well-connected at several of the major monasteries, had trained on Mt. Hiei, and was heavily anti-Taira. He quickly fell in with the opposition against the upstart warrior-nobles and moved to Onjōji to join the rebellion. Because of his anti-Taira activities, Kakumyō was forced to leave Nara during the Heike offensive late in 1180.[88]

As the Minamoto forces approached Kyoto in 1183, Kakumyō wrote a letter to various monks at Enryakuji, including the aforementioned Chinkei and a certain Kōmyō, known as a "great evil monk" *(dai akusō)*. The letter asked, on behalf of Yoshinaka, that Enryakuji disassociate itself from the Heike and support the Minamoto. The *Genpei seisuiki* informs us that those in favor of Kakumyō's proposal managed to persuade the other monks to join the Minamoto cause, a decision that was finalized in a meeting on Mt. Hiei. Kakumyō's education as a mid-level courtier was obviously of great use to him in these endeavors, and the support of the clergy greatly facilitated Yoshinaka's advance toward the capital.[89] As is well known, however, Yoshinaka was soon ousted by Yoritomo's half-brother Yoshitsune, and this development forced Kakumyō to abandon his position in the capital and seek refuge on Mt. Hakone, where he authored a legend of that holy locale, the *Hakonesan engi,* in 1191. Kakumyō must have been pardoned at some point, for, according to the *Azuma kagami,* he appeared in Kamakura, where he lectured and performed ceremonies for deceased nobles, with Hōjō Masako (Yoritomo's wife) attending in the fifth month of 1190. In 1194 he wrote the spiritual vows for a number of high ranking nobles and warrior leaders as part of a ceremony for the *mandalas* performed at Tsurugaoka Hachimangū, and for Yoritomo and Masako during their visit a few days later.[90]

Some of the details in these narratives cannot be confirmed in reliable historical sources, but Chinkei's role is described similarly in contemporary diaries as well as in the *Genpei seisuiki*. Yet even if we disregard the specifics, it is noteworthy that a later war tale does not indicate any hesitation by either side in the Genpei War to recruit support from militant monastics. Whether one reads diaries or later literary accounts, it is easy to get the sense that no warrior-commander could gain or maintain control of central Japan without the support, or at least a promise of non-aggression, from certain of the leading religious institutions. The Kumano Shrine on the southern part of the Kii peninsula became actively anti-Taira early on. Its abbot, Tanzō, is said to have joined the Minamoto in central Japan in the ninth month of 1180 and led warriors in an attack on Taira supporters in Kii in the following year. The gains were temporary, however, since the Taira sent out forces to drive the intruders away.[91] Four years later, Kumano exacted revenge when its substantial fleet, together with ships from nearby Tanabe, played a prominent role in the 1185 battle at the Dannoura where the Taira were finally defeated. Although contemporary sources are mostly silent about why Kumano took such a stance, the *Heike monogatari* offers an imaginary account of how Tanzō, as the head of Kumano shrine and

FIGURE 3. Statue of Benkei and his supposed father, Tanzō, on the grounds of Tōkei Jinja, Kii Tanabe. Photo by author.

widely believed to have been the father of none other than Benkei, had seven white cocks fight seven red cocks to decide whether to join the Taira (red) or the Minamoto (white). The legend tells us that all white cocks won, and so Tanzō arrived with two hundred ships at Dannoura to join the Minamoto, to the dismay of the Taira. To this day, the legend is kept alive in Kii-Tanabe where Tōkei Jinja (The Cock-Fighting Shrine) is located and features a monument showing Tanzō, Benkei, and two roosters fighting (see Figure 3).[92]

In reality, of course, other factors might have persuaded Tanzō to support the Minamoto, not the least of which would have been estates contested by the Taira, or Taira supporters in the Kumano area. In fact, Yoritomo was quite generous to Kumano after the war, granting land donations and other gifts associated with imperial pilgrimages.[93]

The Kamakura age saw a continued escalation of violence, clerical participation in military conflicts, and alternating condemnation and condoning of monastic violence by the secular elites. Prohibitions against monks carrying weapons were continually being issued by both the imperial court and the bakufu, beginning with an edict from Yoritomo himself in 1189 that banned Enryakuji monks from carrying arms.[94] In the third month of 1212, the court issued a twenty-one-article edict, reiterating the general prohibition against monks carrying military equipment.[95] And, when the Enryakuji clergy violated the ban in 1213, warriors from the imperial police and from Retired Emperor Go-Toba's guard were sent to disarm them.[96] Only two years later the Nashimoto and Shōren'in cloisters within Enryakuji engaged in a battle over the abbotship of Heisenji in Echizen Province, which resulted in yet another edict from the retired emperor that ordered the instigators to be arrested and strictly punished.[97] But in a striking turn of attitude, Go-Toba specifically asked for and received support from Enryakuji forces during the short-lived Jōkyū War of 1221. Enryakuji refused to send further reinforcements at a crucial juncture, however, and all the Nara temples remained on the sidelines.[98]

After a return to more peaceful conditions, the bakufu's branch in Kyoto, Rokuhara, issued an order in 1228 stating that members of the Kōyasan clergy must not carry weapons, and the bakufu deputies duly arrested armed monks in Kyoto two years later.[99] In 1235 the bakufu issued an edict that provides an unusually clear picture of the problems facing the authorities and inhabitants of Kyoto:

> Item. The clergy is prohibited from carrying arms.
> As to the martial monks of Mt. Hiei [sansō buyū],[100] they were banned from the mountain's temples after the Jōkyū War. However, we have heard that in recent years, there are many monks who carry military gear, bows and arrows, performing evil deeds in the capital. And when upstanding fellows try to confiscate that gear, quarrels and confrontations ensue. From now on, these groups shall be inspected, whether in Kyoto or in the provinces, their comings and goings shall be observed and recorded. In accordance with these lists, the patron institutions shall be informed of their deeds, and the violators shall be forwarded to the Kantō. This is the order that has been issued, and it shall be executed thus.
>
> Second year of Bunryaku [1235],
> first month, seventeenth day
> Signed: Hōjō Yasutoki, Hōjō Tokifusa
> To: Hōjō Shigetoki, Hōjō Tokimori[101]

The problems were not limited to the Kinai, however, and two more bakufu edicts issued in 1239 and 1242 prohibited monks in Kamakura from carrying arms.[102] In the second instance, the bakufu specifically noted that monks had recruited warriors of questionable character as followers. To prevent such rogues from performing violent acts and killing people, the government stipulated that any followers of monks, regardless of their status, would be prohibited from carrying and drawing swords, lest they and their masters be punished.[103] To note one more proclamation, the imperial court, under the leadership of the assertive Go-Saga, issued an edict prohibiting Enryakuji monks from carrying arms, something hardly surprising considering the retired emperor's frequent problems with the monastic center on Mt. Hiei and his support of Onjōji.[104] While this chronology of prohibitions may seem tedious, it does indicate that, on the one hand, these edicts were issued in specific circumstances, as deemed necessary by the secular authorities, and on the other, they were not particularly effective. The very frequency with which the prohibitions were issued and reissued reflects their lack of efficacy.

The secular authorities also tried to induce the clergy to submit a pledge stating that they would refrain from using weapons. That way, the clergy could be held responsible for upholding the promise—perhaps a more effective way to exert control within the otherwise judicially immune monasteries. In 1131 the ranking monks of Enryakuji submitted a six-article pledge to the court, in which they promised to maintain the ideals of the founder Saichō. The articles indicate that members of the clergy had indeed developed a taste for more worldly desires, such as drinking, dressing in expensive robes and maintaining large numbers of pages. As for the issue of weapons, one article states that the monks would refrain from assembling "evil followers" and that those who carried arms must be detained.[105] Similar pledges were occasionally made at other temples, such as Kaijūsanji, where the scholar-monks signed a pledge vowing to "not carry bows, arrows, or other military gear" in 1234.[106] And the Kōyasan clergy submitted an eleven-article pledge to the bakufu in 1289, whose last article states that "with the exception of warriors [heishi], large swords and glaives are prohibited on the platform."[107] Since warriors were also part of the monastic organization, as will be shown in the next chapter, such promises might have done little to discourage temples from engaging in violence. Still, coincidence or not, we have no records of violence involving those two monasteries in the decade immediately following the pledges.

The Fourteenth Century Transition

Many monastic complexes maintained their armed forces and remained crucial allies of the secular elites in Japan until the late sixteenth century. But the political, military, and cultural setting of the two centuries preceding that crucial juncture was substantially different from that of the late

Heian and Kamakura eras.[108] The changes that occurred in this period had profound effects not only on the composition of the forces and their affiliation with the monasteries, but also on the way those forces were perceived.

The establishment of the Ashikaga Bakufu signified the rise of the warrior class and was the single most important political event of the fourteenth century. Although continued struggles between forces of the Southern and Northern Courts prevented the bakufu from achieving stability until the end of the century, there was little doubt even during the tumultuous years of the early 1350s that it was the warrior leadership, and not the imperial court, that controlled governmental matters. Perhaps nothing proves this new balance of power more clearly than Ashikaga Takauji's ousting of Prince Moriyoshi as shōgun (see also chapter 4) and the emperor's visit to the villa of Ashikaga Yoshimitsu (1358–1408), a compound that rivaled the imperial palace, for the coming of age ceremony of the Yoshimitsu's son in 1394.[109] Moreover, the bakufu had assumed charge of much of the economic jurisdiction that had hitherto allowed Kyoto elites, both temples and nobles, to collect considerable income, even as revenues from the estates declined. In the late fourteenth century, the bakufu began to tax guilds that had until then been tax exempt under the protection of the patron temples and shrines, and it severely restricted the number of toll stations—most under the control of various temples—allowed in the capital area.[110] In the religious sphere, the Ashikaga leadership moved away from dependence on the established schools primarily by promoting Zen, but the spread of populist ideas additionally posed a challenge to the old monastic complexes. As a result, temples such as Enryakuji, Onjōji, and Kōfukuji found themselves on the defensive in the second half of the fourteenth century, staging protests in the manner they had for centuries, but now against a common threat from the new schools of Buddhism. They also came to realize that demonstrations had little effect on the ruling warrior aristocracy. For example, when the Kōfukuji clergy began a protest in the twelfth month of 1371 with the intention of inducing a verdict in a prolonged land dispute, nobody expected that the divine symbols carried by the demonstrators would have to remain in Kyoto for three full years before any resolution was worked out. To contemporary observers and the monks themselves, there could be little doubt that times had changed, and that the warrior elites were now in control.[111]

The fourteenth century thus marks the important political transition to warrior rule, and this shift was also accompanied by social changes. It was an age often signified by the historical term *gekokujō* (the lower overturning those above), in which members of lower social classes managed to challenge their lords in an unprecedented manner. Increased reliance on military might had to a critical degree displaced reliance on social status. The use of arms became significantly more widespread from the fourteenth century as people of various classes, including farmers and merchants and above all "evil bands" *(akutō)* of rogue warriors and farmers, resorted to violence to defend or expand their interests. The established centers still maintained armies, but they were not as tightly tied to the monasteries as before, and their leaders had become warrior commanders known as *daimyō* (big name), with no measure of religious training or administrative responsibilities within the monasteries. Several figures from Enryakuji took part in military conflicts in the early fourteenth century, ranging from the customary burnings of Onjōji to the wars of the 1330s. Even though these men are known to us under monastic names such as Jōrinbō Sagami Gōyō (1310s), Dōjōbō no suke Yūkaku, and Myōkan'in Inaba Zenson (1330s), they are simultaneously identified as "members of the warrior class for generations" *(daidai buke gokenin no yoshi).*[112]

The Ashikaga Bakufu readily recognized the importance of these figures and used them to extend its own influence over Enryakuji by appointing them "Enryakuji envoys" *(sanmon shisetsu)* in 1377, a measure against Enryakuji independence unmatched since the ninth century.[113] There is strong evidence that many of these monastics had as their sole vocation the art of war and owed no administrative duties to the temple under whose name they operated. In 1319 the Enryakuji monk Kōsō wrote a Tendai treatise called *Keiran jūyōshū engi* in which he mentions his masters. Among these, four were "masters of the art of the warrior" *(heihō no shi),* who taught him military traditions.[114] Compared to earlier ages when the armed personnel had other responsibilities, such as administration or menial work, their specialization in the fourteenth century reflected new ways of defining social and political status. As Thomas Conlan has noted, the domestic wars of the Nanbokuchō age (1336–1392) had a profound impact on society in general, where social status now became based on military performance rather than other factors such as political titles and pedigree.[115] The commanders of the fourteenth century relied on military skill to maintain their political and social status within the monasteries, where in preceding ages pedigree and nobility determined one's eligibility for posts as commanders and ranking monks.

These fourteenth-century changes are also reflected in the nature of military engagements. In the preceding ages, monastic warriors fought both warriors and other religious complexes, but battles against temples had all but ceased by the Ashikaga age. Internecine battles still frequently plagued the countryside and warrior families at this time, but inter-temple conflicts between the old schools had been replaced by attacks on the new populist schools. The most notorious actors among the new schools were the "the single-minded bands" *(ikkō ikki)*, groups of lower-ranking warriors and commoners who first banded together under the auspices of the Shinran teachings in the fifteenth century. But other sects, such as the Lotus (or Nichiren) sect, also became more active in central Japan and eventually drew an attack by Enryakuji forces in 1536. Enryakuji's success notwithstanding, other schools could not maintain their forces at such a level. In fact, while the armed monastic forces still appeared to be equal to those of the local and smaller military leaders, they were now increasingly overshadowed by the regional warlords, whose warriors were better trained and frequently more numerous.[116]

The general spread of warfare across social boundaries, both upward and downward, grew out of the new conditions of warfare and the socio-political framework that emerged in the late fourteenth century. First, warfare became more commonplace as military might could now be used as the sole factor in determining leadership status. For the first time since the age before the imperial state, warriors fought without regard for the elites in the capital area, and temples had to stay on their mettle to defend their landed interests. By the same token, since the political system that relied on the noble, military, and religious elites to cooperate in ruling the realm had effectively been eliminated by the third Ashikaga shogun, there was no longer a need for religious rhetoric. Accordingly, Buddhist claims to protect the state became less common, if not obsolete, and references to the mutual dependence of the imperial and Buddhist laws had nearly disappeared.[117] This new ideological climate stands in sharp contrast to that of preceding ages, when the very foundation upon which the military and political power of Buddhist temples rested was their status as co-ruling elites. As a result, temples lost their judicial and economic privileges, and thus had little to offer warriors by way of assistance. Skilled commanders and warriors began to act independent of the temple administration, and often rose to unprecedented heights as commoner leaders within their home complexes. The fourteenth century was the beginning of an age dominated by warriors, with new cultural practices and new levels of violence and warfare determined less by considerations of social and political status. Monastic complexes and armed forces still played an important role in this context, but less as religious institutions than as local and regional powers whose elite status no longer guaranteed any privileges. There was thus little call for warrior-commanders to assume positions within the temple administration, since their sole vocation at this point was warfare, unlike earlier times, when monastic workers and administrators took to arms only as the situation might call for it.

Conclusion

The tendency to compile lists of violent incidents involving monastics that has pervaded the field is understandable. "Religious confrontations" are at least on the surface conveniently recognizable by the presence of monks or other groups associated with temples or shrines. In point of fact, however, such distinct categorization is deceiving, for monks were rarely just monks since they retained, cultivated, and used their social origins and connections to the secular world.[118] And as will be evident in the next chapter, many members of the clergy were no different from their counterparts working as administrators, guards, menial workers, or warriors in the service of nobles. Moreover, all incidents accounted here have their counterparts outside the monasteries and shrines. As with the early instances of monastic violence, there were many cases of individual outbreaks of violence involving warriors, freewheelers and other local strongmen. And besides the parallel emergence of warriors in capital politics and forces serving the monastic centers, the noble elites' treatment of these warriors was identical. Although they often condemned warriors, whether employed by religious institutions or by other nobles, for their lack of respect for the law and tendency to resort to arms to solve the slightest conflicts, the very same elites were never hesitant to endorse arms and violence if it suited their needs. And monastic violence could easily be justified in the name of the state since there was a Buddhist rhetoric that not only allowed violence in such cases but also tied the fate of the state with that of Buddhism, as represented by the idea of a mutual dependence between the Imperial and Buddhist Law *(ōbō buppō sōi)*. Justifying violence by monks was not unique to the Japanese setting, as evidenced also by the often praised resistance by monks and their forces during the Japanese invasions of the Korean peninsula by Toyotomi Hideyoshi (1537–1598) in the 1590s. Unsurprisingly, such monks have been the topic of many appreciative studies in Korea, confirming the importance of the specific political circumstances of monastic violence, not only in the past, but also in their treatment by modern historians.[119]

Naturally, without the prevalence of violence as a viable means of solving conflicts, such rhetoric would not thrive, and Japan was indeed a violent society from the mid-to-late Heian age. As armed men gained influence and control in the countryside, the imperial court had little choice but to try and simultaneously contain and co-opt this trend. Punishments and admonitions were issued to those who could not easily be controlled, and those who could were brought into the system with rewards and titles to help deal with their colleagues. It was violence and armed men that made inroads into capital politics and society in general from the late Heian age, not Buddhist centers that somehow induced or promoted a decline of the imperial court that involved the militarization of temples and shrines. Nevertheless, the evidence for such conclusions has admittedly been rather circumstantial, focusing on the timing of various developments and trends, and comparing their general character. A contextualization and a more detailed analysis of those who fought for and within the monasteries, how they were organized, where they came from and how they became part of monastic armies are crucial for a more nuanced understanding of the armed monastic forces. These are the issues that will be the topic of the next two chapters, one looking at the composition of the forces themselves, the other exploring their leadership.

THREE

The Fighting Servants of the Buddha

The development of Japan's monastic forces has frequently been viewed as inversely related to a perceived decline in the socio-spiritual power of temples and, by extension, of Buddhism in general. There was and continues to be tacit agreement among scholars that religious institutions were not to engage in politics, much less warfare, hence their involvement in both has been promptly imputed to moral deterioration. But even if we were to accept the notion that monks and priests should not take up arms, a more precise definition of terms such as "armed monks" or "monastic warriors" is needed. What exactly makes a warrior a monastic warrior, a *sōhei*, or a crusader for that matter? Is it a question of spiritual conviction, of having taken formal vows, or of what or whom one is fighting for? The failure to unpack these issues sufficiently has resulted in the inclusion or exclusion of a range of warrior types, depending on the personal preferences of each scholar. In the end, one must ask if a broad distinction between religious and secular warriors can be usefully applied to premodern societies. This chapter will address this problem by focusing on those who constituted the bulk of the religious forces. By necessity then, it will explore the social networks and origins of those warriors, but it will also touch on warfare techniques, weapons used, martial strategies employed, all issues related to their social status, as well as other details that may provide clues to their identities, both individually and as groups.

The single most important yet elusive aspect of the temple forces is their complexity. Scholars have tried to pin their origins to one monastic group or another—the "evil monks" *(akusō),* clergy *(daishu),* scholar-monks *(gakushō),* or monastic workers *(dōshu)*—or to fighters of the private estates, known variously as warriors *(heishi* or *bushi),* estate warriors (shōhei), or secular warriors (zokuhei). In these cases, the historian's urge to simplify the past—especially the more distant past—in support of the modern notion that society "progresses" from a simple constellation to ever more complexity has created an erroneous image not only of religious institutions but also of the premodern age in general. As indicated in the introduction, the most disturbing aspect of these simplifications is their assumption that somehow one class or group can act without reference to other groups simply because its members have taken religious vows, or that class conflict, in the Marxist spirit, necessarily dominates all social and religious configurations. What is more important, and what we turn to here, is the network of connections between various groups and the social and ideological framework within which they acted, whether during times of conflict or cooperation.

It is no coincidence that monastic forces emerged about the same time armed conflicts were on the rise in the provinces in the mid-Heian period. The waves of insurgence involving Taira no Masakado, Fujiwara no Sumitomo, and Taira no Tadatsune (967–1031) in the tenth and eleventh centuries were paralleled by violent incidents at Enryakuji, Onjōji, and Kōfukuji.[1] Curiously enough, the close relationship between these trends was for a long time all but neglected because of the desire to view religious violence separately from the general militarization of society, at least until Kuroda Toshio's characterization of the secular and monastic forces as twin products of the same social developments.[2] But even as Kuroda pointed out these common origins, he persisted in viewing monastic warriors as a distinct group. Another important reason for the lack of comprehensive analyses is the overall paucity of records. Even though some of them may have been literate, most of the monastic fighters came from groups and classes that rarely left such extensive records as diaries, wills, transaction records, or court documents. This deficiency notwithstanding, the largest monasteries with armed forces were located in the capital area, and their nobles and abbots did keep records in diaries and chronicles. By critically using these sources we can recover to a considerable extent the historical character of the monastic organizations and learn about the people within them—including those who used weapons—and where they came from.

Temple Warriors

Japanese scholarship has a tendency to argue for one group or another as the breeding ground of the sōhei. In reality, it is not possible to pinpoint a sole progenitor, so we must instead direct our attention to the range of relevant groups and the terms applied to them, depending on the monastery and the age. What becomes immediately clear is that, in contrast to the monastic orders of Europe, warfare was not an elite privilege in pre-Tokugawa Japan. The bulk of the armed forces were comprised of lower-ranking members of the monastic communities and other affiliated commoners. The most general and common terms applied to the large numbers of clerics who acted in unison were *daishu* or *shuto*, which might most appropriately be translated as "clergy." The terms were used intermittently by observers making records of events, frequently high-ranking nobles, and their lack of precision indicates a general unfamiliarity with the personnel associated with temples.

Instructive examples of the broad use of these terms can be found in the diary of Fujiwara no Munetada (1062–1141), which, because of Munetada's position as a mid-level administrator and retainer of Retired Emperor Shirakawa (1053–1129; ruled 1072–1086), contains vital information about court procedures, political factionalism, and general conditions in the Kinai area and in the monasteries. Concerning the 1113 conflict between Kōfukuji and Enryakuji over the Kiyomizudera abbotship, Munetada notes that four to five hundred members of the Enryakuji clergy *(daishu)* came to the capital to demand that the Kōfukuji abbot Jikkaku be exiled for his failure to contain his monks. Later, he also notes that among the protesters were shrine members *(jinnin)* from Hiesha, who seem here to have been counted as part of the clergy, and in yet another place, he uses the term *shuto* interchangeably with *daishu*. Other combinations with *-shu*, such as *jishu* (temple clergy) and *nanboku no shu* (the clergies of the south [Kōfukuji] and north [Enryakuji]), are also used with some frequency.[3] In another case, dated 1092, followers of the imperial police captain Taira no Tametoshi clashed with "lower monks" *(gesō)* from Enryakuji. Strikingly, even though Tametoshi was a ranking warrior and his followers were likely also seasoned fighters, it was the monks who inflicted the most damage before escaping from the scene. Tametoshi was subsequently exiled for the aggressive behavior of his retainers, but he was pardoned the following year.[4] Still, when Fujiwara no Teika (1162–1241) in his diary, the *Meigetsuki*, notes that "the carrying of military gear by the clergy *[sōto]* must be stopped," one does not get a clear sense of just who the clergy is.[5] The difficulties of identifying just who carried arms can thus be a real challenge and frustration.

It must be noted, of course, that the diarists themselves may have been uninterested in where the armed monastics came from, or in distinguishing one group from another within the lower classes, but the mixing of terms in these cases strongly indicates either a complex composition or a poor understanding, or perhaps both. Temple records, however, occasionally offer more precise information about the composition of the clergy. Within

Enryakuji, for example, the *daishu* are divided into three classes, simply called "top," "middle," and "lower" *(jōhō, chūhō, gehō)*, based on their status and role within the monastery. The upper level included learned monks, *gakushō*, who were further divided into four categories. The mid-level can best be described as administrators with managerial and leadership skills. Two important groups can be found in this category, the "hall clergy" *(dōshu)*, more commonly referred to as monastic workers, and the "attendant clerics" *(samurai hosshi)*. The *hosshi*, or *hosshiwara* in the plural, is a term that appears with some frequency, referring not only to attendants of the middle level but also to members of the lower level (the *gesō*); these were clerics who performed menial duties inside and outside the monastery and who frequently kept secular names and wives.[6] Another category within this lower group was the *bōkan* or the *bōjin*, residential retainers who similarly led secular lives while performing services within the monastery.[7] In short, few whom we might call full-fledged monks were included in the ranks of the lower level clerics. Although these men might sometimes be initiated as novices, they worked mainly as support staff, performing general maintenance and cleaning operations or supplying specific products.

Taken together, the various sources demonstrate that the clergy was a complex mix, and that nobles were generally unfamiliar with internal conditions at the monasteries. These factors are most likely connected, for the complex composition of the residents made it difficult for courtiers to recognize differences between various subgroups or their affiliations and ranks. But while the capital elites may have been unable to distinguish between specific subgroups, they did understand that the clergy was not one coherent entity. A record of the confrontation between Kōfukuji and Tōnomine in 1173 provides a particularly telling example. As will be recalled, members of Kōfukuji burned substantial parts of Tōnomine in retaliation for the latter's destruction of a new tollgate. In response to Enryakuji's demands for punishments, the Fujiwara chieftain Motofusa (1144–1230) dispatched one of his chief retainers, Fujiwara no Mitsunaga, to transmit an edict from Retired Emperor Go-Shirakawa. As Mitsunaga was conveying the contents of the edict to the ranking monks, members of the clergy assembled in front of the bath hall (a common meeting place for lower-ranking clerics) to show their displeasure, in effect preventing Mitsunaga from proclaiming the edict to the general clergy. According to the diary of Fujiwara no Kanezane (1149–1207):

> The clergy assembled in the yard of the Golden Hall [Kondō], and there were some four to five thousand people there, all clad

in armor. Seats had been prepared in the front of the yard, and the clergy took their seats. Those remaining [without a seat] stood up. Among those there was a young monk who wore a robe on top of his armor.[8]

At first glance, this eyewitness account seems to indicate a tremendous number of "monk-warriors" at Kōfukuji, but it bears closer examination before we draw any conclusions. First, although it is safe to say that the courtyard must have been full of upset members of the clergy, one must be wary about exaggeration of the numbers. One should not, therefore, overlook the possibility that Mitsunaga may have exaggerated the situation to mask his own failure to effectively convey the order from the regent. Second, it is curious that Kanezane pointed out the young monk wearing a robe over his armor. Does this mean that he was the only one among the monks standing who was dressed in that fashion, or that none of the other participants was dressed in both armor and monk garments? Both readings are plausible, and although I would tend to favor the second interpretation, the fact that this combination is pointed out in either case suggests that it was unusual. With the exception of this young monk, the clergy members who assembled in the courtyard were not, in other words, armed monks, but rather menial workers and other temple associates who may have carried arms. This separation of monks and clergy members suggests a third point, offering an indication of the social distance between the learned monks, who were taken aback by the show of force, and those referred to as *daishu*. Mitsunaga first read the edict to the ranking monks, who in turn were expected to transmit its contents to the clergy assembled to show their displeasure.

The presence of armed fellows among the lower-ranking clergy is indisputable, but the above account still offers no support of the view that they were full-fledged monks. If anything, the note about the acolyte wearing armor together with a monk's robe points in the opposite direction, indicating that armed clerics were little more than monastic employees. In a separate incident just a few months later, when it ordered that estates and branch temples earlier confiscated from Tōdaiji be returned, the court demonstrated its awareness of distinctions within the cleric organization, but without indicating actual knowledge about the roles of the identified groups. The court also stipulated that the "possessions of evil monks and their masters" should be held by the main temple.[9] The implications here are quite clear: While the estates of individual cloisters and monks were to be returned, those belonging to evil elements within the clergy would be transferred to the monastic complex in general.

An even clearer example of factionalism inside the monasteries can be found in records relating to the early stages of the Genpei War, when Kiyomori struggled to contain resistance from elements of the Kōfukuji clergy. In the fifth month of 1180, as the disenchanted Prince Mochihito called the nation to arms against the "Taira usurpers" from his hideout at Onjōji, rumblings of rebellion came from the southern capital as well. Kōfukuji, in particular, was used by anti-Taira warriors as a haven and a point from which to mount resistance. When the Taira-led imperial court met to develop a plan of action against the rebelling warriors and temples, a discussion ensued between Taira supporters who wanted to launch a full-scale attack and conservative courtiers who wanted a more detailed investigation of who the rebels were within each complex. One of the ranking nobles, Fujiwara no Kanezane, opined that the people responsible for the offensive acts were not the general clergy, but evil elements within it, and that the temple's general properties should be spared while the "evil clergy" ought to be apprehended.[10] The Taira leaders were persuaded by Kanezane's reasoning and refrained from attacking Nara at that point, only to burn both Kōfukuji and Tōdaiji to the ground six months later after prolonged bickering and exchanges of threats between the temples and the Taira camp. The wisdom of hindsight tells us that the Taira made crucial mistakes in assuming too much coherence not only within Kōfukuji but also within Enryakuji. There, despite support from the monastery's ranking monks, its forces did not become the ally the Taira had expected because of resistance from the *dōshu*.

Coming to grips with the division of responsibilities, the occasionally conflicting interests of monastic community members, and the monastic population's general lack of homogeneity is crucial to not only understanding the monasteries themselves but also their interaction with other parts of society. Consider the use of the term *akusō*, "evil monks." Although commonly misunderstood to refer solely to armed monks,[11] it was in fact applied to anyone engaging in activities the secular authorities considered subversive to the interests of government leaders, noble abbots, or to the interests of the monastery in general. *Akusō* first appears in early Heian sources, but recurs with increasing frequency from the *insei* period. In 1142, for instance, fifteen "evil monks" from Kōfukuji were exiled to Mutsu Province in the north for engaging in rebellious activities. One courtier noted that many of the monks punished were said to be educated in the way of the Law, which indicates that members of the ranking classes could also earn the "evil" epithet.[12] In another case, a well-educated Enryakuji monk named Yūkei, became notorious as "an evil monk without par within the three pagodas [of Enryakuji]." Yūkei began as an Onjōji monk, but following a transfer to Enryakuji, he became involved in the factional politics surrounding the head abbot Myōun, taking the lead in an 1177 incident in which the Enryakuji monks freed Myōun as he was being taken into exile by court warriors. At that point, he is said to have put on armor and used a *naginata* with a three-foot-long blade.[13]

Although some evil monks were clearly armed, it is less evident just what activities other such monks were engaged in. In fact, the term was commonly used to designate monks who did not perform according to the abbot's wishes, which does not necessarily mean they were armed. An even more persuasive criticism against the old view can be found in an entry from the *Chūyūki,* dating to 1104:

> Tenth month, thirtieth day. Recently, [Minamoto no] Yoshiie and Yoshitsuna, and the imperial police captains have been ordered to secure the eastern and western areas of Hieizan, and to arrest *evil monks and fellows carrying arms who ascend the mountain.* Moreover, they are to arrest evil monks in Kyoto.[14] (italics added)

The distinction made here between evil monks and men who ascended the mountain with weapons is striking, although its meaning is not immediately clear. It is possible that the author was merely distinguishing between monks and secular supporters, and in that case "evil monks" may indicate armed monks. But considering contemporary usage of the term, this is highly unlikely. Rather, the quote seems to indicate two types of actors—monks who behave contrary to the orders of the abbot and are in general unruly, and fellows of any kind carrying weapons.

This interpretation is also born out if we examine entries in the wide range of sources available in databases at the Historiographical Institute at the University of Tokyo, which yields a total of sixty-nine instances of the term in documents and diaries from the mid-eleventh to the mid-sixteenth centuries.[15] Although it is difficult to group "evil monks" in a single category, it quickly becomes obvious that *akusō* was used not simply for monastic members involved in armed confrontations. Twenty-two of the cases concern the illegal appropriation of harvests and intrusions into private estates, eight involve general rowdiness and another seven protests or other politically oriented activities. Of the remaining thirty-two, the causes behind eighteen remain unknown, and only fourteen can be directly related to armed conflicts. Therefore, even though scholars have overwhelmingly identified the *akusō* as armed monks, this is not born out by the record. Rather, the term refers more broadly to unruly elements in the monastic

community who engaged in a range of activities unbefitting monks following the Buddhist precepts.

Akusō were not confined to the monastic complexes but were also present in provincial estates. For example, as Tōdaiji's estates increased in Iga
Province in the twelfth century, the ambitious estate manager *(azukari dokoro)* Kakunin imposed an extraordinary tax in the third month of 1158,
when "evil monks" from the villages who collected the tax claimed that it
was ordered by the estate proprietor.[16] In this record, the *akusō* label indicates the perspective of local resident officials *(zaichō kanjin),* who were un-
happy about the extra tax. The label's charge is reversed in 1144 edicts from
the Tōdaiji clergy encouraging the inhabitants of Kuroda Estate to assemble *akusō* in armed resistance against resident officials, who were attempting to restrict the temple's control over the estate. Despite the contradictory relationship resident officials and the clergy had with local *akusō,* the
term's usage in both cases indicates a top-down perspective that had been
adopted equally by representatives of the provincial government and the
clergy in Nara. In fact, *akusō* was an appellation used not only by capital
nobles and ranking monks, but at times by the lower-ranking clerics themselves. In such cases, the term refers to clerics who acted without the consent or sanction of their larger community.

Community consent played a crucial role in legitimizing cleric activities.[17] For instance, clerics of the largest monasteries, most notably those
of Enryakuji and Kōfukuji, held in common a notion about divine justice. Briefly stated, unanimous agreement among members of the clergy
on a policy or course of action signified, ipso facto, that the divine powers supported their decision and they were sanctioned to carry it out. In
court diaries, this divine justice, in the case of Kōfukuji, was referred to as
"Yamashina justice" (Yamashina *dōri),* stemming from the temple's original location. Studies by the British social historian E. P. Thompson on riots
and the mob in eighteenth-century England show that such ideas were by
no means unique to Japan. Thompson argues that crowds resorted to riots
because of a widely held belief that they were entitled to do so and that they
were acting on behalf of the larger community.[18] The striking similarity between two rather different societies and historical contexts highlights the
importance of the ideological climate in which mass protests and violence
take place, and this certainly deserves more attention in future studies.

Returning to the context of violence in late Heian and Kamakura Japan,
the notion of divine justice, together with the concept of mutual dependence between Imperial and Buddhist Law *(ōbō buppō sōi),* provided both
the main ideological foundations for the forceful protests and a powerful

way to pressure the capital nobles. Where the clergy from a major monastery en toto resorted to protest, there are no references to *akusō*, signifying an acknowledgment by the imperial court that this strategy was a privilege granted to a few temples. But when the term does appear in conjunction with protests, it consistently indicates those in which only certain members of the clergy—that is, the evil elements—acted on their own without the consent and support of the entire clergy. Only such protests were seen as unjustified acts. This kind of distinction is easy to miss, but one case in particular points to not only its validity, but how it could be deployed. In the evening of the seventeenth day of the third month of 1142, several tens of evil monks from Onjōji wearing armor and carrying weapons climbed Mt. Hiei and burned five or six monk dwellings in the Tōtō section. Two monks, named Keichō and Chōjun, were interrogated as ringleaders, but they defended themselves claiming that they had acted on behalf of, and with the endorsement of, their entire monastery. They attempted to justify their attack by invoking divine justice in the spirit of *ichimi dōshin* (fellows of one heart) and thereby deny that they acted on their own as dissidents.[19] The term *akusō,* then, might refer not only to monks who violated the precepts but also to those who acted without the consent of the entire monastery.

But the term "evil" could apply to more than the various monastery residents. Most famously, the expression *akutō,* "evil bands," was used for the fourteenth-century *gekokujō* (the lower overturning those above) movement, in which lower classes challenged their superiors. Specifically, it referred to farmers, warriors, and other locals who banded together to resist tax collection and the rule of proprietors primarily in and around Kyoto. Thus, one must keep in mind that *akutō,* like *akusō,* reflects the bias of rulers and a concern with threats to the social order as conceived in ruling ideologies. Nevertheless, it also offers an important glimpse into the social structures of the period and the changes under way at the time.

Given the central role played by temples in Kamakura and Muromachi Japan, it is hardly surprising that the emergence of evil bands also affected them greatly. Temples were challenged as institutions by the *akutō* since the many intrusions and tax refusals by local bands threatened the temples' financial foundation. And because temple organizations also included a large number of traders, farmers, and administrators with the means and incentives to resist authority, *akutō* were also reported within the monastic communities. For example, among Enryakuji's followers, certain monks engaged extensively in trade, but in reality many of these men were monks only in name and used their religious titles to qualify for judicial protection under the Tendai headquarters on Mt. Hiei. In 1315, having refused to pay the required duty, a band of traders shot arrows at and injured representatives of the military governor at the Hyōgo toll station. We know the identities of these traders from the list of the instigators submitted to the bakufu, which contains the names of twenty monks and seventy-two lay people. Preceptor Ryōkei was considered the leader of the group in his capacity as one of the ranking administrators at Enryakuji, but other educated monks are also listed. Some of the monks had in fact been involved in similar incidents before, and three of them resided close to the toll station, despite the titles indicating that they belonged to specific cloisters on Mt. Hiei.[20]

The account of the conflict also contains details that provide glimpses into how this band fought. The toll station, which was administered by a Tōdaiji manager, provided vital income for the temple. When the traders passed through, they refused to pay the duty, and having driven away the manager, dug in and occupied the station. When the Kamakura Bakufu's branch in Kyoto sent a representative to deal with the situation, he was met by the band members charging out of the barricade to give battle, and in the ensuing fight several of the government warriors were injured.[21] The disturbance was eventually quelled, but it proved to be merely a precursor to more serious and coordinated uprisings and challenges to central authority. Temples and monks were as affected by social upheaval and political changes as the rest of society, and as the gradual militarization of society in the tenth century induced important changes within the monastic communities, so did the social challenges of the thirteenth. Far from being isolated institutions with little connection to the world outside, monasteries were part and parcel of the social developments of the Kamakura age.

Among the many subgroups within the monastery, some were more inclined to use arms than others. We find, for example, references to a group known as *bōjin* (residential people) in Enryakuji in the late Heian period. In 1168 over one hundred *bōjin* of a ranking monk on Mt. Hiei forced their way into a cloister (the Rengazōin) and ravaged the area. This group broke into several temple halls, harassed administrators, and killed two armed guards. The imperial court condemned the behavior of their leader, a certain Hyōe no jō Toyohara Tomomitsu, who lost his official rank as a result of these acts.[22] Tomomitsu was an accomplished warrior, and while it is impossible to tell if all residential retainers could be so characterized, it appears they were at least a crucial part of the monastic communities and that they had the mind and the means to arm themselves. At least one Heian source makes note of such *bōjin*, suggesting that these residents were a permanent feature in the monasteries.[23] *Bōjin* are also noted in association with conflicts between the Daidenbōin and Kongōbuji of Kōyasan in 1140. According to the *Kōya shunjū*, some residential fellows "assembled large numbers of warriors from various estates" for an attack on their antagonists at the Daidenbōin and the Mitsugon'in, who, for their part, were prepared with armor as well, and so battle ensued.[24] Since this account lacks corroboration in contemporary sources, and because of its later compilation date (1718), almost six centuries after the events it describes, one must be cautious about taking all the details at face value. Nevertheless, the mention of *bōjin* in the context of battles and as leaders of other warriors is supported by other sources. For example, in 1173, Kōfukuji asked Iwashimizu Hachimangū for assistance against Enryakuji, whose *bōjin* had, according to the plea, led hundreds of followers in an attack on a Kōfukuji estate, burning residences and shooting at the local inhabitants.[25]

The ability to lead armed people begs the question of the rank and role of the *bōjin*. Arai Takashige has suggested that they were primarily personal retainers of the monks, an observation supported by their frequent involvement in factional disputes.[26] One fourteenth century source explains that scholar-monks at Kōfukuji did not carry arms but did keep *bōjin,* a privilege enjoyed by monks of noble or elite warrior *(buke)* origin.[27] As residential retainers, they would quite naturally develop their own loyalties and priorities, and one must not be surprised to find them embroiled in conflicts with residents of other cloisters. While these men do not appear to have been monks, they maintained the privileges that monastic membership entailed and could freely engage in secular activities in the service of their masters.

In the late Heian age, the *dōshu,* or monastic workers, stand out as one of the groups that resorted to violence most often. Jōmyō Myōshu, the all-but-invincible warrior in the battle of the bridge at Uji, proclaimed himself to be a monastic worker in the *Heike monogatari,* inducing later observers to equate *dōshu* with *sōhei.* Tomikura Tokujirō, an influential translator of the war tale, explicitly makes that assumption and further calls Myōshu "a *sōhei* of Onjōji."[28] Moreover, the prolonged conflict between monastic workers and scholar-monks on Mt. Hiei in 1178–1179 indicates a relatively high level of military training among the workers. It was this conflict in particular that contributed to Hirata Toshiharu's conclusions that those with the most military training were to be found among the monastic workers. The main clergy *(daishu),* he claimed, was not adverse to fighting, but their principal method of exerting pressure was by invoking the powers of the deities, as indicated by their participation in protests in the capital. Granted, some among the general clergy possessed skills with arms that earned them leadership positions, Hirata believes, as well as the name *akusō.* The monastic workers, in contrast, being accustomed to manual labor and using tools, were generally more physical, and thus the taking up of arms was never far away.[29]

Hirata's attempt to find distinctive groups that fit these various terms is ultimately unsuccessful, for, as already demonstrated, *akusō* were to be found at all levels of the monastic organization, ranging from leaders (treated in the next chapter) to provincial clerics with little religious training. Moreover, the terms *daishu* and *dōshu* are not as distinct as Hirata assumes, since their usage in contemporary diaries demonstrates that worker-monks were frequently seen as members of the clergy. What is valuable in Hirata's analysis, however, is his characterization of the monastic workers' responsibilities within the monasteries. Although some members of the *dōshu* may have taken Buddhist vows, they principally handled administration, management, and other menial tasks, and they frequently lived secular lives with their wives and children. Judging from the references we have, most monastic workers came from local villages, as was the case with Jōmyō Myōshu, some even from families of local notables *(dogō)*. For example, when Kōfukuji forces attacked and burned possessions and numerous buildings of Tōnomine in 1173, the attackers are listed as monastic workers, but with distinctively local names and origins. In fact, we do not find a single monk among the commanders, and one must therefore acknowledge the central role played by not only armed workers, but also local strongmen. Engaged mostly in manual labor but with status and skills above the farming population, many of the strongmen were either local warriors or had learned to use arms through their menial work. As a result, they became known in a later source as "the fellows of hard deeds and carriers of bows and arrows," reflecting, in effect, the process of militarization across society.[30]

One of the biggest challenges of investigating the monastic workers is gauging the level of their religious training and status. Were they merely workers granted monk names with shaved heads and monastic robes, or were they involved in both menial work and in ritual practices? The *Genpei seisuiki* informs us that "those called *dōshu* were originally young *hosshi* [clerics] who served the scholar-monks, or they were intermediary *hosshi*," but these men had also performed Buddhist services on their own and taken meritorious Buddhist names. They accordingly challenged the exclusive right of ordained monks to make offerings to the deities. The worker-monks further aggravated the ranking monks by amassing riches through high interests on loans, which gained them a high degree of independence. With this added prestige and wealth, the chronicle explains, the lower-ranking monks ignored the clergy and their masters, and challenged them in battles.[31]

Although it is a literary source of later date, the implications of this passage in the *Genpei seisuiki* are illuminating. It implies, in short, that the *dōshu* were expected to serve ranking monks as servants, workers, and lower-ranking administrators, and were not to perform their own ceremonies and offerings to the Buddha. It is difficult to find other sources that support such claims, but it is certainly conceivable, despite their decidedly secular roles within the monasteries, that some of the monastic workers may have performed their own rituals even though such privileges were not attached to their regular duties. More significantly, of the various groups within the monasteries, the *dōshu* were surprisingly cohesive and independent in a society where the vertical ties tended to be much stronger than horizontal ones. In fact, it would be no exaggeration to claim that class consciousness was weak among non-elites until the fourteenth century, when the emergence of guilds, village bands, and other organizations fostered a more communal spirit. The monastic workers appear to have prefigured that development, no doubt because the influx of nobles into leadership roles added a new level of tension between the privileged abbots and their staff, whose roles as administrators and workers gave them leverage over temple resources as well as a sense of common cause with administrators outside the monasteries. For instance, when the imperial court attempted to isolate the Enryakuji *dōshu* from their estates during the conflict with scholar-monks late in 1179, it was an obvious attempt to not only cut off their resources, but also to diminish their human resources and support beyond the confines of the monastic establishment.[32]

In their role as administrators, the *dōshu* were in frequent contact with other officials in temple estates, but there were also cases when they were themselves appointed to such offices. In a document from 1239, we learn that the land steward *(gesu)* office of Tamai Estate in Yamashiro Province had been given to a monastic administrator.[33] Other examples include Iga's Kuroda Estate and Settsu's Nagasu Estate, which had a seventy-year-long history of appointing *dōshu* as administrators by 1315.[34] Documents in the extensive source collections of Tōdaiji indicate that many members of the *dōshu* had strong ties to and resided in temple estates. This enabled the administrators of a Tōdaiji cloister named Hokkedō to not only steal crops in Nagasu, but also to obtain and maintain their own land in other areas, such as on the nearby Kawakami Estate.[35]

The clerics *(hosshi)*, who have already appeared in a number of the documents cited above, constitute another important group within the monastic communities. In fact, the worker-monks notwithstanding, it was these clerics who were most commonly identified as monk-warriors in later writings, including the encyclopedic work *Koji ruien*, first published in 1901, which explains that "monk-warriors are military clerics *[hosshi musha]* who wrapped their heads in a monk cloth, and put on armor and carried arms. Their armament was barely different from that of other warriors."[36]

The term *hosshi*, while meaning "teacher of the law" could be used to refer to monks of various ranks. Several documents mention monks with the title *dai hosshi* (great master of the law), and we also find the term *chūkan hosshi* (intermediate clerics) that indicate mid-level clerics who were being trained for further advancement. Over time, however, use of the term changed and most *hosshi* appear to have been similar to the monastic workers, since both were lower-ranking clerics who lacked extensive training in Buddhist teachings and had few opportunities for advancement.[37] The best-known members of this group may be the mountain clerics *(yama hosshi)*[38] of Enryakuji, a term used in Shirakawa's famous lament about matters beyond his control:

> The flow of the Kamo River, the role of the dice, and the mountain clerics are things I cannot control.[39]

It is easy to sympathize with Shirakawa's statement given the frequent references to the clerics' unruly behavior. A prime example is the 1040 conflict over Onjōji's plan to establish a separate ordination platform, which spurred Enryakuji followers to gather in Kyoto to wreak havoc:

> The capital is full of people armed with bows and arrows, and violent and evil clerics *[ran'aku no hosshiwara]* are acting wantonly with their swords and rioting, while others keep setting fires.[40]

Hosshi was also used to denote lay people who had taken Buddhist vows without official sanction, or who simply dressed as monks and wandered the countryside. One entry from 1180 in Fujiwara no Kanezane's diary describes a lay monk named Hirata, who led a band of followers in Iga Province, where they harassed the inhabitants, killing sixteen by beheading. This Hirata, referred to as a *hosshi*, further traveled to other provinces in the Kinai, toppling the fortification of another lay monk in Kōga.[41] *Hosshi* is here used, in other words, for warriors who had taken Buddhist vows but still lived secular lives, which offers further evidence for the notion that the *hosshi* within monastic centers were far from monks in appearance and profession, and that many of them had warfare as their main occupation.

The monastic communities of late Heian and Kamakura Japan were complex conglomerates that reflected their contemporary social milieu. Besides trained monks, temples employed a wide range of administrators and menial workers, whose occupations put them in the middle ground between the monastic rules of Buddhism and the secular world. Their duties situated them in the realm of secular occupations, but they benefited from the protection and privileges offered by the monastic communities. In fact, this situation was not unique to Japan. According to the *History of Koryŏ (Koryŏ sa)*, monks in the north of the Korean peninsula raised armies in the early eleventh century, and about a century later monk armies were assembled to defend the northern border against Jurchen invaders. These armies consisted mainly of members of the *sŭngdo* (J. *sōto*), the same group of primarily menial workers referred to as clergy in Japanese sources.[42] The *dōshu* and the *hosshi* were thus central members of monastic communities, whose connections outside the temple complexes reached into areas where there were large numbers of potential administrators, menial workers, and even warriors, for whom weapons were not only accessible but also part of their toolbox.

Estate Warriors and *Jinnin*

In contrast to the complex origins and social standing of those inside the monasteries who carried arms, fighters brought from outside can be a bit more easily characterized as belonging to one of two groups—estate warriors or shrine members *(jinnin)*. Of these, the secular warriors were, as can be expected, the most prominent in violent confrontations. Most of them came to their affiliation with temples through the estate system, where they served as land managers at various levels. As is well known, warriors had a penchant for hoarding larger shares of the crop yields than they were entitled to and used a variety of pretexts to justify their actions, as indicated by the conflict between the Sasaki and Enryakuji mentioned earlier. But temples also became important allies for warrior managers, since they could obtain additional income by "donating" the estate to a temple patron. The temple would be promised a fixed amount of the yield, and the warrior would be allowed to keep a larger share of the taxes. On one occasion, the manager of Kasahara Estate, Motsutaka, failed to deliver rent owed to the Minister of the Left's family and was subsequently removed from his post in the fall of 1106. Motsutaka promptly responded by trying to "donate" the estate to Onjōji or Enryakuji in hopes of using the clergy of these temples as leverage against the rightful landholders.[43] The measure failed and Motsutaka was arrested, but his very attempt demonstrates an expectation that such arrangements could be easily created.

There are several similar cases, such as when the lay monk Morotō donated an estate in Yamato Province in 1145 to both Kōfukuji and Kinpusen (described in the previous chapter) in an attempt to secure as much income as possible. Suffice it to say that local warrior-administrators knew well the advantages and strengths of engaging a religious patron. By the same token, monasteries in general and the clergy in particular were also aware of the value of the private estates and having ties with the warriors residing there. These warrior forces were frequently brought in to aid in conflicts, both by the monasteries as a whole and by individuals. In the Tendai sibling dispute of 1081, when the Onjōji clergy interrupted the Hie Festival, one source notes that they led several hundred warriors. Other contemporary sources contain similar information, repeatedly referring to the large numbers or bands of warriors involved in the disturbance. Enryakuji monks were believed to have led an army of thousands in retaliation against Onjōji's own thousands of warrior-retainers *(sūsen no zuihei)*, clearly indicating the prominent role secular fighters played in inter-monastery confrontations.[44]

During the 1113 dispute over the abbotship of Kiyomizudera, when Kōfukuji followers threatened to engage Enryakuji since the court had been unable to render a fair judgment, one courtier, Fujiwara no Munetada, noted:

> The clergy of the southern capital riot incessantly as the warrior bands *[gunpei]* of Kinpusen and Yoshino, and estate and provincial residents of Yamato, all gather with their bows and arrows and follow [the Kōfukuji lead], amounting to an unknown number. The Fujiwara chieftain has issued an order that there will be severe punishments if these warriors *[bushi]* come to the capital, but I doubt that the clergy will obey.[45]

These armed men were perhaps neither elite nor even professional warriors, but rather locals with access to arms. It is therefore not surprising that when government warriors were eventually dispatched to stop them, they gave only brief battle in which the Kōfukuji side sustained most of the casualties. Munetada noted that more than thirty members of the Kōfukuji clergy had been shot and killed, and about ninety secular warriors *(zoku heishi)*, of whom three were shrine members, were injured. By contrast, only two government warriors were killed, though several tens were injured.[46]

A similar incident involving Kōfukuji and Enryakuji as the disputing parties further indicates the role of secular warriors in the monastic forces. During funeral ceremonies for Emperor Nijō in 1165, a brawl broke out over the seating order, and some of the Kōfukuji monks seem to have destroyed Tendai buildings around Kyoto. The Enryakuji clergy wasted no time in retaliating, as they attacked and destroyed parts of Kiyomizudera, Kōfukuji's branch temple in the eastern part of the capital. Enryakuji also demanded that the several Kōfukuji monks and government warriors who had come to the rescue of Kiyomizudera be punished; this resulted in a demotion of the head abbot and the exile of eight of his followers. In addition, one warrior, Minamoto no Yoshimoto, was also sent into exile. The Nara monks in turn became enraged and began to prepare for an outright attack on Enryakuji. They detained the messenger of the Fujiwara chieftain, ignoring his attempts to calm them. Some Kōfukuji warriors were in fact on their way to Kyoto, camping at the Kizu River in the middle of the tenth month, when the court managed to appease the temple forces by promoting some of its ranking monks. One record states that among those assembling at Kizu were "warriors [heishi] from throughout the province and branch temples."[47]

Further evidence of local warrior involvement in monastic battles can be found in the early stages of the Genpei War when Kōfukuji and Onjōji in particular opposed the Taira control of the capital. Tensions heightened in the twelfth month of 1180, when Kiyomori had decided to return the court to Kyoto after moving it to his Fukuhara Estate. Kujō Kanezane noted the monastic opposition and increased tension in his diary, writing that the Nara clergy were rioting in great numbers and had called together warriors from branches and temple estates.[48] Three years later, following the Taira's initial defeat in the capital region, Retired Emperor Go-Shirakawa pleaded for help with the Kōfukuji abbot as the Taira planned a counterattack to retake central Japan. But the abbot refused out of fear that a rally against the Taira would create a critical mass of "evil monks," who might then engage in various illegal and violent activities. Go-Shirakawa realized the abbot's precarious situation and decided that he would himself issue an order to the clergy, thus invoking imperial authority over unruly elements. "But in the meantime," he stated, "use the power of your office to assemble the warriors [heishi] of the branch temples and estates, and prepare them to be dispatched."[49]

Both temple organizations and their military forces, then, were considerably more complex than scholars have realized. On one hand, we find a noble abbot referring to elements of the clergy he cannot control as "evil monks"; on the other hand, secular warriors with no religious training were brought in to fight for the temple on the basis of their affiliation with a temple estate or local branch temple. These warriors spent most of their time in the provinces but were occasionally called to serve during times of conflict.

Some temples engaged warriors inside the compound in times of peace as well, in part to keep tabs on their men on the various estates. One example of this survives in the records of Daigoji, a Shingon temple in the Fushimi district just south of Kyoto. Apparently, the temple rotated warriors from its various estates to serve as guards. According to a 1151 administrative record, the temple estates were to supply five warriors to serve monthly at the temple. The only exceptions were the last two months of the lunar calendar, which were split between certain estates and officers. Thus, the manager *(gesu)* of one estate performed the guard service for the first half of the eleventh month, while the manager of another was responsible for the second half. The twelfth month was divided into six-to-nine-day rotations among the managers of the other estates. Finally, the document states that this five-warrior service shall continue in perpetuity.[50] Assuming that the detailed division of services in the final two months was based on the specific size, yield, and general conditions of the various estates, it reflects not only detailed knowledge about each estate, but also the close monitoring of the temple possessions and personnel.

Unless Daigoji was an exception, it seems likely that similar service arrangements existed at other temples as well, which in turn offers one explanation as to why secular warriors would be familiar with and often present inside temple precincts. A document from 1325 lists tens of warriors for each estate owing service to Tōji, but since these services included the delivery and stocking of taxes and dues, which required manual work rather than guard duty, they were something closer to the regular duties of warrior-managers at their own estates.[51] In either case, evidence for the presence of warrior-managers working inside monasteries is ample for the late Heian and Kamakura eras.

In addition to the temples' ability to bring in armed men from the outside, individual monks sometimes ventured outside the temple to find armed allies. One Enryakuji monk and a certain Taira no Masahira conspired to break into an estate belonging to Tado, a branch shrine of Tōji, thus also challenging Tōji's rights to Tado itself. The court eventually confirmed the estate and Tado's status as a Tōji branch in 1089, but new problems arose in 1105, when another Enryakuji monk allied himself with the former governor of Izu, Minamoto no Kunifusa, to wrest control of the same estate. Despite summonses from the court, Kunifusa stayed put on the estate, where he harassed and killed some of the farmers. The occupation continued until late in 1107, when it ended only after the court had issued repeated edicts in Tōji's favor.[52]

At Kōfukuji, monk-administrators often allied themselves with estate warriors *(shōhei)* to gain greater control of the estate and its income at the local level. A literary account of these overlapping interests can be found in the *Genpei seisuiki,* which offers detailed information along these lines in connection with an internal conflict at Kōfukuji. Hari-no-shō in Yamato Province was designated to supply oil products for Kōfukuji's Saikondō section, but in 1178 the estate manager Ogawa Tōtada conspired with the Kōfukuji director Kaison to take the revenue meant to cover oil production and delivery for themselves. The worker-monks of the Saikondō responded by allying themselves with Tosabō Shōshun, who led a large force onto the Hari Estate and attacked Tōtada. At this point, Kaison rallied the clergy, drove Shōshun off the estate, and prepared to lodge a divine demonstration in Kyoto to persuade the court to arrest his opponent. Shōshun responded by assembling a large number of followers whom he led to the clergy's meeting at the temple, where they managed to stop the planning and broke the holy branch prepared for the divine demonstration. The clergy naturally became upset and sent an appeal to the court to have Shōshun punished, but he never appeared in Kyoto.[53]

Of the various categories of monks and warriors associated with monastic forces, the mystical mountain clerics *(yama hosshi)* have added a particular burnish to the *sōhei* image, even though they appear only infrequently in Heian and Kamakura sources. On just a few occasions are these figures, who were reputed to wander the mountains and passes and live in isolated areas where they pursued secret practices, actually described as something other than a cleric, or distinguished from the Mt. Hiei "mountain clerics." The best-known account of armed mountain clerics can be found in a chronicle detailing the events of the Jōkyū War of 1221. There clergy from Kumanodera and Kiyomizudera and mountain clerics from the province of Harima are said to have joined the failed challenge to the Kamakura Bakufu under Retired Emperor Go-Toba.[54] One chronicle describes the mountain clerics as wanderers armed with foot soldiers' swords as well as with long swords and *naginata,* who fought bravely like warriors.[55] Like the monk-workers, the mountain clerics were not educated monks, and they frequently performed duties outside the immediate monastic complex; but they also seem to have been less organized than the workers, who worked inside the monastery and functioned more like a coherent group.

Among the followers residing outside the monasteries, the estate warriors were likely the people best equipped to fight, but the shrine servants included warrior-like figures as well. Armed supporters of Kōfukuji, for instance, can be counted as belonging to one or the other of these two groups. On the one hand, we find monastic workers who functioned as local estate administrators, and on the other hand, followers of local strongmen *(koku-min)*, who resembled regular warriors in appearance and were referred to as *jinnin* under the protection of Kasuga.[56] Many of these shrine servants were traders and artisans, and because they provided products essential to the shrines—and by extension the monastic complex with which the shrine was associated—they played a crucial role in the wellbeing of their patrons. *Jinnin* status was highly desirable in that it offered judicial immunity, but many locals also sought it to evade taxes. In 1135 Fujiwara no Atsumitsu complained that "residents of the various provinces evade taxes by calling themselves shrine servants, or by becoming evil monks; they travel around and resist the administration of the provincial officers." Referring to a report submitted by Miyoshi Kiyoyuki, Atsumitsu even claimed that compared to two centuries earlier only one tenth the number of the people in the provinces paid taxes.[57] Naturally, this is a biased observation, and there were also cases in which the governor and his administrators were the offenders, but in their reports to the court they would characterize their victims as the evildoers. This pattern became especially prevalent from the late tenth century on, when many governors saw their appointments as little more than an opportunity to rake in the substantial income necessary to support their lifestyle and careers in Kyoto. Under these abuses, farmers discovered that becoming affiliated with a local shrine connected to one of the major religious centers could gain them a measure of protection. A further motivation was the prestige of becoming part of a powerful organization with links to the very top of the social and political pyramid.

Shrine servants, like warrior-managers, exploited the protection that monasteries and shrines could offer and often disrespected the laws of the court and their monastic patrons. Some scholars have concluded that they were little more than thieves and marauders, who used their judicial immunity to enrich themselves. Although these conclusions are not justified across the board since many shrine servants were in fact artisans and traders who did serve the temples and shrines, cases of rampant abuse certainly did occur. During one 1116 conflict between Kōfukuji and Enryakuji, for instance, Emperor Toba issued an edict to the shrine Iwashimizu Hachimangū in which he condemned the activities of its *jinnin* and monks:

> In recent years, the shrine members [of Iwashimizu] have favored evil behavior, and the monks have made selfishness their foundation. They invade public and private fields and appropriate prop-

erty from high and low. Not limited to the Kinai, not respecting borders, they gather and assemble bands, filling [the regions] with fortifications so that they bristle with barricades. Not only do they cause hardship for local residents, they also engage in battles with their fellows. Throwing away learning, they embrace weapons; they take off their monk's garments and put on armor to burn down hermitages and destroy monk dwellings.[58]

The ultimate benefit for the most ambitious strongmen was the judicial immunity temples could extend. We know of several cases where criminals escaped to temples for protection. One, following an incident that resulted in a death in Nara, recounts that the guilty party quickly escaped to hide out at Ninnaji in Kyoto. When the imperial police were dispatched to the temple, the clergy refused to let them in, claiming there was no precedent for warriors of the imperial police to enter the temple. Thus they shielded the killer from punishment.[59]

Although territorially immune to the jurisdiction of secular authorities, religious institutions were, in fact, expected to hand over criminals when asked to do so. Of course, this principle did not always work in practice, not the least because many members of the monastic and shrine communities had more in common with the perpetrators than with the nobles at court. These bonds are apparent in a case from 1123, when criminals from Echizen were being transported to receive punishment, and "evil monks" from Enryakuji attacked the Taira guard and released them. The court demanded that the prisoners be handed over, but despite urging from the head abbot, the clergy refused to comply, responding that "there is not a single evil monk on Mt. Hiei." In a separate incident, when the court toughened its stance and ordered that murderers among the clergy also be arrested, the abbots of Gion and Kiyomizudera stated that those members had suddenly fled.[60] Even though the courtiers knew that troublemakers and criminals hid inside the religious complexes, unless the community handed them over voluntarily there was little the secular authorities could do. Such was the strength of the judicial immunity enjoyed by the temples, a persuasive reflection of the cooperative and multi-polar political system in late Heian and Kamakura Japan.

Jinnin, then, were far from passive locals recruited to work for shrines. They were ambitious men of some stature and skill who, by combining that power with the status granted them through shrine affiliation, could exploit those privileges—and other people living in the area as well. Most of them may not have had the same training as the elite warriors serving as estate managers or in various guard positions in the capital, but they used weapons as needed to pursue and protect their local ambitions. In the 1081 dispute between Enryakuji and Onjōji, for instance, it was the shrine membership, who, fully aware of the tensions between the Tendai siblings, asked Onjōji for support in resisting the taxes imposed on them. And in 1120 the same shrine affiliates attempted to extend their influence in Ōtsu, which forced a confrontation between Enryakuji and Onjōji followers.[61]

The *jinnin* remained a crucial element of the larger shrines throughout the Kamakura age and they continued to be involved in armed confrontations. During a dispute between warriors and shrine servants of Hiesha in 1314, the warriors destroyed the new Hie Shrine's main building, and several of them also sustained injuries inflicted by the shrine's defenders.[62] Some shrine affiliates resided in estates rather than in communities attached directly to the shrine or temple. In a document from 1321, Tōdaiji listed a total of eighty-nine *jinnin* from its thirty-six branches and estates who owed service in the form of carrying sacred palanquins *(mikoshi)* that belonged to Shintō affiliates.[63] Such lists suggest the operational importance of the shrine affiliates as well as the diversity of their duties. In one case, we also find a subgroup within the shrine affiliates, referred to as *shirōto*, whose duties were generally diverse as well. Like the *jinnin*, this group could be responsible for administering and policing estates and for forwarding taxes to the shrine. In reality, they commonly ventured out on their own and formed warrior bands like those in which the shrine affiliates participated.[64]

If the *jinnin* comprised a diverse group ranging from workers and administrators to local warriors, their special privileges and status made them a group with common interests primarily outside the precincts and purposes of the monastery. They not only performed their trades under a shrine's protection, they also might and did act aggressively, and often violently, on the pretext of patron sanctions. The mountain clerics were not as coherent a group, and therefore had far less impact as a cohort. Most armed men in the monasteries had much in common with non-monastic warriors in terms of social status, but the temple estate warriors stand out as the better trained. Estate warriors could not easily be distinguished from regular warriors, for they used secular names and made no pretense of being monks. Their only distinction was serving a religious patron instead of a noble one. The kinship between secular and religious fighters can be demonstrated socially through analysis of temple and warrior networks, as I have done here, but scrutiny of warfare strategies and techniques additionally reveals important commonalities.

Warfare and Battle Strategies

Because monastic forces are so closely associated with the image of the *sōhei,* there is a general assumption that monastic warriors were clearly distinguishable by their accoutrements—monk's garments, the head cowl and *naginata,* with the occasional complement of a sword. But both contemporary and later literary records tell a different story. In point of fact, the weaponry and warfare strategies used by monastic forces were identical to those of the secular warrior class, and modern images notwithstanding, temple warriors used a range of weapons depending on the circumstances. Among the literary sources, the *Heike monogatari* passage featuring Jōmyō Myōshu describes him and his compatriot worker-monk (named Ichirai) as fighting with bows and arrows, *naginata,* swords, and dirks.[65] The *Heike monogatari* and the *Genpei seisuiki* also include an episode in which one "evil monk" named Eikaku fights with exceptionally large swords and arrows that highlight the same kind of superhuman strength associated with the archery of the more famous Minamoto no Tametomo (1139–1170).[66]

Displays of shooting from horseback and other archery feats are usually associated exclusively with those who are today considered samurai, but monastic warriors also mastered such skills. During the annual Kegon ceremony at Tōdaiji in 1212, a number of adept novices performed feats of mounted archery *(yabusame* and *kasagake).* Given that *yabusame* was a speed event, in which the archer shot arrows in rapid succession, and *kasagake* involved long-distance shooting, both performed on horseback, there is little doubt that these skills required extensive training. These events, staged as competitions near Tōdaiji, drew quite a few spectators, some of whom were monks and novices visiting from Kyoto.[67] Mounted warriors participated in the Wakanomiya Festival at Kasuga in 1136, indicating that this temple's clergy was also a diverse lot.[68] Even later picture scrolls, which have more than other sources been interpreted as supporting the stereotypical *sōhei* image, show monastic warriors sporting a remarkable range of weapons and garments (this topic will be considered in greater detail in chapter 5).

For defensive purposes, monastic forces erected simple barricades, known as *jōkaku,* as did other warriors. These were not major fortifications, nor even the wooden stockades used increasingly in the fourteenth century throughout central Japan. Many were merely heaps of wood and debris, meant to impede or block an opponent's forward progress, while in more sophisticated cases they might be embankments, sometimes with shallow moats and an entrance way with some kind of gate. Accounts of more extended fighting, such as that of the Genpei War, only rarely refer to any advanced constructions, although there is some evidence of "shield walls" *(kaidate)* in later sources.[69] As Karl Friday has pointed out, however, these devices were uncommon at best during the Genpei War, and barricades were the most common strategy to mount a temporary defensive line and slow an enemy's advance.[70]

It is not surprising that barricades are first noted in association with monasteries in the second half of the twelfth century, when factionalism and the tendency to settle disputes through violence had become more commonplace. During a skirmish between the clergies of Tōtō and Saitō in 1167, the Saitō clergy built a barricade to stake out their area on Mt. Hiei. About a decade later, as tensions mounted between scholar-monks and workers, both sides erected barriers, but their effectiveness against larger determined forces was limited. According to a later literary source, the workers of several estates around the Kinai area conspired with thieves and mountain brigands and launched a successful attack on the scholar-monks on Mt. Hiei, before the latter were bailed out by government warriors.[71] Still, such barricades became even more commonplace during the Genpei War. Onjōji forces are said to have erected one to withstand the Heike assault in the fifth month of 1180, and the *Azuma kagami,* a later chronicle, states that "government [Heike] warriors burned the Omurodo in Uji because the Onjōji clergy had built a barricade."[72] Several barricades were also built in and about Nara at the same time, as noted in the *Heike monogatari,* which explains that the Nara clergy constructed barricades at Narazaka and Hannyaji in the fifth month of 1180.[73]

A fifteenth-century picture scroll, the *Aki no yo no nagamonogatari,* contains a scene from the Genpei War in which warriors are seen charging up an embankment defended by another group of warriors with shields.[74] Although the image reflects the strategies and military equipment of its own time as described in the *Taiheiki,* rather than the era it purports to represent, it is of considerable interest because it depicts the Onjōji defenders as warriors rather than monks (see Figure 4).[75] In fact, the stereotypical monk-warrior, the *sōhei,* is nowhere to be found, indicating that even at that time, depictions of monastic warriors were much more varied than assumed.

Although quite common during the civil war of the 1180s, barricades were used even during minor skirmishes, as shown in an account of a conflict in 1203 in which the Enryakuji scholar-monks are said to have again built barricades against the forces of the workers. To quell this disturbance, the court dispatched a force, which was met by the monastic workers at

FIGURE 4. Taira warriors attacking Onjōji barricades during the Genpei War, according to the fifteenth century *Aki no yo no nagamonogatari.* Reprinted with permission from the Metropolitan Museum of Art, New York.

Hachiōji, one of the Hie shrines, where they had also built a barricade.[76] A battle ensued, and while the details are obscure in contemporary sources, the *Azuma kagami,* a later chronicle, provides us with one version:

> Around the fifth month [of 1203] the Shaka *dōshu* of the Saitō were in disagreement with the *gakushō.* All of the *dōshu* began to assemble and lined up in front of the bath hall. On the first day of the eighth month, the *gakushō* prepared a barricade at the Dainagon Hill and at the Minamidani's Tōibō Hall, driving out the *dōshu.* On the sixth day, the *dōshu* led skilled warriors from three estates, climbed the mountain, and attacked those barricades. There were too many injuries and casualties on both sides to count. However, because of an edict issued by the retired emperor, the *dōshu* abandoned the barricades on the seventh and retreated. The *gakushō* left the barricades on the seventeenth and came down to the capital, and for now, the situation is calm.[77]

Not only are the defensive strategies in this account identical to those used by the warrior class, the forces that appear are clearly estate warriors, which offers further evidence for the important presence of such fighters among monastic armies.

Although not reliable in its details about conditions in the early thirteenth century, an image in the fourteenth-century *Hōnen shōnin eden* de-

FIGURE 5. Government forces attack worker-monk barricade at Hachiōji on Mt. Hiei in 1203, according to the *Hōnen shōnin eden*. By permission of Chion'in, Kyoto.

picts the barricade at Hachiōji, with accompanying text that explains how the monastic workers erected defensive walls at Hachiōji and faced off against bakufu warriors dispatched to quell the disturbance. Its description finds some support in contemporary sources, even if the scroll erroneously lists the date as 1192 instead of 1203. But it is the depiction of the forces, with both sides looking every part the secular warrior, that is of greatest importance, since it also contradicts the traditional image of the *sōhei* in monk robes with a head cowl and *naginata* (Figure 5).[78]

To mention another example, a contemporary diarist noted how Kiyomizudera's clerics both dug moats and erected barricades in preparation for a fight with Enryakuji in 1213.[79] According to a later account, the conflict began when Seikanji, a branch of Enryakuji, complained that Kiyomizudera had built a new temple hall on its property. As tensions mounted, the Kiyomizudera clergy built their barricades, inducing the Hiei monks to assemble at Chōrakuji east of the capital in preparation for a possible confrontation. To prevent a disturbance, the court dispatched imperial police captains to destroy Kiyomizudera's barricades. The clerics were told to promptly don their monk robes and assemble in front of the temple, which signaled the end of the disturbance.[80] Again, we find images that stand in sharp contrast to depictions of the *sōhei* stereotype, since, according to this source, the Kiyomizudera clergy were apparently not wearing monk's garments during their military preparations.

Two years after this incident, Onjōji clerics *(hosshiwara)* erected a barricade in the middle of a large passageway bordering an Enryakuji estate in the Ōtsu area just east of Mt. Hiei. The Onjōji partisans then burned residences and barracks *(heishi ya)* on the estate, which caused the court to again dispatch warriors to tear down the barricade. Twelve of the clerics judged to be instigators were punished, which prevented rioting and a demonstration by the Enryakuji clergy.[81] A final example comes from the second month of 1233 when the Mudōji clergy set out to battle members of another cloister, the Minamidani, of the competing Tōtō section on Mt. Hiei. Both sides suffered fatalities in the initial battle, but the Mudōji clergy were ultimately successful in destroying two of their opponents' residences. This dispute came about because lower clerics *(shimo hosshi)* of Minamidani, who appear to have cut down trees within the Mudōji precinct, got involved in a skirmish in which some were injured. Following these initial battles, both sides erected barricades and would clash again early in the fourth month before matters finally settled down.[82]

Similarities between warriors and monastics extend even into the sphere of punishments and in the execution of enemies. It is well known that the nobility was averse to capital punishment, and in fact, no executions were carried out in Heian-kyō for a period of almost 350 years, from the Kusuko Incident of 810, when former Emperor Heizei (774–824, r. 806–809) and his consort Fujiwara no Kusuko (?–810) challenged Emperor Saga (786–842, r. 809–823), to the Hōgen Incident of 1156. It is no coincidence that beheadings and the display of severed heads became "fashionable" again in the mid-twelfth century, when the warrior class had become thoroughly entrenched in and crucial components of factional politics in Kyoto. Capital punishment and infliction of bodily harm were integral to warrior culture, and, more important, to the operation of the monasteries as well, which indicates not only an overlap of personnel but also of customs. One of the more famous examples is the execution of Taira no Shigehira, the Taira commander deemed responsible for burning Kōfukuji and Tōdaiji in 1180. When he was captured at the end of the Genpei War, Shigehira was first brought to Kamakura for punishment, but the Tōdaiji clergy protested, demanding that he be executed at the hands of members of the monastery he had destroyed. As a compromise, he was beheaded at Narazaka, overlooking the river of Kizu, close to Nara, before several attending monks.[83]

Other accounts demonstrate that killings were common even within the monasteries. During a dispute between Enryakuji and Onjōji in 1142, fifty to sixty clerics put on armor and climbed Mt. Hiei to engage in battle. The Enryakuji forces defended themselves well, however, and according to a contemporary source, they retaliated by beheading three of the Onjōji followers.[84] A few years earlier (1138), when the unpopular Ryūkaku was appointed head abbot of Kōfukuji, the clergy objected in a protest. Ryūkaku responded by leading a force of warriors against the clergy, and one literary source describes how Ryūkaku beheaded clergy members and burned down several building in ensuing battles.[85] Since no contemporary sources note these killings, they may in fact be literary fabrications rather than actual deeds, but that is beside the point. The very fact that such accounts are associated with monastic communities as a whole is an important counterargument to the widely held notion that so-called monk-warriors represented one particular type of religious figure.

Conclusion

Those who armed themselves and fought in the name of temples have long been relegated to historical obscurity for two reasons. First, the paucity of sources about the middle and lower classes has made it difficult for scholars to discuss these groups in detail. Even when lower- and mid-ranking clerics were literate, the nature of their work hardly allowed them time to indulge in writing diaries and chronicles. Second, and more importantly, the power and ubiquity of the *sōhei* image have distracted scholars from an empirically based interpretation of the sources in their quest to identify just who was that monastic warrior. Thus, for example, Ōshima Yukio claims that because we have relatively few records of armed confrontations between temples over estates, secular warriors must be considered distinct from "monks with military gear" *(busō sōryo)*, that is, estate conflicts embroiled estate warriors, while intra- and inter-temple fights must have involved mainly monks.[86] The evidence presented in this chapter speaks for itself in exposing Ōshima's analytical errors, induced no doubt by the addictive idea that monastic and secular warriors somehow belonged to separate categories. Even Kuroda Toshio's interpretations, revisionist and counter-*sōhei* as they were, suffer from similar limitations. When he concluded that the armed monks and the samurai were twin figures born from the same sociopolitical developments in Heian Japan, he still failed to appreciate the complex composition of the monastic forces. Similarly, Hirata Toshiharu's observation some forty years ago that warriors *(heishi)* and secular warriors *(zokuhei)* were the pillars of the temple forces does not explain the presence and activities of other groups among those forces.[87]

War tales commonly invoke an image of professional warriors, the samurai, but they ignore the range of people who actually carried or used arms. As the various sources I call on here demonstrate, many lower-class commoners who engaged primarily in other professions might take up arms to extend their influence or to protect their rights. The same was true of "the Buddha's warriors," who were not of one kind, but consisted both of monastic workers with little or no military training and professional warriors. In fact, they had far more in common with other warriors than with educated monks in the monastery they served. The boundaries between these cohorts were hardly crystal clear, as we noted in the inconsistent use of a wide range of terms haphazardly applied across contemporary records. Secular warriors and clerics alike participated in displays of martial skills at shrine and temple events, reflecting a shared culture of knowledge and skill in the use of weaponry. If one were to classify the many groups associated with shrines and temples, it is perhaps most useful to consider where they lived. Those residing on temple estates or close to various branches away from the main monastic complexes appear to have had more military training, perhaps because local conditions required the use of arms more frequently. Monastic workers and shrine servants, in contrast, were employed full time by their institutions in other duties and were therefore only rarely as skilled. While both groups participated in battle, the estate warriors are not mentioned in the incidents that can best be classified as riots. Men living close to the monasteries and shrines were naturally easier to recruit for and more likely to participate in such events, since they had a greater stake in the privileges and status of their institutions.

But it was the combination of these two large groups—secular warriors, primarily recruited from temple estates, and monastic workers, the *dōshu* and the *jinnin*—that comprised the monastic forces. It is inaccurate to describe them as "monks," even if we allow for a broader interpretation of the term that includes anyone associated with a monastery. That would in fact be tantamount to calling the provincial warriors nobles because they served high-ranking courtiers. The epithet "monk-warrior" is thus doubly incorrect. It labels as monks men who were involved in distinctly secular trades with no religious duties, and it implies that monastic warriors somehow trained as both monks and warriors with skills based in mystical powers or techniques associated with religious doctrines. Instead of labeling these forces with the anachronistic term *sōhei*, it might be more appropriate to see them as *jihei*, "temple warriors." *Jihei* does indeed appear in a few contemporary sources, specifically in the *Sōchiki*, in an entry from 1081 referring to mounted warriors on the Onjōji side.[88] This term is not as common as the others treated in this chapter, but the fact that it does appear indicates an awareness on behalf of contemporary observers that monastic forces were just that, warriors serving the temples.

When criticism of these forces appears in the sources, it seems to arise more from the particulars of the circumstances than from views about the proper relationship between monasticism and arms. Temple warriors were repeatedly recruited by warring factions at the court throughout the late Heian and Kamakura eras, and when edicts were promulgated against monks and their followers carrying arms, they represent the warning of a victor to an upstart rather than a principled view of religious communities. Other cases point to what the monastic communities themselves considered exceedingly selfish behavior, but punishments or admonishments in these instances were no different for those serving monasteries than for those serving nobles. The key to maintaining some measure of control over either type of force hinged on the leadership's ability to motivate their retainers. But, given the social distance between ranking monks and the menial workers, administrators, and warriors of the temples, how can we explain the investment of the latter in court factionalism and their participation in internal confrontations based on politics in the capital? It is here that the monk-commanders, aristocratic warriors at the other end of the spectrum, came to play a crucial role in the organization and growing importance of monastic forces in Japanese society. With the emergence of such leaders, monastic forces could for the first time mount a real challenge to and rival military forces employed by the imperial court.

FOUR

The Teeth and Claws of the Buddha

Noble Monks and Monk-Commanders

In his 1974 opus on the rise of the warrior class, Jeffrey P. Mass asserted that it was the noble commanders, whom he described as "bridging figures," who played the most crucial role in linking the provincial warriors to the capital elites. In short, whereas warriors had been prominent members of local society for much of the Heian age, it was only through the leadership of nobles, who became commanders over groups of local warriors (sometimes referred to as *bushidan* by historians), that armed men were brought into the foreground of national politics.[1] Likewise violent elements had always been present in the monasteries and religious estates, but only when the monk-commanders emerge in the late eleventh and twelfth centuries do we see monastic forces joining the factional frays of the capital. If, as shown in the previous chapter, the monastic forces were largely comprised of menials among the clergy and warriors from the estates in the provinces, then whence came their commanders? Are these the figures that best correspond to the received image of the *sōhei*? To address these questions, it will be useful to explore the careers of several monk-commanders as they have come down to us in the sources.

The Belligerent Monks of Mt. Hiei

Jōjin (1037–1118) was one of the most belligerent monks of Shirakawa's era. He was the son of Fujiwara no Yoshisada, a mid-ranking member of the Northern Fujiwara, who served as governor of Bingo Province in the 1040s and early 1050s.[2] The family had a history of pursuing ambitious careers, but met with little success owing to its comparatively low status within the

Fujiwara. Jōjin took Buddhist vows on Mt. Hiei, perhaps in hope of escaping the limitations of his family, but even as a cleric his promotion through the ranks was fairly slow. Despite counting two of Enryakuji's most influential leaders among his teachers—Genshin, the famous author of *Essentials of Salvation*, and Shōhan, both of whom served as head abbots—Jōjin only reached the level of preceptor in 1085, at the age of 47.[3] This belated promotion did, however, allow him to participate in ceremonies performed for the imperial court, such as the Godan-no-hō in 1092, with regent Morozane in attendance, and the following year with the new regent Moromichi. Late in 1095 he was promoted to minor assistant prelate *(gon no shō sōzu)* in reward for his services. In fact, he appears to have been so busy in the capital that he did not return to Enryakuji for four or five years prior to this promotion.[4] But Jōjin began to pay increasing attention to matters on Mt. Hiei soon after his promotion early in 1096, when he became involved in a dispute over the abbotship of Saitō, one of the three main sections of Enryakuji, where his teachers had served as abbots before becoming Tendai heads.

Jōjin had been dismayed at the selection of the previous abbot, which may have contributed to his decision to remain in the capital for several years. Now, with that abbot gone, he saw an opportunity to himself become head of Saitō, and he suddenly ascended the mountain to confront his opposition. Battles ensued until the Tendai head abbot, Ninkaku, stepped in to award the prestigious abbotship to Eijun, a non-ranking monk of Jōjin's own cohort. There was more than just religious politics behind this decision. The head abbot was well connected among the capital nobles—he was a descendant of Michinaga's line of the Fujiwara and the uncle of the chancellor Moromichi (1062–1099). The latter, in particular, disliked Jōjin, whose family was in general on poor terms with the Regent's. At one point, Moromichi's grandfather (Yorimichi, 992–1074) referred to Jōjin's branch as a family "with evilness deeply rooted in their hearts."[5] One can certainly not deny that Jōjin was ambitious, but it is the intensification of the factional tensions that deserves our attention more than the monk himself. Contemporary diaries call the clashes he was involved in "battles" *(kassen)*, which suggests a new level of violence, strategies, and leadership compared to skirmishes that occurred earlier in the eleventh century.

Following his initial failure to wrest control of Saitō through force of arms, Jōjin returned to the capital, where he resumed his career as a celebrant of Buddhist rituals. But when Eijun died in 1100, and Jōjin was again overlooked in favor of Chōkyō, another disciple of Shōhan, Jōjin enjoined warriors on Mt. Hiei to express his objection, and the new appointment was enforced only with some difficulty.[6] Then, when the Tendai head abbot Ninkaku died in the third month of 1102 at the age of fifty-eight, he left the court with a difficult succession decision. The seventy-six-year old Keichō, who had retreated entirely from ceremonies and official religious titles at one point, was the compromise selection. For Jōjin, this was a stroke of good luck. Keichō was his maternal relative and, perhaps more important, the two monks lived close to one another in the capital. In fact, they both participated—Keichō as lecturer and Jōjin as reader—in a ceremony at Hosshōji in Kyoto sponsored by Retired Emperor Shirakawa in 1103.[7] When Chōkyō died the following year, Jōjin moved again to assume control of the Saitō section. His forces were, however, outnumbered, since members of the Tōtō section had joined his opponents. The fighting spread throughout the Enryakuji complex, and this time several tens of dwellings were destroyed over the course of four or five battles before heavy rains interrupted in the middle of the sixth month of 1104. Fujiwara no Munetada wondered in his diary if this was not a sign that Buddhism had entered an age of decline and that Shintō deities had become fed up with the recurrent disturbances at Saitō. "It appears," he stated, "that every time the monks fight at the Saitō section, it begins to rain heavily."[8]

A few days later, the Tōtō side submitted an appeal to the imperial court, stating that the battles were mainly the work of Jōjin, who headed a large number of warriors on Mt. Hiei, and that he should be exiled for his crimes. Although most nobles were also concerned with the presence of Tōtō supporters, who wreaked havoc on their own in Kyoto, they generally agreed that Jōjin caused much of the violence.[9] Yet, Jōjin was clearly not the only cleric capable of leading forces and fighting. One noble remarked:

> The law codes specifically prohibit the assembly of more than twenty warriors without proper reason. However, the clergy on Mt. Hiei have recently brought together thousands of warriors to battle from dawn to dusk, and [as a result] there are too many fatalities to count. Mt. Hiei and Kyoto are like one, located not far apart. Thus, even if the mountain monks do not appeal [to contain the fighting], order should be imposed. But there is no such decree, and we are therefore pressured by the clergy's demands and forced to hold a meeting like this for the first time. At this point, there is not much we can do, except to heed the advice of the emperor.[10]

The court thus seemed to lack the ability and determination to confront the clergy through traditional means, yet it was unwilling to resort to force. In part, this lack of determination was due to the premature death of regent Moromichi in 1099, which left the court without the powerful leadership of its resourceful Fujiwara chieftains. Moromichi's dealings with religious institutions as they had became increasingly active in the 1090s were merciless and unforgiving. He had decisively dispatched several warriors under the command of a Minamoto no Yorinao to stop one of the earliest demonstrations staged by Enryakuji in 1095 and ordered that the sacred palanquins brought from Hiesha should under no circumstances be feared. As a result, Yorinao's warriors shot and killed some of the shrine servants carrying the palanquins, an act that was widely considered sacrilegious. He also rejected a petition from the monks of Kōfukuji in 1096 even in the face of that clergy mobilizing, and he was responsible for dispatching imperial police to contain fighting at the Saitō section on Mt. Hiei that same year. Such decisive measures against temples essentially ceased when Moromichi suddenly died from a rash of boils on his face in the sixth month of 1099 at the young age of thirty-eight. The Enryakuji clergy was quick to declare that his death was caused by the local deities *(kami)* of Mt. Hiei as punishment for the violent measures he took against the protesters a couple of years earlier.[11] It seems plausible, therefore, that the imperial court was reluctant to challenge the deities so soon after Moromichi's unexpected death.

To return to the disturbance of 1104, Tadazane inquired with the emperor about the clergy's plea to have Jōjin exiled. The court eventually decided that Jōjin, who stood accused by his opponents of having killed 198 people on Mt. Hiei, was indeed the culprit and stripped him of his rank within the Office of Monastic Affairs. It would not go as far as to exile him, however, which may have been part of the reason the problems were not resolved. When Head Abbot Keichō climbed Mt. Hiei shortly afterward, in the eighth month of 1104, the clergy accused him of having endorsed Jōjin's actions and drove him off the mountain. Not only was his dwelling destroyed in the process, but the clergy also managed to steal his head abbot's seal.[12] In the tenth month Enryakuji's ranking monks were called to Kyoto to explain the clergy's behavior against their head abbot. As these talks progressed, supporters and disciples of Jōjin and Keichō struck again, attacking more monk dwellings within Saitō and killing some of its members. It is also clear from the explanations submitted by Enryakuji that the monastery was now severely divided. Although a large number of the clerics there had been behind the ouster of the head abbot, a separate statement from the Ryōgon'in of the Yokawa section claimed that the act had been carried out only by certain clerics and was not endorsed by everyone on Mt. Hiei.[13]

The courtiers had grown frustrated with the aggression of the unruly monks as well as with their own inability to contain such violent outbursts. It was not merely the incident at Enryakuji that bothered them, but also what appeared to be a general rise in encroachments and illegal behavior associated with the monastic communities. Efforts were made to stop "evil monks, who carve up the various provinces by calling properties there branch temples or temple estates," and prohibitions were issued against "armed supporters on Mt. Hiei and monks carrying weapons within Tōdaiji, Kōfukuji, Enryakuji and Onjōji." To contain the monks on Mt. Hiei, several government warriors, including Minamoto no Yoshiie and Yoshitsuna, were ordered to "besiege Mt. Hiei in the east and the west, arrest evil monks, and detain and bring supporters trying to ascend the mountain to Kyoto."[14] But even these measures proved insufficient.

Since the Tendai head abbot Keichō had been ousted in the eighth month of 1104, a certain Hōyaku Zenshi, one of the ringleaders in the coup, had handled the administration of Enryakuji. Hōyaku Zenshi was in every way as belligerent and ambitious a man as Jōjin; he was commonly known as a "rough monk," who was "extremely skilled in the way of the warrior, led tens of warriors in various battles, and engaged in thefts and killings in the Kyoto area."[15] Nothing is known of his origins, but references in the diaries suggest that he was a son of a low-ranking courtier or provincial elite with only limited religious training. Once in command on Mt. Hiei, his main concern was to maintain and expand Enryakuji's control of estates and branch temples. One of his first acts was to send lower-class temple servants and service people of Hiesha, many of them his own personal retainers, to Kamadoyama Shrine located in Chikuzen Province (present day Fukuoka Prefecture) in an attempt to obstruct the administration of its new abbot, Kōsei.[16] This shrine was a local branch of Daisenji (Hōki Province, present day Tottori), which in turn had been a powerful branch-temple of Enryakuji since the late ninth or early tenth centuries. Shirakawa had appointed Kōsei, who also was the head of the rival shrine-temple complex of Iwashimizu Hachimangū, administrator of Kamadoyama even though the right to make such appointments belonged to the patron temple. The appointment of Kōsei was, unsurprisingly, interpreted as a direct threat to Enryakuji, and Hōyaku Zenshi's ousting of Keichō was in part related to the latter's unwillingness to protest the appointment on Enryakuji's behalf. In any case, Hōyaku Zenshi's troops encountered resistance in Chikuzen, where a local Kyushu official aided Kōsei's followers. Enryakuji eventually emerged victorious in this dispute late in 1105, but by that time, Hōyaku himself had already been eliminated. The details are not known, but he was arrested sometime around the twelfth month of 1104 and disappears as suddenly from the sources as he had appeared only a few months earlier.[17]

Keichō returned to Mt. Hiei to resume his duties as Tendai head abbot, but he found the clergy opposition too stiff and resigned in the second month of 1105. An Onjōji monk named Zōyo was appointed on the fourteenth day of the second month, but he was forced to resign after only one day. He was succeeded by Ningen, who, as the son of Fujiwara no Morozane and the uncle of Regent Tadazane, appeared to have sufficient court backing to stabilize matters. But the sound of swords clashing could still be heard on Mt. Hiei, and Jōjin managed to be appointed abbot of Saitō in the ninth month of 1106 at the age of 69, after years of striving and struggle. Jōjin was now the most influential man on Mt. Hiei.[18] Even so, he was unable to sustain his position for long. One of his retainers apparently killed a messenger of Retired Emperor Shirakawa close to the palace sometime in the second month of 1107. Shirakawa understandably became enraged, and fingers soon pointed in the direction of Jōjin, who was taken into custody and interrogated by the imperial police. Although it is not clear if the slaying was carried out with the support of Jōjin, he refused to name the person responsible for the crime, and a substitute was eventually forwarded to be punished.[19] Shirakawa was not satisfied, however, and had Jōjin banished from the capital province of Yamashiro in the first month of 1108.[20] Jōjin's strength clearly lay with his followers, and that the actions of one of them proved his undoing in the end only seems fitting.

Several people in the capital area appear to have felt relieved by Jōjin's exile, and Fujiwara no Munetada, the retired emperor's retainer, commented that "Jōjin is a very evil person, and he has been an instigator [of trouble] among the clergy many times, performing exceedingly evil deeds for years. It is for this reason that he is punished like this." By contrast, Jōjin's longtime adversary, Kankei, who himself led forces against Jōjin in 1104, was generously promoted and frequently employed in prestigious Buddhist rituals in the capital. Kankei's loyalty to the court during these struggles is no surprise, since he was the older brother of another of Shirakawa's entrusted retainers, Fujiwara no Munemichi.[21] It is not clear where Jōjin went during his exile, but he probably spent most of his time in neighboring Ōmi Province, in Higashi Sakamoto, on the eastern face of Mt. Hiei. At some point, the aging monk was pardoned and invited back to the capital, where he was reinstated as a ranking monk in the Office of Monastic Affairs and participated in a ceremony at Hosshōji in the second month of 1114, with Shirakawa himself in attendance.[22] It is difficult to know exactly why Jōjin was permitted to return and participate in a ceremony with the retired emperor, considering the criticism he faced from many nobles. Perhaps with the complete dissolution of his faction, coupled with a confiscation of his estate rights, he was considered powerless enough to be allowed to return.

Or perhaps the Onjōji abbot Zōyo, who was also Jōjin's cousin, pleaded on his behalf with Shirakawa. In either case, most exiles of offending courtiers and monks in the Heian age proved to be only temporary. Jōjin spent his final years in reclusion close to the capital, and died at the age of eighty-one in 1118. Even at that point, he was known among many courtiers as a violent monk, who, as Munetada noted in his diary, had been involved in several tens of battles on Mt. Hiei.[23]

As the best-documented monk-commanders of Enryakuji during the *insei* age, Jōjin and Hōyaku Zenshi provide important clues to the social and political backgrounds of such leaders during Shirakawa's times. While Jōjin sought ranking monastic titles and was deeply involved in factional politics both on Mt. Hiei and in the capital, Hōyaku was an administrator with ambitions centering on landed assets. Both men commanded substantial forces and used them to further their own interests. Most importantly, the sources reveal that their retainers were recruited from among provincial warriors, which further reinforces the conclusions of the previous chapter that monastic forces must be understood in the larger context of the warrior class and the nobility rather than that of religious institutions alone.

Kōfukuji's Shinjitsu:
"Japan's Number One Evil Martial Monk"

Among the belligerent monks of Heian Japan, Shinjitsu (1086–?) must certainly be reckoned one of the most notorious, given that two historical sources call him "Japan's number one evil martial monk."[24] Shinjitsu has become the ultimate representation of the greedy and violent *sōhei*, and by extension of the degeneration of Buddhist institutions and their negative impact on legitimate rulership by court nobles. But such interpretations rely on predetermined negative views of the Buddha's monastic warriors, views that neglect to put monks like Shinjitsu into their proper historical context. An examination of Shinjitsu, his alliances, and his involvement in various incidents is thus crucial in obtaining a more empirically based understanding of the origins and role of the monastic force commanders.

Shinjitsu came from a branch of the Seiwa Genji (Minamoto), a family of warrior background. He was a descendant of Minamoto no Mitsunaka (912–997), an influential general serving the Fujiwara who had been instrumental in the so-called Anna Incident of 969, which strengthened the Fujiwara chieftain's position in the imperial court. From that time on, the Minamoto retainers became known as "the teeth and claws of the

Fujiwara."[25] Following this tradition, Shinjitsu's grandfather and father (Yoriyasu) became commanders of some stature, but they were also exceedingly ambitious and aggressive figures who were known to have appropriated lands for their own gain. Indeed, Yoriyasu earned a reputation as "a well-known warrior troublemaker of the realm." Still, he had no aversion to Buddhism, since he sponsored or himself performed the meritorious act of copying out the Lotus sutra.[26] Shinjitsu appears to have inherited both of these traits from his father, making for himself an unprecedented career as a military leader within the Kōfukuji clergy. We can surmise from his appointment as assistant head administrator of the Hossō center in 1121 that Shinjitsu was born in 1086, the very year Shirakawa retired as emperor and a little more than a decade before he would begin an era of rulership behind the throne.[27]

Shinjitsu was promoted to head administrator (jishu) of Kōfukuji in 1129, which gave him authority over a large portion of the clergy. But Retired Emperor Toba, who took control of the imperial court following the death of Shirakawa that year, favored and attempted to promote the monk Chōen, who had ambitions to become abbot of Kiyomizudera, one of Kōfukuji's most important branch temples. Several members of the clergy disapproved of Chōen and attacked him on his way back to Kyoto after an appearance in Nara. About two hundred "evil monks" assaulted him and his entourage, ripped off his monk's robe, and inflicted severe wounds to his head. In addition, they destroyed the carts he and his party traveled in, and some of his young disciples were killed or injured. Chōen was then detained by the enraged clergy and taken back to Nara, where the Kōfukuji head abbot, Genkaku, eventually persuaded the unruly monks to release Chōen, who quickly fled to Kyoto.[28]

Toba responded assertively, sending government forces to Nara, headed by several renowned warriors such as Mitsunobu, Yoshinari, and Tameyoshi of the Minamoto, along with Fujiwara no Morimichi and Taira no Masahiro. These measures were the strictest ever taken against one of the elite temples and resulted in several skirmishes with the "evil monks." One confrontation resulted in the deaths of three retainers of the imperial police captain and ten Kōfukuji supporters. Toba's fierce pursuit of the Kōfukuji monks can in large part be explained by his patronage of Chōen, who was supported by one of the retired emperor's consorts.[29] The central figure in the beating and detaining of Chōen was a monk named Egyō (1085–1164), who first escaped but was later captured in Iga Province by one of Taira no Tadamori's retainers. Toba subsequently deposed Genkaku as head abbot, blaming him for not controlling his clergy and also stripping him of his official monk rank. Egyō was exiled to Harima, and more than ten other monks were sent to various provinces. As contemporary observers noted, the imposition of such punitive measures against one of the elite temples was unprecedented. Chōen, in the end, got what he wished, since he was appointed abbot of Kiyomizudera.[30]

Shinjitsu was not directly involved in this series of events, but he was nonetheless pursued and arrested by Minamoto no Tameyoshi (1096–1156), who also seems to have burned down the monk's residence. Perhaps realizing too late his innocence, Tameyoshi shielded the besieged Shinjitsu instead of handing him over to the authorities. Shinjitsu subsequently escaped to the mansion of Regent Tadamichi (1097–1162, regent 1121–1158) for protection. But Tadamichi betrayed Shinjitsu and handed him over to Toba in a strange reversal of loyalties.[31] Tameyoshi, Toba's retainer, attempted to help Shinjitsu, while Tadamichi, the Fujiwara chieftain, made no effort to protect one of the clan temple's ranking monks. The explanation, as in so many cases in Heian and Kamakura Japan, can be found in the factional networks, for Shinjitsu was supported by Tadamichi's estranged father, Tadazane (1078–1162) and his younger brother Yorinaga (1120–1156).

Shinjitsu eventually confessed under pressure to committing crimes during the incident, but Toba limited his punishment to house arrest, acknowledging that Shinjitsu was not part of Egyō's faction and thus not one of the instigators. By the third month of the following year (1130), Shinjitsu had been pardoned and was allowed to return to Nara.[32] Two years later, Genkaku was also pardoned and subsequently re-appointed head abbot of Kōfukuji. With this, Shinjitsu was once again reinstated at the top of the administrative hierarchy at the Hossō center.[33]

In 1137 Shinjitsu was promoted to assistant head administrator *(gon no jōza),* confirming and further enhancing his status within Kōfukuji. It was not merely Shinjitsu's military prowess that allowed him to rise through the monk ranks, but also his connections with ranking members of the Fujiwara regent's line, especially Tadazane who appears to have begun to align himself with the belligerent monk at this point. For example, in the eleventh month of 1136, Shinjitsu and his disciple Genjitsu—Shinjitsu's younger brother and adoptive son—hosted the young Yorinaga, whom Tadazane favored over Tadamichi, when he visited Kasuga. Some observers found it inappropriate that two known troublemakers should be bestowed such honors. The monks must have been important associates of the Fujiwara for Yorinaga to ignore precedent during this pilgrimage. In light of his powerful connections then, it is not entirely surprising that Shinjitsu was, in a highly unusual move, allowed to handle the affairs of Kōfukuji upon the death of head abbot Genkaku on the twenty-first day of the ninth month (1138).[34]

A new head abbot, Ryūkaku (1074–1158), was appointed about a month later, but he was unpopular with the clergy. Ryūkaku attempted to appease the monks by bringing rice to be distributed among them from his Suita Estate. Some of Ryūkaku's own followers disagreed with the gesture, however, and stopped the distribution before it started. At this point, Shinjitsu led a force that confronted the spoilers and engaged them in a battle close to the gate of the nearby Hokkeji, after which the Kōfukuji monks, with Shinjitsu's blessing, simply appropriated the rice.[35] Tensions ran high between the clergy and its leadership at the Hossō center, eventually sparking another conflict that caused serious problems and concerns in Kyoto. When a monk named Eiken was killed in the first month of 1139, the clergy, probably under Shinjitsu's leadership, blamed it on the head abbot. They attacked and burned down his cloister along with dwellings belonging to some of his deputies. The Kōfukuji clergy then marched toward Kyoto to stage a divine demonstration and pressure the imperial court to depose Ryūkaku. Approaching the capital from the south, the clergy camped on the western shore of the Uji River before crossing. The court responded immediately by sending government warriors, led by Taira no Tadamori and several Minamoto generals, who fortified the eastern shore to prevent the protesters from actually entering the capital. Unable to break through, the clergy sent an appeal to Regent Tadamichi through a messenger, before returning to Nara. Shinjitsu and another ranking monk, Kan'yo, were deemed responsible for the mobilization, and although they were called to Kyoto for a hearing, both were pardoned.[36]

Needless to say, the monks' connection to two of the Fujiwara leaders (Tadazane and Yorinaga) played an important role in their eventual exoneration. But the tensions were far from resolved. In the eleventh month of 1139, Ryūkaku brought government warriors to Nara to retaliate for the humiliations he and his followers had suffered. When battle ensued, the defending Kōfukuji clergy managed to fend off the attackers, with both sides suffering casualties. Fifty of Ryūkaku's warriors were captured by the opposing monks and later handed over to the imperial police captain. Two days after that, Shinjitsu was, despite his involvement in the fighting, promoted to director, and Ryūkaku was deposed for his belligerent acts in favor of a new head abbot named Kakuyo (1086–1146).[37] But promoting Shinjitsu may not have been the best way to curtail the violence, since elements of the clergy also opposed him. In fact, certain "evil monks" from Kōfukuji went to the Kangakuin, the Fujiwara headquarters in Kyoto, to petition that the aforementioned Minamoto no Tameyoshi—a supporter of Shinjitsu—be exiled. The court obliged regarding Tameyoshi's punishment, but the Hossō center was after this plagued by internal tensions and brawls, which eventually resulted in the exile of fifteen "evil monks." Shinjitsu was actively involved in these altercations, but was shielded from punishment, owing to his connections with Tadazane. He was even accused of sending up the fifteen monks from Kōfukuji to be exiled. It is certainly no coincidence that the banished monks belonged to a group opposing Shinjitsu, which suggests that Tadazane had at this point chosen to align himself entirely with the latter.[38]

Controlling most of Kōfukuji, Shinjitsu set out to expand his, and his temple's, authority in Yamato Province. One stubborn obstacle was, as noted in chapter 2, Kinpusenji, located on the border toward Izumi in the Yoshino Mountains. Shinjitsu attacked this temple in the seventh month of 1145 in a campaign fittingly known as the Yoshino Battle (Yoshino *kassen*). A contemporary account notes that Shinjitsu headed these forces as a "great general" *(daishōgun)*, proclaiming his capabilities and station as a warrior leader. But Shinjitsu could not subdue Kinpusenji, and he was forced to retreat after two weeks, although sporadic attacks continued into the ninth month.[39]

In the twelfth month of 1146, the incumbent head abbot Kakuyo died and was replaced two months later by Kakusei (1090–1148). Kakusei's tenure as head abbot was cut short by his death in the fifth month of 1148, which resulted in another edict from the Fujiwara chieftain, stating that Shinjitsu should handle Kōfukuji's administration.[40] When, remarkably, no head abbot was appointed for three full years, Shinjitsu with the help of Genjitsu, his disciple and adopted son, maintained complete control of the monastery. It was during this time, more specifically in 1149, that these two monks were accused of a rather bizarre offense, which involved stealing rocks from the tomb of Emperor Shōmu (r. 724–749). Tōdaiji, which acted as the manager of the tomb and the adjacent area, complained that the two Kōfukuji monks had taken rocks from the tomb for a hall in the Hossō center in Nara. Shinjitsu and Genjitsu responded that they had taken material from a hill known as Nahoyama, which housed the tomb of Empress Genshō, and not from Sahoyama, where Shōmu's tomb was located. Since the tombs are more than two kilometers apart and Nahoyama was the more distant from Nara, it appears unlikely that Tōdaiji's accusations were unfounded. Furthermore, the value of using rocks from Shōmu's tomb provides a motive for Shinjitsu's actions. By the late Heian age, a Shōmu cult had emerged that linked him with both Kannon and the Shōtoku Taishi cult. Rocks from his tomb could thus be used as relics to enhance the spiritual presence and prestige of the planned temple halls. Shinjitsu's statement accordingly seems to be nothing more than a smoke screen, since he counted on the court's unfamiliarity with the area and the similarity of the place names to defend himself. Unfortunately, the imperial officials charged with resolving the conflict never visited the actual site, relying instead on the statements from the conflicting parties.[41] An examination of the adjoining hills would certainly have indicated if there was any truth to the accusations, so why did the officials not simply inspect the sites? Tsunoda speculates that Shinjitsu's forces were so feared that the officials, perhaps convinced of his guilt, simply chose not to pursue the matter further.[42] It seems more likely, however, that Shinjitsu's powerful supporters in the capital objected to an investigation to protect their monk-ally.

Ryūkaku was reappointed head abbot by the Fujiwara chieftain—now Tadamichi, the estranged son of Tadazane—in the eighth month of 1150, despite objections from Shinjitsu. This was clearly a setback, but he was, as we should expect, far from helpless, and he remained the most influential monk in Nara. The head abbot did not have as many adherents within the monastery, and, moreover, Shinjitsu continued to draw support from Tadamichi's opponent, the scheming Fujiwara chieftain emeritus, Tadazane. It was in fact this alliance that prompted Shinjitsu to join Tadazane in the 1156 coup d'état with Retired Emperor Sutoku against the newly enthroned Go-Shirakawa that would become known as the Hōgen Incident. Contemporary sources are unfortunately of little help when it comes to the size and composition of Shinjitsu's forces, but it must have been considerable since his allies in the capital decided to wait for his arrival before making their move. According to a later war tale, the *Hōgen monogatari,* the capital leaders, Yorinaga (Tadazane's son) and the disenchanted Minamoto no Tameyoshi, headed some six hundred warriors, to which Shinjitsu was to add one thousand from Nara. The recruitment of monastic troops was in fact not a sudden decision at the time of the coup. Tadazane had instructed Yorinaga to pardon men from Kōfukuji, Kinpusen, and Tōnomine in the eleventh month of 1155 in an obvious attempt to secure greater support for his faction. In the end, however, Emperor Go-Shirakawa, who managed to recruit more extensive support, preempted his opponents by striking first in the capital, where he succeeded in driving his enemies away. Shinjitsu and Genjitsu thus did not make it to the capital on time, and instead joined the beaten warriors, including Tadazane himself, in their flight to Nara the day after the debacle.[43]

One of the most astonishing facts of the failed coup is the lenient punishment the monks received, especially considering the central role Shinjitsu's forces might have played had they arrived in time. Shinjitsu,

Genjitsu, and one of their followers lost their official monk titles and their estates were confiscated and transferred to Kōfukuji, which implies that the monks had acted without the endorsement of the entire monastery. Other rebels were banished and some even executed, but the monks escaped with only a loss of social status and financial foundation.[44] What lay behind this lenient treatment? The answer is crucial for our understanding of the monks and also of the court's perception of their roles. First, we must of course note that such leniency probably reflected the victorious faction's consensus that the monks were not ringleaders in the failed uprising. Rather, they were allies who had responded to the summons of more exalted nobles in Kyoto. And, although Shinjitsu had chosen the wrong side, the court may have elected to punish him more lightly because his forces had never engaged in any fighting.[45]

Second, Tsunoda suggests that the court still feared Shinjitsu's forces and wished to avoid the more common punishment of exile to avert further disturbances and perhaps even battles with the monk's followers.[46] But how would Shinjitsu have managed to muster such forces after losing his estates? As a Minamoto warrior with a foundation of resources in the provinces, Shinjitsu lost most of his power through the confiscation of his lands. The connection between estates and power is clearly indicated in the last recorded incident involving Shinjitsu, dating from the seventh month of 1158. The imperial court had decided to perform a survey of public land in Yamato Province, most likely in an attempt to protect it from further carving up by influential estate patrons there, such as Kōfukuji and Kasuga. The surveying group included the provincial governor and, unexpectedly, Shinjitsu, whose participation was not popular with the clergy. The clerics attacked Shinjitsu's residence, forcing him to call up his faithful retainers in self defense. Tens of fatalities and many injuries occurred on both sides, and the battle managed to frighten the government officials away and interrupt the survey.[47] Shinjitsu's dramatic switch of loyalties must surely be understood in the context of the failed coup's aftermath. Having sided with the losing faction, Shinjitsu probably managed to escape severe punishment by cooperating with the victors. Thus, when he gave up managerial control of the estates, he may additionally have promised, as part of his surrender agreement, to cooperate with the provincial governor. That this would include surveys aimed at limiting the landed interests of Kōfukuji may not have been clear at the time, but such terms provide the most plausible explanation for Shinjitsu's unexpected participation in the survey and the subsequent attack on him by the clergy.

Were it not for his monastic status in Kōfukuji, it would be easy to dismiss Shinjitsu, like his father and other members of his lineage, as an overly ambitious warrior-commander, who used his military skills, control over land and retainers, and his patrons in the capital simply to further his own interests. Can we in fact describe him as anything but a warrior? Should we even bother to state that his involvement in the Hōgen Incident marks the first time in Japanese history that members of the imperial court called temple forces to battle? Although there can be no doubt that Shinjitsu does not readily fit the stereotype of the "monk-warrior," his case is important, not because he fought as a monk, but because he made his career within Kōfukuji as a warrior-administrator. His case speaks, in other words, to the inseparability of the monastic, noble, and military worlds of late Heian Japan.

Kakunin: The Great Buddha's Estate Manager

Owing to the vast source collection of Tōdaiji, the life and activities of Kakunin are well documented. His name first appears in the record on the twentieth day of 1127, when his service as administrator of Tōdaiji estates earned him the rank of assistant temple provost (gon no tsuina).[48] By 1133 Kakunin had advanced to assistant temple head administrator (gon no jishu), involving himself in protecting and expanding Tōdaiji's possessions in Iga Province against the local official class.[49] His methods became increasingly aggressive, however, and by 1147 an edict relating to complaints from Ise Province and the Iwashimizu and Kasuga shrines refers to him as an evil monk for the first time. Then, in 1149, the governor of Iga lodged a complaint against him, charging that he had joined forces with local landlords to appropriate harvested rice from a village within the boundaries of the public domain. Unsurprisingly, since Kakunin "could not prove beyond any doubt the rights of Tōdaiji," the dispute ended in favor of the local officials.[50]

These activities—the cooperative efforts of local landlords and Kakunin to exclude a larger portion of the harvest from provincial taxation—continued well into the 1150s. In particular, his efforts in Kuroda Estate appear to have been relentless. In 1158 provincial officials again accused him of appropriating tax grain and trying to wrest control of land from the public domain in collusion with mid-level landlords. This document quotes the local timber laborers' complaint that Kakunin, "an evil monk from Nara," endlessly sent messengers to exert pressure and harass them. It states that their situation had been unbearable ever since the monk took control of the estate.[51]

Kakunin's behavior indicates that he treated the temple's assets as his own and felt entitled to expand his personal interests in the name of Tōdaiji. It is not surprising, then, that he would eventually encounter resistance from within Tōdaiji itself. Problems came to the fore only a few months after the complaint against him in 1158, when another ranking monk named Nōe attempted to reestablish his cloister's control of the estates under Kakunin's management. The sources do not reveal how these tensions flared into a more serious dispute or what other issues were contested, but Kakunin was eventually accused of having stolen 194 horses. Kakunin did not have much support among other monks within Tōdaiji, a strong indicator that his main power base was in the estates. Yet Kakunin defended himself well, and managed to retain most of his rights. He was important to Tōdaiji's ranking clergy as an able manager and as an influential member of the temple's administrative corps with extensive knowledge of litigation procedures.[52]

Kakunin relied primarily on his local contacts, not on patrons in the capital, to promote his career within Tōdaiji. He was born a Taira, and derived much of his personal power and prestige from his family's background in the provincial class of officials *(zuryō)*. Pedigree and blood relations were useful to sons of aristocrats, who could usually expect a fast-track career as clerics with active support from their relatives. But, as noted in the case of Shinjitsu, one's lineage also helped in securing support and followers in the provinces. Indeed, it was not unusual to see coordinated efforts by warriors and monks from the same family as they attempted to expand their influence. Kakunin entered local estates supported by several followers, many of whom had been armed and recruited, not as servants of Tōdaiji, but as retainers of the Taira.

Kakunin's position was strengthened in the third month of 1159, when a new head abbot named Kanpen was appointed at Tōdaiji. Kanpen must have been on good terms with Kakunin, because he promoted him to the highest level *(jōza)* within the temple's executive organ (the *sangō*) less than a month later. As a ranking member of the *sangō*, it is hardly surprising that Kakunin's signature appears with increasing frequency on Tōdaiji documents.[53] Kakunin had been heavily involved in administration within Tōdaiji, but he now had even more clout in land matters. As the ranking estate manager of Kuroda-no-shō, he not only held judicial rights over the estate, as indicated by his adjudication of disputes over office fields in 1159 and 1169, he also continued to appropriate its assets for himself. Appeals, accusations, defense statements, and skirmishes were all part of the daily management process. A verdict issued in 1162 by the imperial court provides yet another account of Kakunin's local influence and human resources. The provincial officials stated:

> When this Kakunin was appointed land manager, he began to perform evil deeds. He assembled a band of over three hundred armed men [*gunpei*] and drove away the hamlet manager Toshikata. The latter even fled together with the farmers, because Kakunin tried to kill him. As a result, this district has now been removed from public taxation. These are evil deeds beyond words. To disobey generations of imperial decrees and gather armed men to plan killings reflects the utmost lack of respect for the law of the imperial court.[54]

Kakunin's aggressive land policies also led to a conflict with Kōfukuji, which filed a complaint against him in 1161, stating that he had performed various illegal deeds, such as detaining messengers and stealing oil and rice.[55] This dispute lasted for several years, with Kakunin applying his usual strategy of asserting a strong local presence, which forced the next Tōdaiji head abbot, Ken'e, to submit letters in defense of him to the Fujiwara chieftain's headquarters in 1167 and 1168. To divert the charges, Tōdaiji accused Kōfukuji supporters of appropriating taxes from Tōdaiji's Takadono Estate and claiming that certain fields belonged to Kōfukuji. The Fujiwara administrative headquarters was unable to reach a decisive verdict in the case, and merely stated that taxes should be collected as before, which undoubtedly disappointed both sides. The Kōfukuji monks then took matters into their own hands and went to the estate to stake claims to several residences and harassed the representatives from Tōdaiji. Kakunin responded by going straight to the capital to lodge another complaint, this time to the retired emperor Go-Shirakawa, in the fourth month of 1170. But he neglected to appear for a "trial confrontation" at which the court attempted to settle the dispute, preferring instead to continue applying pressure directly on site.[56]

Kakunin masterfully employed force, local pressure, and his own status within Tōdaiji while manipulating his contacts and the litigation system in Kyoto to remain a powerful presence in Nara. He was never punished, despite accusations from the Kōfukuji clergy that it was Kakunin, and not Tōdaiji, who was behind the complaints against Kōfukuji. He remained active into the mid-1170s, with no indication that he was ousted or punished for his aggressive managerial strategies. In fact, his legacy lasted beyond his death in more than one respect. In 1201 Tōdaiji disputed some of Kakunin's land rights with the nun Shinmyō, who was Kakunin's widow. Shinmyō and her son, Taira no Chikatoki, the governor of Ōmi Province, continued employing Kakunin's strategies, appropriating titles for themselves and using military force to collect taxes and expand their local influence. In an attempt to regain control of one of the estates Tōdaiji lodged a complaint that explained how Shinmyō had assumed managerial rights from Kakunin despite the temple's longstanding right to administer the estate. Perhaps more noteworthy is the claim that representatives of the nun, just like those of Kakunin, had harassed their adversaries in the area.[57]

Kakunin was not only a Taira descendant with significant armed support but also part of the large contingent of low- to mid-ranking nobles with knowledge of the legal procedures of the Heian court, as demonstrated by his appearances in Kyoto in judicial hearings both to appeal against his opponents and to defend himself against various accusations. His combined use of legal procedures, his authority as a ranking Tōdaiji manager, and his leadership of a band of warrior-followers made him one of the most successful monk-commanders of the twelfth century. Factions, blood lineages, and family alliances all played as much of a role inside the walls of Japan's monasteries as outside them in the late Heian age. Kakunin's position, like Shinjitsu's was based more than anything else on social status and kinship organizations. Both men played the same role in the monasteries as other mid-ranking nobles who rose through the court ranks to become important retainers of the retired emperor or the Fujiwara chieftain—by commanding armed forces while serving as aggressive administrators. The fact that they served a religious elite did not change anything in their *modus operandi* as commanders and warriors.

Sōken: The Dress Code Enforcer on Mt. Kōya

Kōyasan's location at some distance from Kyoto and Nara spared it from much of the factional infighting until Kakuban's (1095–1143) meteoric rise within Shingon. Supported by Toba and his consort, Bifukumon'in (1117–1160), Kakuban's Daidenbōin grew quickly, and the monk attracted an enviable number of estates. As if more proof is needed regarding the key role of court factionalism in the increasing violence in the monasteries, it was precisely during Kakuban's time that Kōyasan became embroiled in violent internal disputes. Details of those battles cannot be substantiated in contemporary sources, but Kakuban's close relationship with Minamoto no Tameyoshi (1096–1156), one of the retired emperor's prime commanders, is revealed in a pledge and donation from Tameyoshi, indicating that Kakuban was well aware of the possibility of military conflict.[58]

A short respite from fighting followed Kakuban's death, but arms were again brought in during a dispute in 1162. Six years later, Kongōbuji monks attacked the Daidenbōin. According to an appeal submitted by the Daidenbōin clergy, the incident began during the annual New Year's ceremonies, held in the first month. The ringleader was none other than the master of ceremonies, a ranking Kongōbuji monk named Sōken (?–1183) who, on the fourth day of the rites suddenly brought "armed evil-doing fellows with him, and entered the various halls at Daidenbōin." Apparently, Sōken and his armed followers cut and slashed in every direction as they made their way through the complex, causing the Daidenbōin monks to run for their lives. Once they had cleared the area, Sōken's group rampaged, stealing a variety of Buddhist images, sutras, and other valuable objects. They tore down dwellings and repositories, and also made off with relics and food items reserved for the residing monks.[59]

What triggered this outbreak of violence, led by the master of ceremonies no less? There can be no doubt that envy of the patronage the Daidenbōin enjoyed was the prime factor. Just prior to the New Year's ceremonies, the Daidenbōin had been renovated, making it look even more glorious than before. In addition, the Daidenbōin monks had decided to wear silk robes instead of the black hemp robes prescribed by Kūkai for the ceremony, further causing envy and anger among the Kongōbuji monks. Following the brawl, monks from both sides were called to Tōji, the Shingon center in Kyoto, to explain themselves. Seventeen monks went to Kyoto, but instead of admonishing them himself, the head abbot handed them over to the imperial police, and three of the monks were swiftly exiled for their role in the incident.[60]

Sōken's case took more time, perhaps because he did not fit the typical description of an "evil monk." He came from a village not far from Mt. Kōya in Kii Province and did not have anything close to the kind of following that a Taira or Minamoto warrior would have. Still, he was most certainly a figure of some local stature, since, according to a later source, he traveled back to his home area on several occasions as a monk and on those trips spearheaded the construction of Buddhist halls and donated sutras to local shrines.[61] Although these activities cannot be confirmed in contemporary sources, Sōken does not appear to have made fighting and the commanding of armed men his prime vocation, since we have no other records of his involvement in similar events. Nevertheless, he was sentenced to exile early in the fifth month of 1168 under orders from Retired Emperor Go-Shirakawa. Sōken was sent to Satsuma on the southern island of Kyushu under armed escort, while his accomplices Genshin and Kakuken were exiled to the islands of Iki and Tsushima, respectively.[62] Exile was undoubt-edly a severe punishment for anyone with ambitions in late Heian Japan, especially if it were a lengthy sentence, and it seems to have been effective in Sōken's case. His fate immediately following his banishment is not well documented, but he was eventually pardoned and allowed to return to Mt. Kōya to resume his duties. He appears to have stayed out of trouble until his death in 1183.

Even though Sōken's case is itself informative, the aftermath of the inci-dent provides us with a more vital piece of information. Concerned about their safety and position on Mt. Kōya, the members of the Daidenbōin clergy submitted an appeal to the court in the eighth month of 1168, ask-ing that a prohibition against the use of arms on the mountain be issued. Although such decrees were common in the twelfth century, this one is un-usual for the rare description it provides of how the armed men who in-vaded the monastery were brought together:

> A group of evil monks, with malice of forethought, planned a dis-turbance to chastise the monks residing at the Daidenbōin. They called together the resident administrators of the temple head-quarters, assembling and employing warriors *[bushi]* from nearby provinces and districts. They performed evil deeds day and night, and both youngsters and elders now carry arms [on the summit] to defend themselves.[63]

Although the term *akusō* appears in many court diaries, this impor-tant document supports the notion presented in the previous chapter that the men who actually fought in the major monasteries were rarely monks, often not even in name. As for the appeal, Retired Emperor Go-Shirakawa granted the request by issuing a decree warning the clergy on Mt. Kōya about misbehaving, promising that anyone who disobeyed the Buddhist precepts would be banished just like Sōken.[64] While the tensions between the clergies of Kongōbuji and the Daidenbōin did not wane until the latter left the mountain to found their own branch at Negoroji in the thirteenth century, the severe punishments of Sōken and his accomplices were suffi-cient to discourage further outbreaks of violence on Mt. Kōya for decades.

Aristocratic and Imperial Monk-Commanders

The monastic organizations of the Heian period were founded on hierar-chical principles, but contrary to the system of ranks at the imperial court, position and status there were based on religious training, experience, and seniority *(nenrō)* rather than pedigree. However, these ideals proved impractical in a world where temples functioned as extensions of court structures, with monks performing important ceremonies on the court's behalf, where the temple's survival depended on the patronage of nobles, and where surplus nobles saw holding office in a monastery as a lucrative career path. Accordingly, as the political and religious influence of the largest monasteries increased in the mid-Heian period, sons of ranking nobles started to pursue careers as ranking monks, not only performing important ceremonies for the court and their own families, but also gaining control of temple assets. Sons of Fujiwara received head abbot appointments at Enryakuji from the late tenth century, soon to be followed by princely monks, who rose to top monk ranks while still in their twenties. By the eleventh century, as sons of ranking nobles became central figures in the religious world, abbots of the largest religious centers without exception came from noble and imperial families.[65]

The effects of this "aristocratization" must not be underestimated, for the noble monks brought everything from their courtier world with them. Rather than living in austere temple halls on Mt. Hiei, they built their own noble cloisters, known as *monzeki*, in the hills surrounding Kyoto. Not only did this keep them closer to the action in the capital city, but they also lived more like nobles than monks in their *shinden*-style mansions, with gardens and other luxuries. And while the estates donated to the *monzeki* might theoretically add to the wealth of the larger monastery, such assets in fact remained under the control of the cloister. But most importantly, since the noble abbots first and foremost identified with their secular lineages, they additionally brought with them the factional tensions and competition of the imperial court to the dismay of monks from lower classes who, until the eleventh century, could at least theoretically have climbed the occupational ladder within any given monastery.

The influx of nobles thus introduced new conditions to the elite monasteries. First, it intensified existing tensions within the major complexes, most notably the Tendai and Shingon establishments. Second, it caused new conflicts in other monasteries as the clergy increasingly identified with one *monzeki* or another, as indicated by competition between the Daijōin and the Ichijōin for the abbotship of Kōfukuji. Third, and most significantly, the presence of nobles considerably widened the gap between the larger mass of menial clerics, such as the worker-monks *(dōshu)*, and the ranking scholar-monks, all of whom came from noble families by the twelfth century. Ryūkaku's failure to assume and retain the abbotship of Kōfukuji in the mid-twelfth century offers one example of the problems created by these new conditions. As the son of Minamoto no Akifusa, a mid-ranking courtier, Ryūkaku's appointment in 1138 disturbed many members of the Kōfukuji clergy, especially the belligerent Shinjitsu, who came from a less exalted branch of the Minamoto, who saw in him a factional opponent. Thus, when Ryūkaku brought warriors with him to Nara in 1139, Shinjitsu bested him by simply outnumbering his forces, a feat quite conceivable given the size of the forces he was supposed to lead in the Hōgen Incident.[66] Both Shinjitsu and Ryūkaku aspired to control Kōfukuji, and both used military means to wield their authority and reach their goals, but only Ryūkaku had the lineage necessary to become head abbot.

Just a few years later, another Kōfukuji head abbot, Eshin (1124–1171), experienced similar problems while trying to subdue an armed resistance. The son of Fujiwara no Tadamichi, who was on the winning side in the Hōgen Incident, Eshin had greatly benefited from his pedigree, rising through the ranks at the expense of more experienced monks when he was appointed head abbot in 1157 at the age of thirty-three. Until that point, he had not even resided in Nara, preferring instead the Kyoto environment. There can be no doubt that his loyalties lay with his own ancestry within the Fujiwara rather than with the monastery, and so, when he failed to support the clergy in an appeal in 1163, the latter attacked his Nara residence.[67] Following Ryūkaku's example, Eshin tried to subdue the clergy by bringing a significant force of warriors and other supporters to Kōfukuji. These forces were quite skilled, since they were headed by the *daishōgun* Minamoto no Yoshimoto and Minamoto no Tadakuni, but the clergy somehow managed to hold them off for three days before the Eshin forces retreated.[68] Although unsuccessful is this effort, Eshin tried again to impose his will on the Kōfukuji clergy in 1167, when he and his warriors attacked and destroyed a temple hall and several monk residences in the middle of the night. Perhaps the clergy was unprepared this time, for it did not put up much of a fight, choosing instead to appeal to the imperial court for punishment. Eshin was eventually ordered into exile, but spitefully remained in Nara until the imperial police finally escorted him to Izu where he died a few years later.[69]

Blessed with status, education, and wealth, it is curious that both Ryūkaku and Eshin failed in their attempts to control the clergy. It deserves to be pointed out that many noble monks served successful tenures, but the records on them amount to barely more than a few footnotes. What seems to separate the former from the latter was their blunt and confrontational styles, which demanded some means of enforcement for successful leadership. The importance of leadership skills is demonstrated by the Tendai monk Sonshō, whose life and career highlights the specific problems associated with leading Enryakuji. Sonshō was born in 1194, the son of Retired Emperor Go-Takakura (1179–1223) and Princess Jinshi, the daughter of Go-Shirakawa. Despite his rank, Sonshō seemed to have lacked the proper backing to be a candidate for the throne, and so he took Buddhist vows in 1209 at the age of fifteen and entered the Myōhōin cloister of Enryakuji. When his younger brother, Go-Horikawa (1212–1234, ruled 1221–1232), was chosen to be emperor by the bakufu following the Jōkyū War of 1221, Sonshō also received a princely rank *(shinnō)*. In 1225, at the age of thirty-one, he was appointed abbot of Shitennōji and only two years later became head abbot of Tendai, a tremendous position of power for such a young monk.[70]

Sonshō's tenure was anything but peaceful. His time at Shitennōji was marked by several violent outbreaks close to the temple, and the same occurred on Mt. Hiei. In fact, the very appointment of Sonshō to Shitennōji was beset with problems. When the incumbent Tendai head abbot Jien, the well-known author of the *Gukanshō* and standing abbot of Shitennōji, died in 1225, Enryakuji and Onjōji, both of whom had claims to the abbotship, proposed different candidates to the court.[71] Sonshō was the compromise candidate his brother, Emperor Go-Horikawa, selected—to the dismay of the clergy at both temples. Moreover, the monks at Shitennōji were also dissatisfied, and they demanded that the Enryakuji candidate (Ryōkai) be appointed. Sonshō initially managed to endure the opposition, but tensions erupted in outright violence late in 1229. Sonshō, hearing rumors that the monks planned to set temple buildings on fire and steal relics, responded by stationing warriors to protect the compound.[72]

It is unclear where these particular warriors came from, but Sonshō was obviously well connected. Besides the advantages of his relationship with his brother, the emperor, he was also on good terms with the bakufu, which had become more involved in civil matters in Kyoto following the Jōkyū War. Perhaps this explains why the Fujiwara regent, Kujō Norizane, asked the bakufu to send warriors to defend the temple precinct and protect Sonshō when the Shitennōji clergy began to riot and demand Sonshō's removal. The bakufu, probably fearing that the "evil fellows" assembled at Shitennōji might set the ancient temple on fire if a confrontation with its warriors took place, instead recommended that Sonshō should resign. Given his connections with the bakufu, Sonshō must have expected more support, and in disappointment at its recommendation, he stubbornly refused to resign. Instead, he assembled his own troops of "brave non-government warriors" *(hikan no yūshi)* and sent them to battle the "evil band" at

Shitennōji, which resulted in several fatalities. He could not, however, oppose the bakufu for long and was replaced by Ryōkai in the twelfth month of 1231.[73]

Two years later Sonshō was reappointed to Shitennōji, which may in fact have been part of the bakufu's plan. Sonshō was also head abbot of Enryakuji at this point, something that proved to be yet another challenge. Early in 1233 clerics of the Mudōji and the Minamidani sections on Mt. Hiei clashed numerous times. Several accounts of these skirmishes and battles survive, but according to the *Kachō yōryaku,* the dispute began when Mudōji monks injured lower-ranking monks of Minamidani in a fight. As the latter were planning to retaliate, a Mudōji monk happened to pass by, and the Minamidani clergy pursued him. The monk escaped, but a servant was apparently killed, which greatly angered the Mudōji clergy, even more so since the head abbot Sonshō refused to act on their appeal that the Minamidani perpetrators be punished. While the head abbot employed a laissez-faire strategy, the two groups of clergy again engaged in battles later the same month, resulting in the destruction of several Mudōji buildings and equally devastating retaliation against Minamidani. The record notes that during this prolonged conflict the Minamidani clergy apparently operated at a disadvantage because they dressed in white robes.[74]

Other contemporary sources confirm many of these details, so there is good reason to accept the credibility of this account.[75] The view presented by a contemporary observer, Fujiwara no Teika (1162–1241), who blamed much of the violence on Sonshō, is also noteworthy:

> Everybody knows that when princely monks are appointed head abbot, it leads to Enryakuji's decline. This princely monk [Sonshō] is especially fond of warriors, and when the clerics enter the capital, they are all accompanied by fellows who carry arms.[76]

Accurate or not, many courtiers in the capital opined that much of the violence at temples was caused by the monopolization of abbotships by imperial descendants who lacked the support of their clergy. At any rate, new confrontations that resulted in fatalities took place early in the fourth month of 1233, before the clergy finally calmed down under pressure from the court. Several of the instigators were arrested and interrogated in Kyoto, and the barricades that had been erected were finally torn down, an act that truly signaled the end of the conflict.[77]

The next year, Sonshō became involved in a fierce dispute over land and borders with Sumiyoshi Shrine. This time, Sonshō did not send his own troops, but immediately sought the help of warrior government representatives in Kyoto, the Rokuhara tandai, who obliged by having the Sumiyoshi perpetrators arrested.[78] Only two months later at Shitennōji, the temple's former executive officer *(shugyō)*, Enshun, brought his band to attack the current officers, Myōshun and Ryōkaku, both of whom were killed in the confrontation. Enshun and his followers dug in at Myōshun's residence, at which point Sonshō again asked for the bakufu's help. Battles between the factions continued, however, until the court negotiated a peace by offering Enshun a pardon.[79]

Whether it was because of his contacts with the bakufu, or more likely because of his distance from the clergy, Sonshō found it increasingly difficult to function as the Enryakuji head abbot. When he failed to support punishment of a land steward who had killed several clerics, the clergy rioted in the intercalary sixth month of 1235. With this bout of violence, Sonshō announced his resignation, but the imperial court would not allow it. In response, the Enryakuji clergy prepared to stage a protest, which caused the bakufu to threaten to punish the rowdy members of the clergy. When the protest went forward in the seventh month, the clergy was met by warriors, and a skirmish ensued in which several demonstrators were killed. Chaos reined at Enryakuji for months, but Sonshō's attempts to resign were continuously rejected, and in the meantime it was left to the bakufu to calm the clergy, which it eventually managed to do by early 1236. Sonshō remained head abbot until 1238, and he died some eighteen months later.[80] As a monk-commander, Sonshō may not have been especially successful since he failed to control his own clergy. However, his contacts with and support from the bakufu is instructive for the narrowing distance it suggests between the aristocratic and military classes, a trend that culminated with the appointment of Prince Moriyoshi (also known as Morinaga, 1308–1335) as shogun in 1333.

As is well known, Moriyoshi's father, the emperor Go-Daigo (1288–1339; emperor 1318–1339) had aspirations to topple the Kamakura Bakufu in order to secure his line's grip on the throne, but he was caught plotting and, after several battles over the course of 1331, was exiled to Oki Island early the following year. As part of the build-up to this confrontation, Go-Daigo had spent much time and energy recruiting the support, both spiritual and military, of the major monasteries in the capital region.[81] Besides making visits and donations to various shrines and temples, Go-Daigo also had two of his sons, Moriyoshi and Muneyoshi (1311–1385) take Buddhist vows and make careers within Tendai. Moriyoshi, taking the Buddhist name Son'un, became head abbot at Enryakuji in the twelfth month of 1327 at the tender age of nineteen, but he resigned in the second month of 1329. Some records indicate that his resignation was voluntary, but there are signs that the bakufu, which had removed another imperial prince from the Enryakuji cloister Shōren'in just before, may have been behind it. Nevertheless, he was reappointed in the twelfth month, but again resigned in the fourth month of the following year. The details surrounding his second resignation are also unclear, and while one source claims that the Enryakuji clergy forced Moriyoshi to resign, the *Taiheiki,* a later war chronicle, states that he stepped down to lead his own forces in support of his father's rebellion against the Hōjō. Of course, the *Taiheiki* may not be entirely reliable in its details, nonetheless it is of some interest that it claims Prince Moriyoshi "threw away the holy life of learning, to devote himself day and night to military exploits," in hopes of toppling the bakufu.[82] Yet another chronicle praises his skills with a bow, and a later scroll indeed shows him riding out to battle so armed.[83] Considering Go-Daigo's frequent visits to Enryakuji during Moriyoshi's tenure, there can be little doubt that the abbotship was a means to recruit support and control valuable resources.

Go-Daigo eventually managed to depose Moriyoshi's replacement in favor of Muneyoshi, who used the Buddhist name Sonchō, late in 1330.[84] Go-Daigo's interests in controlling Enryakuji are understandable, given its assets, both landed and military, but it also seems like Go-Daigo had planned to use Mt. Hiei as an outpost for his anti-bakufu activities. But when the Hōjō began arresting his allies, both nobles and monks, and then heavily attacked Enryakuji in the eighth month of 1331, both Go-Daigo and Muneyoshi fled Mt. Hiei for nearby Mt. Kasagi.[85] This betrayal, which forced the Enryakuji clergy to endure an extended siege with no outside support, resulted in many temples in the capital area withdrawing their support for Go-Daigo.[86] When Go-Daigo was exiled in the third month of 1332, Muneyoshi, already deposed as head abbot, was sent away to Sanuki Province. Moriyoshi, however, escaped and continued fighting with support from warriors associated with Kinpusen in Yamato, where he established fortifications. In the course of these developments, he renounced his monkhood, yet retained his monk's signature—Ōtō no miya (Prince of the Great Pagoda)—and in the sixth month issued a proclamation asking for support in the central provinces.[87] Although few other religious complexes would offer their support outright, nevertheless, the document became a tool for many warriors opposing the Hōjō, such as Kusunoki Masashige (1294–1336). When the prince-commander won an important victory against local bakufu supporters late in 1332, he gained strength and the support of some temples, such as Kokawadera in Kii Province and Daisenji in Harima.[88]

Following Go-Daigo's escape from Oki early in 1333, the tide turned in favor of the anti-Hōjō forces. Moriyoshi and local warriors continued to reap success in central Japan, while warriors in other parts of the country heeded the call to rebel against the bakufu. To gather support, Moriyoshi continued to issue edicts, over forty of them in the first five months of 1333. Seeing these developments, the Enryakuji forces, despite their disappointment at Go-Daigo's treachery four years earlier, now began to assault bakufu warriors throughout the region, perhaps less in support of the returning sovereign than to avenge the earlier attack on Mt. Hiei. When Ashikaga Takauji (1305–1358), a powerful general from the east, dramatically switched sides in the fourth month, Go-Daigo was able to re-enter the capital in triumph, and the bakufu fell a month later.[89] Attempting to reassert his control of temples and ceremonies, Go-Daigo returned to his religious agenda, which included bringing Muneyoshi back from exile and reappointing him head abbot of Tendai. More importantly, late in the fifth month Go-Daigo appointed Moriyoshi shogun, a title the prince coveted to complete his view of himself as an aristocrat-commander. He soon changed his signature from Ōtō no miya to Shōgun no miya (the Prince Shogun), and when he entered the capital in the middle of the sixth month, a large number of warriors, most of them from the Kinai area, accompanied him.[90] As Mori Shigeaki has argued, between his flight from Kasagi in the tenth month of 1331, when he had few followers of his own, many of whom were known under monk names, and his entrance into Kyoto, he had not only recruited more supporters, but had also made the transition from imperial monk-commander to aristocratic general.[91]

Unfortunately, Moriyoshi's appointment and ambitions put him on collision course with Ashikaga Takauji from the outset. The *Taiheiki* notes that Takauji arrested and executed twenty of Moriyoshi's followers, who had broken into storehouses in Kyoto and stolen goods in the fifth month of 1333, the very same month that Moriyoshi became shogun. In addition, Takauji is supposed to have spread rumors to Go-Daigo that Moriyoshi had his eyes on the imperial throne.[92] These points of tension notwithstanding, it was clearly leadership of the warrior class that was the main issue. This competition stemmed back to early 1333, when both Takauji—then still a bakufu supporter—and Moriyoshi recruited warriors in Kyushu, and Takauji had been the more successful in rallying local warriors around him. Takauji's plans to pit father against son seem to have met with success, since Moriyoshi's relationship with Go-Daigo apparently deteriorated and he was quickly deposed as shogun in the eighth month of 1333. A new crown prince (Tsuneyoshi) was designated in the first month of 1334, and another young prince was made shogun in the eighth month of 1335. Moriyoshi was exiled to Kamakura, a move veiled as an appointment, in the eleventh month of 1334, while several of his followers from the Kii peninsula were beheaded in Kyoto. The reasons behind this banishment are not entirely clear, but it appears that Takauji's machinations may be at least a part of the explanation. Moriyoshi, for his part, was certainly not innocent. There are strong indications that he had planned an attack on Takauji's residence in Kyoto in the sixth month of 1334, causing sufficient alarm that Go-Daigo ordered his son arrested in the tenth month and exiled the month after.[93] In the seventh month of 1335, less than a year after Moriyoshi had arrived in Kamakura, one of the Hōjō descendants started a rebellion in an attempt to regain control of the Kantō. Ashikaga Tadayoshi, supreme commander in the east at the time and younger brother to Takauji, set out to quell the disturbance and used the general chaos as a cover for assassinating Moriyoshi.[94]

Thus ended the short life of a prince whose activities had substantially contributed to the military toppling of the Hōjō. Although less committed, or restricted, to a career as a monk-commander than others treated in this chapter, Moriyoshi represents the completed joining of three political spheres—noble, religious, and military. A ranking noble, he became head of the largest monastery in Japan, and he commanded enough training and status to lead warriors, not just monastic ones, in battle. This combination seemed destined to succeed in the mid-fourteenth century, had his father not sided with Takauji, a general who joined him late in the conflict. In hindsight Go-Daigo's decision seems anything but wise. Takauji eventually used the resurgent Hōjō as a pretext to assume command of the warrior class and challenged Go-Daigo as battles broke out in the Kinai late in 1335. Enryakuji sided with Go-Daigo anew, but none of the other temples would lend any support, with Tōdaiji and the cloisters attached to Kōfukuji and Kōyasan all choosing to remain on the sidelines.[95] After losing a crucial battle in the capital area in the summer months of 1336, Go-Daigo sought protection on Mt. Hiei, and the Enryakuji forces became more involved in the battles than ever before. After enduring a siege, the temple's forces struck back at Kyoto with tremendous force, and took control of the capital for a short period. Although contemporary sources are scarce, it is noteworthy that the Enryakuji armies at this point listed among their warriors the "mountain clerics" (yama hosshi) discussed in the previous chapter.[96] In the end, however, the Hiei forces were cut off, Go-Daigo was forced to surrender, and Muneyoshi just managed to flee the mountain to Ise. Muneyoshi eventually joined his father, who escaped from Kyoto to the Yoshino Mountains to set up the Southern Court, marking the beginning of the Nanbokuchō era (1336–1392).

Bridging the Gap

Despite the criticisms of contemporary nobles, imperial princes did not initiate the increased levels of violence in the temples they oversaw. Armed men were a presence in many temples and shrines well before we can identify any monk-commanders. But with the appearance of monk-commanders, monastic warriors became a force outside the religious centers themselves and grew capable of affecting political developments in general. In short, like the Minamoto and the Taira—bridging figures between the court and provincial warriors—monk-commanders availed themselves of the manpower and resources of their institutions and succeeded in channeling the broad and growing trend toward violence into their own factional struggles. Since warriors possessed little class consciousness before the establishment of the Kamakura Bakufu, it was to these figures that ambitious strongmen, whether professional warriors or armed menial workers, looked to further their own interests. It was this confluence of interests that incited the formation of organized warrior bands in the religious institutions of late Heian and Kamakura Japan.[97] But at the same time, we find no evidence anywhere that these commanders either considered it somehow unethical or inappropriate to head such forces, nor did they seem to use religious rhetoric in their efforts to rally the support of the clergy. As the accounts around Shinjitsu and Kakunin in fact attest, they were commanders no different from other ambitious nobles and aristocratic warriors.

The monk-commanders' social status also provided a measure of protection for local warriors. Social organizations in the Heian and Kamakura ages relied heavily on vertical ties, and the notion of reciprocity was central to those bonds, even if it was not always adhered to in practice. Specifically, the monk-commanders were expected to use their social status and the judicial immunity of the temple to protect their followers. The records show that when the imperial court demanded criminals be turned over for punishment, temples and ranking monks often refused. In cases where monks without much social capital became commanders, as in the cases of Hōyaku Zenshi and Sōken, who based their power on local rather than capital elites, their careers tended to be short-lived and less successful, reflecting their lack of pedigree and allies in the capital. With fewer resources to draw on, these men also lacked military training, and without these tandem tools, they were hard pressed to exert influence over an extended period. More importantly, the further we progress toward the fourteenth century, the more critical military skills become, to the point that they began to take precedence over pedigree. Prince Moriyoshi perhaps epitomizes this trend, for while he stands out as the most influential of the monk-commanders, it is fair to conclude that he was less of a monastic leader than a military man. The fact that monk-commanders were essentially aristocratic leaders within their institutions again calls into question the concept of a separate category of "monk-warriors." Like the secular warrior-commanders, they managed, when successful, to combine their aristocratic status and training to command local warriors and monastic workers, both in the name of their temples and for their own benefit. Accordingly, they were not monks who became warriors, but aristocratic warriors who applied their skills within the context of monastic and political factionalism.

FIVE

Constructed Traditions

Sōhei *and Benkei*

Despite the prominence of monk-warriors in popular culture and the ubiquity of *sōhei* in Japanese academic works, no searches will yield any occurrences of this term in pre-1600 sources, literary or historical. It is no surprise therefore that none of the historical figures among the monastic forces match the "monk-warrior" image. Rather, as the preceding chapters have demonstrated, temple warriors were a diverse group, some of whom might share individual features with the *sōhei* stereotype, but all of whom had more in common with the warrior class and their leaders than any other group in society. Some Japanese scholars noted early on that monastic fighters were provincial warriors working as managers on the various temple estates, but since those figures fit the *sōhei* image poorly, they were ignored. Evidence in the historical record was simply not sufficient to overturn misperceptions that had become entrenched in Japanese scholarship.

Besides the provincial warriors, many who carried arms came from comparable cohorts inside the monasteries—from administrators down to menial workers—while others, including shrine servants, were based outside the monastic complexes, usually in the communities and villages surrounding their shrines. Primarily engaged in trade, construction, and other services, and sharing origins similar to the monastic workers, they were familiar with weaponry and handy in a donnybrook. Even given their clergy status or affiliation with religious institutions, these men cannot simply be classified as monks. They may be referred to as such, but few of them seem to have followed monastic rules, and it is my contention that reliance on such labels is much less useful than examining the social contexts and behavior of these groups. In short, the view of monastic warriors as something fundamentally different from other warriors is based more on the constructs of the observer than on the societal circumstances in which those figures actually lived. Needless to say, this argument is at odds with the *sōhei* interpretations sustained by a vast majority of scholars to this day, and so the question of how the *sōhei* image came to be dominant begs to be answered. While some might find the monastic warriors of Heian and Kamakura Japan fascinating in their own right, it is perhaps the persistence of the *sōhei* and Benkei images that will prove the more valuable issue to those interested in Japanese studies and the writing of history in general. The emergence, construction, and perpetuation of these images are the topic of this chapter.

Constructing Benkei and *Sōhei*

The *sōhei* image is perhaps most popularly represented by the well-known Benkei (?–1189), a giant of a monk who, as we are informed in literary sources, came to serve the tragic but brilliant Minamoto no Yoshitsune (1159–1189). Very little is known about the historical Benkei, except that he trained at the Saitō section of Enryakuji before eventually joining forces with Yoshitsune. Literary and theatrical accounts inform us that he set out on a quest to collect one thousand swords to melt into a monastic bell. After having collected 999 blades, he hesitates to confront a young and frail man he meets on the Gojō Bridge in Kyoto, hardly a worthy foe. Yet in a legendary duel mirroring Robin Hood's first encounter with Little John (which, incidentally, also took place at a water crossing), Benkei challenges him and is to his own amazement defeated. That youth turns out to be the well-trained Yoshitsune. Impressed with and humbled by his opponent, the youngest surviving son of Minamoto no Yoshitomo (1123–1160), Benkei found his life's purpose, and after pledging loyalty to Yoshitsune, followed him in battle after battle during the Genpei War. When Yoshitsune became the target of his older brother Yoritomo's envy and was chased throughout the realm, it was supposedly Benkei who saved his master on several occasions. In the end Benkei held off a vastly superior force to allow Yoshitsune to commit an honorable suicide in the north in 1189.[1] Of course, few of these events can be confirmed in historical sources, but, as these stories indicate, it is not the historical Benkei, but the remembered Benkei that has played such a prominent role in popular culture. From the late Muromachi and Tokugawa ages, his loyalty and devotion to Yoshitsune were frequently interpreted on stage and his image was reproduced in prints. In today's Japan his image can be found on a variety of products, ranging from souvenir dolls to Pachinko parlors and restaurants.

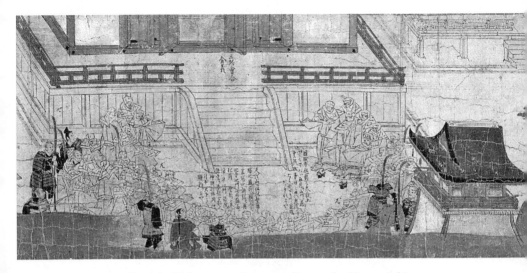

FIGURE 6. Enryakuji clergy meeting according to the *Tengu sōshi.*
Courtesy of Tokyo National Museum. Image by TNM Image Archives
(source: http://Tnm.Archives.jp).

Benkei is seen as a hero because of his devotion to an even more famous warrior, but other monastic fighters have not been so kindly treated.
Even though they have been dealt with variously by later generations, all
sōhei images have one thing in common: their attire, which commonly
featured cleric robes, head cowls, and possibly clogs. They are also consistently armed with a *naginata,* sometimes in combination with a sword. It
deserves to be reiterated that these images are not just recycled in popular
culture, they are also uncritically used by Japanese scholars. Thus, for example, Hirata Toshiharu, Katsuno Ryūshin, and Hioki Eigō all rely on these
images in their extensive *sōhei* works, as does the encyclopedic *Nihon rekishi daijiten.*[2] But their analyses fall short of explaining how this image corresponds to the monastic forces mentioned in contemporary diaries and
documents, nor do they explain the contradictions and differences between
those accounts. For example, when Hirata addressed the emergence of military powers at various monastic centers, he devoted considerable attention
to violent incidents within and between temples, but he did not examine
the actual style of fighting or equipment used, and he referred to later picture scrolls uncritically as illustrations.[3]

The *sōhei* image used in this manner does have a historical origin that
can be traced to picture scrolls from around the turn of the fourteenth century. Needless to say, these scrolls are of great value to both art historians and

FIGURE 7. Enryakuji clergy meeting according to the Hōnen scrolls.
By permission of Chion'in, Kyoto.

historians in general for the cultural and artistic preferences they reflect. But, by the same token, they must be used with caution, for they were produced in a specific setting for a targeted audience. In fact, it is in their reading of these scrolls that Japanese *sōhei* scholars have failed to exercise the most basic rules of source criticism. At best, they interpret them as showing conditions at the time of their production. At worst, the scrolls are seen as representative of the times they claim to portray. One of the most damaging of such misinterpretations is the common view that later picture scrolls accurately represent clergy meetings of the late Heian and early Kamakura eras. The notion that assembled monks dressed in full armor and in the robes and cowls that would identify them as *sōhei* is particularly strong.[4] Such interpretations are based on works such as the oft cited *Tengu sōshi*, painted in 1296, which shows a clergy meeting at Enryakuji where armed men, some with shaven heads to indicate that they have taken Buddhist vows, surround monks all neatly dressed in white robes and cowls (Figure 6, opposite).[5]

Another detailed "depiction" of a similar meeting can be found in the *Hōnen shōnin eden,* a fourteenth-century scroll dedicated to the life of the founder of the Jōdo sect. Although the content is similar to that of the *Tengu sōshi,* several of the monks are here shown to be armed, mostly carrying swords, while the surrounding followers carry a range of weapons including *naginata* (see Figure 7).[6] Another piece of the Hōnen scrolls shows a similar meeting at Kōfukuji, and while no secular followers are visible, the monks are all dressed in the hooded robes and several are carrying swords.[7]

Both the *Tengu sōshi* and the Hōnen scrolls are rich and important sources for those looking for early *sōhei* images because of their focus on what might have been considered by patrons and artists the inappropriate activities of monastics. But scholars' failure to distinguish artistic representations from historical conditions, while ignoring the contradictory evidence in both the textual and visual sources, has resulted in grave misunderstandings. For instance, even if we were to accept the notion that all monks wore cowls during clergy meetings, should we then interpret them all as *sōhei* when the vast majority of them are in fact unarmed? Moreover, the bias in these sources is often overlooked, as is the case with the *Tengu sōshi* scrolls, which have a marked tendency to portray Onjōji in a positive light, as in the depiction of a clergy meeting at the temple, where no armed fellows are visible. Recently, scholars have suggested that an Onjōji monk authored the scrolls, which is more than plausible considering their themes and bias.[8] The *Hōnen shōnin eden*, a vehicle for promoting the beliefs of the sect founder, must have been conceived to portray the Enryakuji clergy as malicious and degenerate for reasons in line with the interests of its patrons.

Failing to address the symbolism of the cowls in these scrolls, scholars have persisted for decades in equating hooded participants with *sōhei*, leading to rather untenable conclusions. For instance, based on the *Tengu sōshi's* use of cowls as a trope for clerics, later observers labeled all monks *sōhei*, even when they carry no arms. But above all, scholars have had difficulties identifying the many visitors to temples and shrines who are dressed in brightly colored robes, their long hair peeking out from under a cowl. For example, in the *Emakimono ni yoru Nihon jōmin seikatsu ebiki*, a compilation of genre scenes from various picture scrolls, an image from the *Tengu sōshi* describes two figures with long hair clad in monk robes and cowls as *sōhei* even though they carry no arms. Equally odd is the description of one of them as a "woman clad in the garments of an armed monk."[9] Other images have suffered similar misinterpretation. Volume 2 of the *Kasuga gongen kenki e* features a scene with Retired Emperor Shirakawa visiting Nara in the third month of 1093. Shirakawa is met by a group of cowled monks, three of whom are smaller figures with long hair also wearing the same garment (Figure 8).

One explanation of this scene claims that these figures are women, who "by dressing in the garment of monk-warriors thus managed to enter the

FIGURE 8. Hooded clerics and visitors assemble during Retired Emperor Shirakawa's pilgrimage to Kasuga in 1093, according to the *Kasuga gongen kenki e*. Courtesy of Tokyo National Museum. Image by TNM Image Archives (source: http://Tnm.Archives.jp).

world of men." It goes on to explain that a woman is also depicted among monk-warriors in the *Hōnen shōnin eden*. But in volume fourteen of the *Zoku emaki taisei,* in which the Kasuga scrolls were reproduced, these same figures are described as young pages.[10] To note one more example, the *Emakimono ni yoru* series also claims that a young warrior depicted in the *Bokie,* a ten-volume scroll produced under the patronage of the Honganji head, Kakunyo (1270–1351), and completed shortly after his death by his son, is in fact female. Having labeled a figure as female in one scroll, the editors have extended this identification to a number of scrolls and drawn the faulty conclusion that women were common among monastic warriors.[11] Such interpretations fly in the face of conditions in the monastic communities and the images themselves, bespeaking not only of weak source analysis, but above all the paradigmatic power of the head cowls in *sōhei* imagery.

Only recently have Japanese scholars begun to acknowledge and wres-
tle with that paradigm. For instance, Kuroda Hideo has offered a detailed
analysis of the figures with cowls and long hair represented in various temple scenes. He examined a number of picture scrolls, paying particular attention to the *Hōnen shōnin eden, Ishiyamadera engi, Kasuga gongen kenki
e,* and *Kitano Tenjin engi,* and concluded that these figures were not women
but boys, who by wearing robes and cowls disguised themselves as members
of the clergy so they could attend restricted rituals.[12] The use and symbolism of the cowls are indeed of great importance for our understanding of the
sōhei image. As Kuroda Hideo noted, they were used primarily to conceal
the identity, whether from the gods and buddhas or the imperial authorities. Not only monks, but any member of the monastic community might
use them, a point on which scholars in Japan now seem to agree. Gomi
Fumihiko, for example, analyzed the representations in the *Ishiyamadera
engi,* an early fourteenth-century scroll dedicated to the founding myths
and history of Ishiyamadera, which in one scene shows young acolytes both
with and without cowls. His explanation for this differentiation is that
those who wore cowls were visitors and not supposed to be in attendance,
while those shown without headgear were young monks participating in
the ceremony.[13] Whether women used the cowls or not during visits to temples cannot be that easily determined based solely on an analysis of the visual sources, but there can be no doubt that all records, written or otherwise, make it clear that there were no female *sōhei.* In addition, the very
presence of distinctly non-military figures among hooded monks suggests
that cowls were not symbolic of military function or a subset of monk-warriors at the time these scrolls were produced. One particularly interesting
example can be found in the thirteenth-century *Kitano Tenjin engi,* which
shows a small figure in a brightly colored robe and a cowl with long hair,
accompanied by three hooded monks and a warrior with a *naginata* (see
Figure 9).[14] It is the warrior, wearing no cowl, and not the monks who represent the element of physical protection for the young visitor, while the
monks appear to be spiritual attendants.

Perhaps it is the multiple reasons for using cowls that have caused so
much confusion. Whenever an unordained or lower cleric wanted to engage in clandestine activities without the approval of ranking monks, it was
simply a matter of donning the cowl, which, among other things, allowed
them access to restricted ceremonies. Then there is the case of monastic
workers, who used cowls both as a sign of group loyalty and of insubor-
dination. For example, in 1130 when hooded monks from Mt. Hiei performed "evil deeds," it became apparent that they came from the ranks of

FIGURE 9. Hooded visitor accompanied by monks and warrior, according to the *Kitano Tenjin engi*. Reprinted with the permission of Kitano Tenmangū, Kyoto.

the community's monastic workers. To resolve these problems, the Tendai head abbot ordered the ranking monk, Seimei, to ensure that monastic workers not cover their heads with cowls. While the message was conveyed in general terms to the workers, the implication was clear that if they covered their heads it would signify their intent to violate temple regulations. The senior workers were responsive, promising that they would respect the command. But their junior compatriots disagreed, claiming that "restricting cowls is contrary to custom," and proceeded to accuse Seimei of evil schemes, then attacked his dwelling. At this point, the secular authorities stepped in and ordered the senior monks to name the perpetrators. But the court was apparently impatient, for the imperial police were dispatched to arrest the accused workers without further investigation and exile them to provinces outside the immediate Kyoto area. In addition, various temple administrators *(shoshi)* were expelled from the mountain, while the heads of the various sections were held responsible for the actions of their followers and for arresting those involved in the incident.[15]

The cowls not only worked poorly in protecting the identities of the monastic workers in the 1130 incident, they in effect also became the means by which the court identified and punished anyone involved, although it must be noted that apparently no weapons were used. In any case, cowls figure in a variety of situations, as explained in the *Nanto sōzoku shikifuku ki*, a record detailing the division of responsibilities and clothing habits among the clergy in Nara. It notes that clerics *(daishu)* employed at various annual ceremonies at Kōfukuji and Tōdaiji normally wear a heavy white robe and a black cowl. We also learn that members of this group included both those who had taken vows and shaved their heads and warriors, "devoted *bushi*," further supporting the notion that hooded garments were used by clergy and secular figures alike.[16] The date and authorship of the *Nanto sōzoku shikifuku ki* are not known, but other sources also suggest that a range of people were associated with wearing cowls, including lay monks from the warrior class.

Another telling instance of cowl wearing occurred in a conflict between the clergies of Tōdaiji and Kōfukuji on one hand, and a noble Tōdaiji monk and the court on the other. In 1235, possibly sensing that his failing health was not going to improve, Abbot Jōhan bequeathed Tōdaiji's Tōnan'in to an imperial prince-monk at Ninnaji, attempting, in effect, to transfer possession of an important cloister to a different temple. The Tōdaiji clergy was understandably outraged and demanded that the court stop the transfer, which, however, it was not inclined to do. In the twelfth month the clergy not only threatened to stage a divine demonstration and close the temple, they also claimed they would burn the great Buddha statue at Tōdaiji if the court did not give them satisfaction. As if these threats were not enough, the Kōfukuji clergy uncharacteristically weighed in on the side of their Tōdaiji compatriots.[17] A later chronicle explains that the clergy took the divine *sakaki* branches to Uji and left them there before returning to Nara and closing the gates of their temples. All religious ceremonies were cancelled, and the clergy members showed their unhappiness and unity by covering their heads and wearing a particular kind of clogs.[18] The sources do not reveal whether these measures worked or not, but Tōnan'in remained an important part of Tōdaiji, so we must assume that the court eventually was obliged to acknowledge the temple's control over the cloister. Here again, cowls were worn as a way to demonstrate the clerics' solidarity and so put additional pressure on the court. It cannot be ruled out, however, that they might also have felt the need to hide their identities during the protest and closures. Still, even in this large protest, there were no weapons in sight.

The connection between weapons and the cowls remains spotty and

FIGURE 10. Kitano jinja silk screen painting from the mid-thirteenth century, showing a *bugaku* performance, with armed clerics attending. Courtesy of Kitano Tenmangū, Kyoto.

inconsistent at best, and neither contemporary nor literary records mention that cowls were worn in actual battle. The specific uses and situations in which cowls appear seem almost exclusively limited to inside the temple precincts since it was there that they served their symbolic purpose. That cowled clerics were not necessarily violent and did not necessarily use arms is strongly suggested by the oldest extant visual image of such figures—a mid-thirteenth-century screen painting kept at Kitano Shrine. The oldest known image of a court dance *(bugaku)* performance, the painting is well known among art historians, but it also deserves the attention of *sōhei* scholars (see Figure 10).[19] Among the more than forty monastics dressed in robes and cowls, the observant viewer will note that in this important image only about half a dozen of them carry swords, indicating in this case no ironclad association between cowled clerics and fighting monks. The artist is unfor-

FIGURE 11. Heisenji armed monks according to the Yugyō scrolls.
Courtesy of Konkōji, Kyoto.

tunately unknown, and it is therefore difficult to judge its accuracy concerning customs in the thirteenth century. The uniform garments of the visiting clerics appears to be an artistic trope, reflecting what noble patrons might have associated with monastic commoners. But besides issues of aristocratic bias and taste, the painting may reasonably be assumed to describe the clerics' appearance with at least partial accuracy. Perhaps most surprising is that despite the painting's uniqueness in depicting armed clerics and its status as the oldest image of its kind, Japanese *sōhei* scholars have neglected it in favor of a few select artistic works whose images better fit the paradigm.

It is thus primarily within the religious communities, which included both temples and shrines in their close affiliation with one another, that hooded clerics are depicted, a point that has been overlooked by *sōhei* scholars. Besides the Kitano painting, we find a number of scrolls containing the same symbolism. In the *Yugyō shōnin engi e,* for example, several armed monks are shown in white monk robes and cowls, and wearing tall clogs, representing a rare instance in early picture scrolls of the complete *sōhei* image (see Figure 11).

The Yugyō scrolls were dedicated to the founder of the Ji School (Ippen, 1239–1289) and produced only ten years after his death. They focus on the founder's life and struggles to promote his faith with the aid of his main disciple, Ta'amidabutsu Shinkyō (1237–1319), who also commissioned the work.[20] As such, these scrolls can be expected to assume a particular perspective, and it is therefore not surprising that in them we find one of the few stylized *sōhei* images, whose figures seem to be trying to drive Shinkyō and his disciples away from Heisenji, a Tendai temple in Echizen Province (present-day Fukui Prefecture). But the aggressive actions of the *sōhei* types must not obscure the fact that their attire is, even here, associated with the religious precincts, not the battlefield.

Textual accounts also suggest that clerical attire was not intended for, or worn on, the battlefield. When the Kiyomizudera clergy erected a barricade during a conflict with Enryakuji in 1203, and the imperial court dispatched its warriors to stop a confrontation, the clergy was told to "promptly put on their monk robes and assemble in front of the Buddha." This order indicates that such garments were not worn during preparations for armed conflict.[21] As noted in chapter 4, when three decades later the Mudōji clergy successfully attacked Minamidani in retaliation for the destruction of several buildings, one record attributes the Minamidani defeat to the white robes they wore.[22] Both textual and visual sources thus suggest that monk's garments were reserved for ceremonies and other activities within the monastic precincts, and it is clear that they were not especially useful in battle situations, later images notwithstanding.

It is my contention that this oversight is a general weakness in previous studies, where later artistic images have been recycled as "evidence" or truthful illustrations of the *sōhei* by numerous scholars. The failure to properly scrutinize the symbolism of cowls, the locations where armed clerics have been depicted, and the particular biases in the visual sources themselves has also led to a failure to mark and analyze the sheer variety of warriors found in picture scrolls and other pictorial representations. Indeed, an in-depth analysis of the array of temple warriors represented pictorially has yet to be attempted, because the focus has remained squarely on figures in robes and cowls, figures that scholars have already predetermined to be *sōhei*. But if such figures represent the *sōhei,* what are we to make of the monks' armed retainers, who in most cases appear much fiercer and more warrior-like? For example, in one scene in the *Tengu sōshi* (Figure 12), we find a single monastic warrior dressed in regular warrior gear, armed with a *naginata* and a sword.

Besides his shaven head, there is nothing else to indicate that he serves a monastery. He appears to be a member of the lower-class of warriors or a menial worker, as does his comrade. In either case, he fights on foot and wears simple sandals instead of the clogs often associated with the *sōhei* stereotype.[23] To describe him as a full-fledged monk who also specializes in

FIGURE 12. Monastic warrior in the *Tengu sōshi*. Courtesy of Tokyo National Museum. Image by TNM Image Archives (source: http://Tnm.Archives.jp).

warfare seems quite misplaced, and instead we must conclude that he is a simple warrior or an armed commoner serving a temple.

Other pictorial representations similarly show a variety of monastic warriors. The *Ishiyama engi,* painted in the 1320s, contains several informative illustrations of monks, commoners, and warriors. In one scene (Figure 13), we find two agitated clerics chasing three commoners, all poor and scantily dressed, away from temple property where they appear to have been hunting despite prohibitions against it inside the religious estates.[24] The clerics are armed with *naginata*—but no cowls—and the headbands they wear on shaven heads announce their monastic affiliation. Another section of this scene (Figure 14) also shows monastic supporters dressed in full warrior attire, indicating again that various types of armed members served in monastic communities, but notably, here there are no *sōhei* types to be found. Perhaps it is no coincidence that we do not see any cowls, since the Ishiyama scrolls are dedicated to the temple itself. Its monks are pictured protecting the sanctity of the temple precinct and fulfilling their vows against killing living beings by chasing away the hunters, and within the narrative and symbolism of temple legends, they were completely justified in their behavior. So the absence of *sōhei* types, who were often considered dissidents within the monastery, makes perfect sense in this type of work.

FIGURE 13. *Ishiyamadera engi* scene showing two monastic warriors driving away hunters from the temple precinct. Reprinted with the permission of Ishiyamadera, Ōtsu, Shiga Prefecture.

FIGURE 14. Temple warriors chasing hunters away from the temple domain, according to the *Ishiyamadera engi*. Reprinted with the permission of Ishiyamadera, Ōtsu, Shiga Prefecture.

FIGURE 15. *Naginata* play at Enryakuji, according to the *Ishiyamadera engi.*
Reprinted with the permission of Ishiyamadera, Ōtsu, Shiga Prefecture.

Another scene in this same work shows a lay person skillfully twirl-
ing his *naginata*, to the delight of onlookers loitering in front of a building (Figure 15). Two clerics in robes are seated nearby, and one of them also
has a *naginata*. But two of the three figures carrying the weapon here are lay
people. This is a playful scene, with one young page in long hair and a color-
ful robe apparently teasing an older monk. The subject here seems to be the
range of activities that would take place in the busy area around the temple
hall of an Enryakuji monk.[25]

A later scene depicting the 1078 destruction of Ishiyamadera by fire
shows a few monks running toward the temple in an attempt to rescue its
treasures. Three of them carry swords or *naginata*, but they are dressed in
simple monk's robes and we see no sign of cowls.[26]

Based on these images, one has to conclude that the *sōhei* package appears rather infrequently even in the visual sources used most often by
Japanese scholars. First, the clogs appear in only one section of the Yugyō
scrolls and in a scene from the *Kitano Tenjin engi* showing a young page and
three monks in cowls and robes.[27] In both cases, the scene is set within a tem-

FIGURE 16. Temple warriors according to the Yugyō scrolls. Courtesy of Konkōji, Kyoto.

ple precinct, where clergy members were likely to wear the clogs to move between buildings. Clogs were practical in residential areas, where people picked their way over grounds and paths that were often wet and muddy, but they would be a tremendous drawback in battle situations, as would cowls and robes. The clogs in later representations of monastic warriors in battle, then, would seem to be more a creation of artistic imagination, a trope, than a reflection of conditions in fourteenth-century Japan or earlier.

Second, when it comes to weaponry, these scrolls indicate that the *naginata,* though seen as the typical weapon of the *sōhei,* was in fact used by a wide variety of commoners, and, more importantly, other weapons were just as common. For example, in the Yugyō scrolls, Shinkyō and his followers are shown crossing a river before arriving at Heisenji, while a number of warriors wait on the other side to stop them from preaching in their district (Figure 16). This scene is possibly the most eclectic of all the temple warrior representations, since we find nine warriors in head cowls variously armed with bows and arrows, *naginata,* clubs, swords and shields. This image is unique in depicting all the warriors in head cowls, no doubt to symbolize their affiliation with Heisenji, for in all other respects, they look like secular warriors.[28]

In point of fact, picture scrolls of the fourteenth century do not show the *naginata* to be the weapon par excellence of the armed monastic forces. Rather, it was a weapon used by foot soldiers for cutting enemies at a distance, especially when combating multiple opponents. Perhaps no visual source supports this notion better than the *Kasuga gongen kenki e,* a scroll from the early fourteenth century dedicated to Kōfukuji's main shrine affiliate. The Kasuga scrolls are believed to have been commissioned by Saionji Kinhira (1264–1315) around 1309, with the text passages written by several members of the Fujiwara. The images have been credited to Takashina Takakane (n.d.), an accomplished writer and painter of the late Kamakura age. Taken together, this combined authorship indicates that the viewer sees and reads what can only be described as the court's view of the incidents depicted.[29] Still, the scrolls are of considerable interest, not so much for the images that concur with those in other scrolls, but rather for those that do not.

Monks depicted as participants in the various ceremonies at Kasuga usually wear white robes and cowls and occasionally carry swords, as might be expected within religious precincts.[30] But one section describes the famous 1113 conflict between Enryakuji and Kōfukuji, in which Nara monks set out to Kyoto to retaliate for the burning of Kiyomizudera, Kōfukuji's main branch in the capital. Retired Emperor Shirakawa dispatched government troops to stop the Kōfukuji supporters, which resulted in a violent confrontation. The scroll shows several tens of warriors, both mounted and on foot, battling it out in a bloody melee where one can hardly distinguish the Kōfukuji troops from those of the imperial court (Figure 17). That government and temple forces look all but indistinguishable and use identical weapons suggests that the distinction between samurai and temple warriors was less clearly marked than hitherto assumed. Some of the mounted warriors are obviously part of the Kōfukuji forces, but this is indicated only by the direction in which they are riding and not by their armor or weaponry. Other warriors fight on foot, some of them wearing part of the *sōhei* attire, such as cowls, but most of the forces are secular warriors, a few of whom even carry shields. The battle scene also shows the *naginata* being used by a number of warriors on both sides. Only three figures can be clearly associated with the monastery, because they are wearing cowls (Figure 18). One is on foot in straw sandals, fighting with a *naginata,* and the other two are mounted and armed with bows, quivers, and swords.[31] While images of mounted monastic warriors are unusual in picture scrolls from this period, their presence in the Kasuga scrolls reflects perhaps more than any other image the lack of distinction between the archetypal samurai and the *sōhei*.

The presumed link between the *naginata* and the *sōhei* is thus not obvious even in fourteenth-century visual sources, though some scrolls portray that combination more than others, which indicates not only an emerging trope but also an artistic milieu of competing images, in which the association between monastic warriors and the *naginata* was only one of many such tropes. Moreover, it must be pointed out that the *naginata* was not used before the middle of the twelfth century, and records of that period do not, in fact, mention its usage in earlier times.[32] Thus, one must be wary of the graphic account in the 1398 *Daisenji engi emaki,* a picture scroll celebrating the history of Daisenji in Hōki Province (Tottori Prefecture), which shows demonstrators surrounding a sacred palanquin in the foreground being carried to the capital during a protest in 1094. Some of the protesters wear robes and cowls and brandish swords, while their secular followers are fully armored and carry *naginata* (see Figure 19).

Scholars have traditionally trusted this account, despite the three hundred years between the events portrayed and the making of the scroll, as well as the sharp contrast it presents with contemporary and textual sources. If the appearance of the *naginata* is due to later artistic license, then one must also question the accuracy of its representation of armed protesters generally.

Other accounts showing monks with *naginata* in the early twelfth century, including the Kasuga scrolls, the *Hōnen shōnin eden* and the *Tengu sōshi,* must similarly be subjected to more careful scrutiny. The widely neglected details in these graphic portrayals of armed clerics offer compelling evidence that the warfare techniques of secular and monastic warriors were more similar than scholars have assumed. In fact, even according to fourteenth-century artistic representations, monastic warriors were proficient in the use of the bow and arrow, a point that finds support in both contemporary sources and later literary accounts. Regarding the 1113 conflict between Enryakuji and Kōfukuji, we learn from one document, partially cited in chapter 3:

In recent years, the shrine members [of Iwashimizu] have favored evil behavior, and the monks have made selfishness their foundation, invading public and private fields or appropriating property from high and low. Not limited to the Kinai, not respecting borders, they gather and assemble bands, filling [the areas] with fortifications and overflowing with barricades. Not only do they cause hardships for local residents, they also engage in battles with fellow monks. Throwing away learning, they [the shrine members] embrace weapons, *take off their monk garment and put on armor,*

FIGURE 17. Above, *Naginata* usage in the 1113 confrontation, according to the Kasuga scrolls. Courtesy of Tokyo National Museum. Image by TNM Image Archives (source: http://Tnm.Archives.jp).

FIGURE 18. Below, mounted armed monks in the *Kasuga gongen kenki e.*
Courtesy of Tokyo National Museum. Image by TNM Image Archives
(source: http://Tnm.Archives.jp).

FIGURE 19. Daisenji protest of 1094, as represented in the *Daisenji engi*.
By permission of the Historiographical Institute, the University of Tokyo.

burn down hermitages and destroy monk dwellings. They carry
bows and arrows on their left and right, and throw rocks and
shoot arrows to practice morning to night. And so, the open areas
of mountain retreats have become battle scenes and the places of
learning and Buddhist practices have become military encamp-
ments.[33] (italics added)

Naginata are not even mentioned in this detailed account, and one cannot help but wonder how this weapon came to be so closely identified with
monastic warriors. To pursue this problem further, consider the *Tōdaiji
zoku yōroku,* a temple record of the thirteenth century, which confirms that
some members of the clergy excelled as mounted warriors. It describes how
monks who came from Kanshūji in Kyoto to attend a Tōdaiji ceremony
in 1212 were enthralled when, after the ceremony, they saw Tōdaiji novices practice target shooting from horseback; they decided to stay on to
watch what seems to have been a brilliant display of mounted archery by
the young monks.[34]

Literary accounts offer additional support for a "warrior" reading of
the monastic forces. Recall, for example, the belligerent and highly skilled
Onjōji worker Jōmyō Myōshu, who, according to the *Heike monogatari,*
fought bravely at the Uji Bridge in Kyoto during the Genpei War, killing off
tens upon tens of enemies before *switching* to his monk's gear and calmly
walking away. Here again, monastic garb seems hardly to have been worn
into battle but was instead used to mark very different circumstances or settings. In McCullough's translation, following the battle, Myōshu "wrapped

his head in a cloth, donned a white clerical robe, broke his bow to make a staff, shod his feet in low clogs, and set off toward Nara."[35] In fact, the more thoroughly one analyzes documentary and literary sources of the time, the less monastic warriors in battle look like monks. Thomas Conlan made a similar observation in his analysis of a battle between Enryakuji and Onjōji forces described in the late-fourteenth-century picture scroll *Aki no yo no nagamonogatari,* noting that "most priests were virtually indistinguishable from warriors," and that they wore identical armor.[36]

While this brief survey is not exhaustive, it reveals a surprising absence of the *sōhei* symbols—especially in full combination—in early sources describing battle situations. This is sufficient to warrant serious reconsideration of the figure scholars have described as the mainstay of Heian and later monastic forces. Late Kamakura and Muromachi literary and artistic sources offer two competing images of those forces, and sometimes both are apparent within one and the same source. On one end of the spectrum, we find figures from which the stylized monk-warrior emerged. They appeared inside monasteries, carrying swords under their monk's garments, but populating a setting that was distinctly non-combatant. It is difficult to speculate about their social status, since both ranking monks and monastic workers may have worn such garments, but the symbolism surrounding the cowls suggests that they would more likely have been lower-ranking clerics, whose presence at certain ceremonies was restricted. On the other side, we find warrior-like figures in battle situations, using a wide range of weapons, but never dressed in full monastic gear. Some of these warriors are portrayed in cowls and carrying *naginata*, but they are few and far between and by no means pervasive.

In light of these observations, one must first conclude that the stylized *sōhei* image has little support in visual sources, and even less in contemporary records and literary accounts. While this does not necessarily mean that the image of the temple warrior in picture scrolls is more accurate, it is the only depiction that finds support in textual sources. Moreover, *sōhei* types appear most frequently in sources critical of the military, financial, and political powers of the old monastic centers, or in works far removed in time from the events they recount. Political, religious, and social changes in the fourteenth century presented major challenges to the old conglomerate of religious and courtier centers. New populist ideas that criticized the older Buddhist schools for their secular involvements gained momentum. In addition, warrior-aristocrats, who saw themselves as the new leadership, were similarly critical of the military and secular power of temples. A partial expression of this new configuration, the picture scrolls commissioned by the new populist schools were sponsored by leading warriors and some nobles. And as the warrior class continued to dominate Japanese politics and culture, this kind of artistic production increased, and the *sōhei* representations grew ever more stylized.

The *Sōhei* and Benkei Images Evolve

Images of monastic sources evolved as a direct result of the rise of the warrior class to national prominence. In the *sengoku* age (1467–1573), when there was little or no control over who could be armed, there were armed fellows within monasteries and shrines, just as they were to be found within villages and cities. It is hardly a coincidence that it is in this context that artists came to rely on an increasingly stylistic image of monastic warriors to distinguish them clearly from the professional members of the warrior class and assert their separate identity. Perhaps the most fascinating image from this era can be found in the *Kiyomizudera engi,* believed to have been composed by the well-known artist Tosa Mitsunobu (?–1522) around 1517. This scroll, which focuses on legends surrounding the main deity, the founding of, and various events associated with the temple, shows a scene in which every armed monk is dressed in the stereotypical *sōhei* outfit (Figure 20). It depicts a quarrel between the clergies of Enryakuji, Tōdaiji, and Kōfukuji that occurred at the time of the funeral procession of Emperor Nijō, who died at the young age of twenty-two in 1165. Apparently, the clerics argued over their positions and roles in the ceremonies and began to break one another's temple plaques. As the procession approached the funerary location, each temple brought armed monks to keep the opposing clergies at bay.[37] It is a scene that makes one wonder at the transformation of monastic forces—from the mix of warriors and armed clerics in fourteenth century picture scrolls to a uniform contingent of *sōhei*-types two centuries later. It is also of considerable interest, and certainly no coincidence, that Mitsunobu's works were commissioned by nobles and affluent warriors.[38]

Mitsunobu lived and produced artistic works at an important historical juncture that involved the codifying of cultural traditions in ways that suited the emerging warlords. He became a court painter in 1469, when Benkei was becoming a revered character in the *Gikeiki,* an anonymous fifteenth century narrative focusing on Minamoto no Yoshitsune. But it was above all through the stories of his sacrifice and loyalty in *nō* plays that the heroic monk became widely known and admired in Muromachi and Tokugawa society, where such themes were the main focus in many cultural productions. In the *nō* play *Hashi Benkei* (Benkei on the Bridge), also dat-

FIGURE 20. Monastic warriors in the *Kiyomizudera engi*. Courtesy of Tokyo National Museum. Image by TNM Image Archives (source: http:// Tnm.Archives.jp).

ing to the fifteenth century, as he prepares to face the young Yoshitsune at the Gojō Bridge, Benkei proclaims:

> I gird my armor on;
> I fasten the black thongs of my coat of mail.
> I adjust its armored skirts.
> By the middle I grasp firmly
> My great halberd *[naginata]* that I have loved so long.
> I lay it across my shoulder; with leisurely step stride forward.
> Be he demon or hobgoblin, how shall he stand against me?
> Such trust have I in my own prowess. Oh, how I long
> For a foeman worthy of my hand![39]

In the *Gikeiki* account of the same event, Benkei only uses his sword and brings out his *naginata* in a later scene.[40] While this may indicate a diversity of symbolism associated with the Benkei figure, it also reflects the difference in the mediums of theater and visual art. In the world of *nō* drama, already heavily reliant on the symbolism of specific attributes, the *naginata* served its purpose by separating a secular warrior from a monk-warrior, hardly a surprising choice considering that *nō* was primarily patronized by members of the warrior class.[41]

By the sixteenth century, Japan was all but dominated by a new kind of warlord, and only a few enclaves remained under the control of monastic strongholds such as Enryakuji, Kōyasan and Negoroji, and the Jōdo Shinshū followers. Unsurprisingly, motifs from wars and war chronicles became increasingly common in artistic works, not only for picture scrolls but also in folding screens designed to decorate the otherwise cold environment of castles. One well-known and much-admired screen depicting six battle scenes from the *Heike monogatari,* now kept at the Kanagawa Prefecture Historical Museum, shows a monastic protest with several armed men surrounding the sacred palanquin (Figure 21), most of whom are represented in the *sōhei* style.

Since this work was made in the late sixteenth century under warrior patronage, it is perhaps to be expected that a demonstration is included among such scenes, even though neither armed warriors nor *sōhei* took part in such events.[42]

As Japan emerged from an age of general warfare and disorder, its new elites favored a definition of the warrior class that distinguished it from the rest of society. Thus Kyoto warrior-aristocrats patronized many of the traditional arts and customs of the nobility, but they also promoted other cultural activities and images that supported their status. As in previous ages, the consumption and display of cultural items, familiarity with modes of reading and stories, and the presence of a heritage, whether constructed or not, were crucial to establishing and maintaining the warrior elites' cultural and political capital. It was in part for this reason that we find schools teaching swordsmanship established in substantial numbers from the late sixteenth century. This was especially true for Kyoto, where several schools operated and competed. But they were not primarily educating warriors to fight on the battlefield, since sixteenth-century warfare no longer centered on one-on-one combat but rather on the clash of large armies of foot soldiers supported by privileged warriors on horseback. The purpose of these schools was instead to provide privileged warrior scions with training and skills that could elevate them above the status of menial soldiers, and so the training offered there was in fact part of a package of constructed cultural traditions.[43] Some monasteries attempted to establish their own niches in this trade, but this effort seems to have been a business decision rather than

FIGURE 21. *Heike monogatari* folding screens showing a *gōso*.
Courtesy of Kanagawa Prefecture Historical Museum.

one based on specific marital traditions, despite later claims to that effect.
For example, Nara's Hōzōin, part of the Kōfukuji complex, was only a small
temple hall with a miniscule number of monks in attendance. Yet it managed to market itself as a center of expertise in spear handling, becoming
the best-known monastic martial arts center. The founder was a certain In'ei
(1521–1607), who is said to have liked using an extraordinarily long spear,
and who traveled around the country to various schools to study and develop his fighting skills before becoming a student of the renowned master Kamiizumi Hidetsuna (?–1577).[44] In'ei eventually established his own
school (Hōzōinryū), later continued by his disciple Inshun (1589–1648),

FIGURE 22. Long spear demonstration at Kōfukuji, September 26, 2004.
Courtesy of Mr. Ichiya Junzō, Hōzōinryū Sōjutsu School.

who had the honor of showcasing his skills in martial arts performances
before the third Tokugawa shogun Iemitsu (1604–1651) in 1639 and 1646.
The school and its later masters, who came, interestingly enough, from renowned warrior families, remained well known throughout the Tokugawa
age, performing occasionally before the members of the shogunate. The
temple was effectively demolished, however, in the mid-nineteenth century, and today nothing remains but a few foundation stones and a plaque
indicating its location next to the Nara National Museum.

The Hōzōin martial art masters themselves never seem to have been associated with the *sōhei,* and there are few indications that any connections
were made between Kōfukuji's once militant forces and the Hōzōin. But
one is inclined to wonder whether In'ei's choice of the spear may not have
been at least partially motivated by the perceived connection between monastic forces and the *naginata.* In any case, a society committed to "pre-
serving the culture of spearmanship for later generations" formed in 1991,
in a cooperative effort by "Nara City, Kōfukuji, and supporters of tour-
ism, Kendō, and the *naginata.*"[45] The society's main event is an annual martial arts demonstration held on the steps of Tōkondō, one of the remaining temple halls within Kōfukuji. Such displays of spearmanship, which
are also held at other locations associated with military traditions in Japan,

FIGURE 23. Enryakuji protests, according to a Kanō school folding screen. Property and courtesy of Shiga kenritsu Biwako bunkakan.

such as Kyoto's center for martial arts, the Budōkan, serve as a supreme illustration of how the premodern past (Kōfukuji's military power) and later images and traditions have blended for the sake of the modern martial arts and tourist industry (see Figure 22, opposite).

The need for a symbolic and actual distinction of the warrior class from other fighters led to standardized images of both the *sōhei* and the samurai themselves. Tokugawa images of monastic warriors built on representations from earlier ages, but their progression toward a more uniform representation is clearly evident—by the Tokugawa period, few images show monastic forces in any attire other than that now associated with the *sōhei*. In other words, the more fluid representations of fighters in the fourteenth and fifteenth centuries had been replaced by one that clearly disassociated monastic warriors from *bushi* in an age when the warrior class dominated politically as well as culturally. There are too many images to treat comprehensively here, but a few deserve to be noted to demonstrate this trend. A pair of folding screens belonging to Enryakuji and the Lake Biwa Cultural Museum offers another depiction of a temple protest. The pair, most likely painted by artists of the Kanō School in the mid-Tokugawa, shows *sōhei* types, all in head cowls, carrying *naginata,* and even armed with shields, following a procession in Kyoto (see Figure 23).[46] It hardly bears mention that the ratio of armed monks increases the more removed we are from the Heian and Kamakura eras. Where early picture scrolls show a mix of figures in cowls and monastic warriors who are all but indistinguishable from war-

FIGURE 24. Monk-warriors attack the Jōdo shinshū headquarters at Ōtani in Kyoto, according to the *Rennyo shōnin eden*. Reprinted with the permission of Saigonji, Nagano Prefecture.

riors fighting for noble patrons, later depictions have transformed all monastic warriors into *sōhei* types.

A slightly different, yet equally transformed, representation can be found in a set of four large hanging scrolls, produced, it is believed, in the late eighteenth century to commemorate the 300th anniversary of the death of Rennyo (1415–1499), the eighth Jōdo Shinshū patriarch. These scrolls, kept at Saigonji in Nagano Prefecture, show scenes describing the destruction of the Shinshū headquarters at Ōtani by Enryakuji forces in 1465. The artists have made the identification of the two sides quite clear by depicting the defending Shinshū believers in simple garments, barefoot, and armed mostly with swords. The attacking forces, in contrast, are shown in full armor and wearing sandals, and two symbolic pieces of their apparel betray their association with Enryakuji—cowls and *naginata* (see Figure 24).[47]

In the subsequent scene, the Ōtani complex is set ablaze, and we see monastic warriors raging across the area, all of them equipped with the typical *sōhei* gear, most commonly the *naginata* and head cowls.

These artistic simplifications and embellishments are almost too obvious to be mentioned, leaving no doubt as to the perspective and historical knowledge of the artist. His emphasis of the superior monastic warriors attacking the forces fighting for the Shinshū sect belies the historical reality. In fact, the Shinshū forces consisted mainly of lower-class warriors and self-armed commoners, like most *daimyō* armies at the time, and by all ac-

FIGURE 25. Benkei *ema* from the early Edo period. Courtesy of Kitano Tenmangū, Kyoto.

counts they should have been portrayed in a manner similar to their attackers, rather than as defenseless clerics and their supporters.[48]

Pictorial representations of Benkei also show development toward a more uniform monk-warrior representation, although this development emerged more gradually. A painting on wood *(ema)* from 1608 by the well-known painter Hasegawa Tōhaku (1539–1610) depicts Benkei in full warrior attire on horseback, having just captured Tosabō Shōshun, a warrior in Yoritomo's service sent out to arrest Yoshitsune (Figure 25). Hasegawa chose the artistic warrior trope rather than the monastic one in this representation, suggesting that both were still prevalent in the early seventeenth century. It might be added, of course, that Benkei's cultural status as a loyal retainer of Yoshitsune was vastly different from the common monk-warrior by this point, and warrior attire would therefore be more justified. In later representations, however, the *sōhei* attire became increasingly common in Benkei portraits, as demonstrated in countless woodblock prints and other images.

It is in conjunction with such cultural production that we find the first documented occurrences in Japan of the term *sōhei*. The earliest, found in a little-known Confucian text authored by a warrior-scholar in 1715 and known as the *Kansai hikki*, states:

> In the middle age of our country, the *sōhei* were extremely prominent. The monks of Enryakuji and Onjōji, the mountain monks *[santō]* of Negoroji and Yoshino, and the black-robed monks of Tōdaiji and Kōfukuji all neglected the duties of their temples. [Instead] they devoted their energy to archery, swordplay, and battles. Is this not wickedness personified? A long time ago, when Tai Wudi of the Wei dynasty went to Chang'an, he entered a Buddhist monastery and became greatly angered when saw weapons there. He said: "Monks should not use such things as weapons, unless they want to create chaos." He proceeded to kill the monks of several temples. Perhaps this is what Lord Oda [Nobunaga] and Toyotomi [Hideyoshi] thought when they destroyed Enryakuji [in 1571] and Negoroji [in 1585].[49]

Lacking any earlier occurrences of the term *sōhei*, this rather sudden appearance induced Kuroda Toshio to conclude that it must have been an import from Korea. A Korean origin does indeed make sense, since there are records of monastic warriors in *The History of Koryŏ* (compiled between 1445 and 1451), which notes the existence of monk armies in an account of the 1217 defense against invaders from the Khitan kingdom. And in 1359 the term *sŭngbyŏng* (J. *sōhei*) is specifically applied to monastic fighters who assisted King Kongmin (r. 1351–1374) against members of the Red Turban movement.[50] Unless we are to believe that the term was reinvented by Japanese thinkers in the Tokugawa age, it seems likely that it was imported from Korea, although perhaps not at that time, since, given the weakened state of temples in Japan, Korean envoys would hardly have discussed monastic forces. Moreover, even if the earliest written reference dates to the eighteenth century, the term may still have been known and used earlier.

As most Koreans are aware, some of the fiercest resistance to foreign invaders in the fifteenth and sixteenth centuries was mounted by monk armies (K. *sŭnggun*), which were by then a crucial component of the armies of the Chosŏn dynasty (1392–1910) and frequently employed in defending the coastlines against Japanese pirates. During the Hideyoshi invasions of the 1590s, two monks, Sosan Hyujong (1520–1604) and Samyŏng Yujong (1544–1610) were specifically put in charge of recruiting and organizing clerics into armies in the defensive efforts and guerilla fighting.[51] It was inevitable that the Japanese warriors and commanders would become familiar with the Korean monastic forces, and they might have brought the terms back to Japan at the very end of the sixteenth century. It should also come as no surprise that in Japan, given the opposition warlords of the period faced from temples such as Enryakuji, Kōyasan, and Negoroji, and the resistance Japanese armies encountered from monastic armies in Korea, the image of the monastic forces was anything but positive. The stylized figure of the Japanese armed monk thus met its match in the term for its Korean counterpart. By the Tokugawa period this conceptualization had jelled and become a central element in various pictorial and textual representations. Its most authoritative use undoubtedly occurs in the *Dai Nihon shi* (The History of the Great Japan), compiled in the spirit of "national learning" *(kokugaku)* between 1657 and 1906. In the section on Buddhist matters, it notes the *Konjaku monogatari* tale of how Enryakuji incorporated Gion Shrine into its network with warrior help during Ryōgen's tenure in the late tenth century. It also cites the *Sange yōki senryaku* (1399) account of Ryōgen allegedly stating that monks of high talent should focus on the sutras, while those with less should learn the path of the warrior. These accounts lack support in contemporary records, and neither of them actually uses the term *sōhei*. Nevertheless, the *Dai Nihon shi* concludes that "the beginning of *sōhei* can be traced to Ryōgen, who assembled evil monks, trained them with weapons, and called them clergy."[52]

Modern *Sōhei* Imagery

The *sōhei* image was bought wholesale by writers and modernizers of the late nineteenth century, for the image of evil, degenerate, and armed monks suited Meiji oligarchs and scholars quite well. With Buddhism put on the defensive, Imperial Shintō was promoted, and the two belief systems were forced into institutional separation. Thus losing state support and, it would seem, even their public raison d'être, many temples declined to the point that they were forced to close, and some monks even experienced persecution at the hands of zealous modernizers.[53] The professionalization of historical study, supremely represented by the many collection and publication projects sponsored by the Historiographical Institute, came to sustain this trend.[54] Contrary to the ideals of this new social science, the sources and reference works produced under the Institute were not unbiased or unaffected by the conditions of their time. For example, the outstanding collectanea *Dai Nihon shiryō*, which has been publishing volumes of primary historical materials for more than a century and may continue for yet another, contains brief titles for each entry, a few of which include the term *sōhei*, even though not one of the documents quoted contain it.[55] Moreover, in the 1901 encyclopedic publication *Koji ruien* we find a substantial num-

ber of pages devoted to the *sōhei,* in which they are defined as armed clerics *(hosshiwara),* and a discussion that also includes a long list of incidents
of monastic violence. A number of textbooks followed suit, and these notions—based not on analyses of historical sources, but on creations of the
Tokugawa age—have shaped interpretations of monastic forces to the present day.[56]

The *sōhei* continue to play an important part of the imagined past of
Japan in various ways and in different spheres. Negative connotations per-
sist among intellectuals, who appear to see in influential monasteries and
monks something ancient, antimodern, and inappropriate. The 1985–1986
tourist tax controversy in Kyoto, noted in the introduction, remains one
of the most fascinating examples of this continued bias. The conclusion
from that event and its public fallout, that "Kyoto is a historical city that is
still tied to its medieval heritage" is striking.[57] And such notions are all but
uncontested in the realm of popular science, as indicated by Ishinomori
Shōtarō's *Manga Nihon no rekishi* (An Animated History of Japan), which
belongs at once to the worlds of comics, popular science, and history. It
owes much of its popularity to the beautiful and sometimes imaginative illustrations, but its focus on traditional topics that reinforce cultural stereo-
types, such as heroic images of warriors and negative portrayals of monastic
fighters, also contributes to its broad appeal. Volume 13 is fittingly entitled *Insei to bushi to sōhei* (Warriors, Monk-Warriors and Rule by Retired
Emperors) and contains, as might be expected, numerous scenes depicting
monastic protests in which each and every demonstrator appears in *sōhei*
attire.[58]

In the sphere of popular representations, we also find the works of
painter Maeda Seison (1885–1977), which frequently deal with historical
themes in the received tradition, even though they are executed in modern
painting techniques. One painting shows a sacred palanquin being carried
through the narrow streets of Kyoto in a protest, accompanied, of course,
by stereotypical *sōhei.* Interestingly, it was this scene that was chosen to decorate the ticket stubs of a 2001 exhibit held in his honor in Kasaoka City,
Okayama Prefecture (Figure 26).[59]

In the West these images are similarly featured in publications that
straddle the domains of popular culture and academe, as demonstrated
most convincingly—or perhaps deplorably—in Stephen Turnbull's work,
Japanese Warrior Monks AD 949–1603. Despite his self-proclaimed expertise as "the world's leading English-language authority on medieval Japan
and samurai warfare," there is very little one can commend about this work,
with the possible exception of the sheer inventiveness with which the illus-
trator has created images of monk-warriors in battle (Figure 27). Relying

FIGURE 26. Painting by Maeda Seison, as represented on the ticket stub in a 2001 exhibit.

entirely on a few Japanese works on the *sōhei,* the author eschews any analysis of the stereotype or of the monastic forces themselves and bases his representations almost exclusively on Tokugawa images, as indicated by the unsubstantiated claim that monastic warriors carried *naginata* around the year 1100.[60]

FIGURE 27. *Sōhei* representation from around the year 1100, according to
Turnbull. Courtesy of Osprey Publishing, Oxford, England.

In contrast to the negative image of monk-warriors generally, Benkei
has continued to enjoy a favorable reputation, but not so much for his martial skills as for his devotion and loyalty to Minamoto no Yoshitsune, one of
the grandest warrior legends in Japanese history. Benkei images now adorn
the Japanese landscape, his statues towering over pachinko parlors, Benkei
dolls are sold at souvenir stores, and numerous restaurants and even a brand

FIGURE 28. Benkei statue, featured in clogs, in Kii Tanabe during the Benkei Festival. Photo by author.

of *sake* have been named after him. In Benkei's supposed birthplace, Kii Tanabe, a small port city on the southern tip of the Kii peninsula, his statue commands the plaza in front of the train station (Figure 28).

There can be no doubt that the inhabitants of Kii Tanabe take great pride in Benkei. According to later literary accounts, Benkei was the product of an affair between a beautiful court lady and Tanzō, the abbot of Kumano Shrine.[61] While the veracity of such claims cannot be confirmed, the desire to connect Benkei with one of the most powerful religious institutions in the area during the Genpei War is noteworthy. To further celebrate and preserve his historical memory, a Benkei Festival is held in early October every year. The festival, which was first held in 1986, is a superb example of a constructed tradition that perfectly mimics the Hōzōinryū performance in Nara. It is funded entirely by the local chamber of commerce to attract business and attention to an otherwise remote region, and the main attractions in 2004 included a flea market, aerial acrobatics, and a dance

FIGURE 29. Members of Team Kumano Suigun Yōheitai at the Benkei
Festival in Kii Tanabe, October 1, 2004. Photo by author.

contest between over a thousand contestants performing in amateur groups
from across the region.[62] Despite the festival's theme, most performances
have little to do with Benkei, but the *sōhei* image is still common and a few
groups are considered the centerpiece of the event for their *sōhei*-inspired
performances (see Figure 29).

These images follow the Benkei legend closely, and the basis of his popularity has not changed much over the centuries even as new traditions are
invented. For the *sōhei*, however, a change can in fact be detected in popular culture, perhaps in part as a byproduct of Benkei's popularity. They now
seem to represent something more positive in local communities, in sharp
contrast to their reputation among historians. There are now *sōhei* dishes
to be eaten at restaurants, perhaps together with Benkei *sake*, and various
sōhei figures appear in video games and other media. And at the Historical
Museum of Ishikawa Prefecture, visitors can dress up as various charac-

FIGURE 30. Yunoyama *sōhei* sold at stores in celebration of the *Sōhei matsuri*. Photo by author.

ters to "experience history," and the *sōhei* are part of that recreated experience.[63] It should come as no surprise, therefore, that two *sōhei* festivals are also held every year in Japan. One takes place in February at Hōsenji in the Nakano ward in Tokyo, but it is little more than a display of costumes set in a local community. Another is held at Yunoyama, a hot springs resort in Mie Prefecture, every fall. This festival is no less commercially oriented than its counterpart in Kii, although it is connected to a temple, Sangakuji, a former branch of Enryakuji and once a stronghold for some of its provincial warriors. Today the temple in northern Mie is overshadowed by hot springs hotels constructed in gray concrete, but it is scenically nestled in hills that seem to emerge from the rice fields as one approaches by train. Instead of Benkei, this festival takes its theme from the Yunoyama *sōhei* (Figure 30), and participants dress in the "traditional" monk-warrior attire and play *sōhei taiko* (monk-warrior drums).

The festival culminates with designated carriers parading a palanquin through the crowds that is then set ablaze by hundreds of torches. This event probably refers to the protests historically staged in Kyoto, even though Sangakuji never was involved in those. One would be hard pressed to find any meaningful symbolism behind the use of the *sōhei* images, except that one senses a certain localism and, in some cases, even anti-authoritarian-ism. Popular culture in modern Japan seems to offer an experience of sepa-ration from the group that may not be readily available to many Japanese in the work place or educational environment. Whether on a local or individ-ual level, the *sōhei* seem to have attained new status as a symbol of indepen-dence and uniqueness that many Japanese seek outside everyday life.

Monastic forces are usually ignored in English-language college text-books, but the *sōhei* image is not unknown among fans of "Japanimation" and Japanese culture in general. They appear every now and then as support-ing characters in video games and *manga,* and in one series a *sōhei* figures as the central character. In a marvelous blend of orientalism and invented tra-ditions, Chris Claremont's graphic novel, *Shi: The Way of the Warrior,* pub-lished in the early 1990s, begins with a telling introduction:

> They were called *sohei [sic]*, the greatest warriors of feudal Japan. Originally they were monks of the great temple Enryakuji, built in the year 788 among the cypress groves of Mt. Hiei to protect the emperor's new capital of Kyoto from evil spirits. But the pressure of constant attacks by marauding samurai intent upon the trea-sures of their temple forced them to take up arms, and eventually the Sohei *[sic]* abandoned the teachings of the Buddha to follow the path of war.[64]

While historians might criticize the *manga* for its many factual errors, it would be meaningless since it is a work of fiction. What is noteworthy, however, is how the *sōhei* image has made the leap to the world of under-ground comics in America.[65] Of course, the image inevitably undergoes changes as it enters a Western cultural sphere, as do most adapted stories, but those too are of great interest. The story focuses, ironically enough, on a woman named Ana Ishikawa, a Japanese-Caucasian, who has been trained in the secret warfare techniques of the *sōhei* by none other than the head abbot of Enryakuji (Figure 31).

Although she lives in the present, she uses primarily the weapons of old—above all the *naginata*—to combat evil on the streets of New York. She fights as skillfully in a bikini-like gear as she does in kimono, and so we see in her the perfect blend of the exoticism of the Tokugawa *sōhei* and the eroticism of twentieth-century orientalism. If one wishes to go beyond the world of imagination, a Sohei Society in Louisiana offers martial arts de-grees, even as its website declares that "the Sohei Society merely borrows the name of the Warrior Monks of Japan," claiming "no legitimate associa-tion or historical connection with the Authentic Sohei."[66] Apparently, even

FIGURE 31. The evil-battling Ana Ishikawa of the comic *Shi*.

though any historicity is denied, the image of the *sōhei* remains attractive enough that martial art schools will use it to peddle their classes. It is unclear, however, whether one has to wear the outfits of Ana Yoshikawa to reach the level of "Sohei godan" (fifth-stage *sōhei*).

One of the most recent cultural reproductions of the *sōhei* image in Japan can be found in the well-known NHK TV series *Taiga dorama*, which aired the story of Yoshitsune in 2005. In the very opening scene of this widely viewed series, the producers have chosen to show Yoshitsune's famous attack on the Taira troops down a steep hillside at the Ichinotani battle of 1184.[67] Benkei is hardly mentioned in early versions of the *Heike monogatari* or in contemporary texts, but in the TV account he is prominently featured right next to Yoshitsune on his own steed. Dressed in armor over a monk robe and sporting a head cowl, Benkei's main weapon is, unsurprisingly, the *naginata*. Even if the modern Japanese public is unaware of how unwieldy the *naginata* is on horseback or that this combination does not occur in pre-1600 sources, the awkward acting of Matsudaira Ken as he tries to swing the large glaive should send enough signals, one would hope, to raise questions about the appropriateness of that sequence.[68] Matsudaira

FIGURE 32. Benkei as depicted in the NHK *Taiga dorama: Yoshitsune.*

will hardly win any Japanese Emmys for his acting, but the producers certainly deserve accolades for doing their best to make the film a celebration of the fabricated *sōhei* image (Figure 32).[69]

In this way, Benkei, the lone hero among monastic warriors, unites the two constructed images: that of Benkei himself and that of the *sōhei* swinging his *naginata*. The power of the *sōhei* image has long resisted critical analysis by historians, even when they have noted that monastic forces commonly came from the warrior class. As has been demonstrated in this chapter, monastic forces and the *sōhei* cannot justly be seen as part of the same history. The former has a past that involved divergent groups who had the opportunity and ability to use arms to their own benefit as part of a monastic complex, or as followers of monastic commanders. The *sōhei* had its origin in a discourse that aimed to set apart those fighting for religious institutions from those who saw themselves as a distinct and distinguished cohort of professional warriors.

SIX

Sōhei, Benkei, and Monastic Warriors— Historical Perspectives

The *sōhei,* monastic warriors, and Benkei images can be described as three strands that, even though they came out of the same historical context, should be treated and understood separately. First and oldest are the monastic warriors, who emerged and developed as part of the social, political, and military milieu of the late Heian and Kamakura ages, not because of the deterioration of conditions within religious complexes, but as part and parcel of the increased tendency to settle disputes with the help of warriors. This "militarization" may be attributed to two separate trends that ultimately merged in the late Heian age: First, the dominance of local warrior-managers in the mid-Heian had become so overwhelming that Kyoto elites had no choice but to abandon many of the imperial state's bureaucratic principles in favor of forging more direct ties to local strongmen. Second, the involvement of warriors in religious disputes followed developments at the imperial court, mirroring factional competition among the leading power blocks. Nobles and warrior-aristocrats played a role in leading monastic forces, and as these leaders became bridging figures between capital factions and the provincial warrior class, temple warriors were drawn onto the national stage.

But religious violence was not a new phenomenon in eleventh-century Japan, since individual clerics had resorted to arms from the very introduction of Buddhism. Monks and monasteries were never disassociated from the imperial court or from politics in general, either in Japan or in the continental contexts from which Buddhism was introduced. Isolated instances of cleric violence in the pre-*insei* period thus reflected conditions in society generally, as did the militarization of the monasteries from the tenth century onward. More importantly, monastic violence was often considered justified, since in Buddhist discourse, as represented by sutras, sculptures, and ideological rhetoric, service to the state was equal to protecting the faith itself. The tensions between Buddhist religious precepts and the right to defend the faith resulted in an ambiguity that could be used to suit the needs of the elites. Accordingly, while Japan's rulers frequently condemned clerics for carrying arms in the late Heian and Kamakura eras, these same rulers on numerous occasions asked for and received military support from the temples. This ambivalence about monastic forces is certainly not unique to Japan or to the Heian and Kamakura ages. The Ashikaga shogunate encouraged Jōdo Shinshū believers to rebel in 1506, less than two decades after it had ordered the sect's head to stop such activities,[1] and European kings and counts alternated between condemning and courting the Church and its armies. In their quest to discredit religious institutions for their secular power, many scholars in both the West and Japan seem to have neglected evidence that secular leaders enlisted the military support of temples almost as often as they opposed it.

Monastic forces were complex in their composition. Most fighters came from lower- to mid-level classes, with some serving as menial workers or administrators within the temple communities and some attached to shrines in various capacities. Still others were warrior-administrators of estates and branches away from the temple compounds. Monastic forces were, in short, constituted by a wide spectrum of armed men, from full-time mounted warriors to workers who armed themselves only as the situation called for it. For these clerics, the label "monk" carries little religious meaning. They were no more monks than their brothers and cousins serving in the capital were nobles. Moreover, the warfare techniques and strategies of monastic warriors, from the weapons they used to the barricades they built, were characteristic of the warrior class in general. For every instance of violence involving religious institutions there are equivalents and parallels in the world of nobles and their warrior affiliates, and the increase of monastic violence from the tenth century was not unique to temples, but rather reflected more general trends in Heian Japan. Social and political conditions generally encouraged the capital elites to co-opt and incorporate monastic forces into their own organizations. This became fully possible only with the injection of noble warrior-commanders into the monastic mix, where they served as important links between secular forces and the temples. It is in this context that commanders such as Shinjitsu and Chinkei were recruited and courted by nobles and aristocrats during the turbulent years of the late twelfth century, and it was only at that stage that monastic warriors became a force to be reckoned with outside the temple precincts. Naturally, these monk-commanders were not only interested in organizing and controlling monastic manpower with its potential to carry arms, they also had their eyes on other resources, whether it be land or control of important religious ceremonies. They went beyond merely organizing warriors already associated with the monasteries and brought their own retainers and warriors with them, in effect speeding up the militarization process. Commentary from contemporary observers, who frequently criticized aristocrats for assuming high religious office on the basis of warrior support, provide ample evidence of this trend.

Japanese monk-commanders and the roughly contemporary knights of the monastic orders in Europe have generally been viewed differently, but there are noteworthy similarities. Both were of aristocratic origin, though not of the top tier, and had warfare as their professions, frequently functioning as ranking administrators within their institutions. In most cases their main motivations seem not to have been merely religious, but rather centered on control of land, trade routes, and sacred sites. Their main differences are rooted in their respective historical contexts. In Japan no external force or faith threatened the state. Even though the Mongol Invasions of 1274 and 1281 boosted shrine worship and the economy of many temples, they did not have much impact on the monastic forces or the disputes that threw them into battle. In Europe the "other" was most commonly identified as a foreign and religious enemy. He could be easily defined as an outsider and intruder, even if that was not always the case, as suggested by the Albigensian Wars in southern France in the early thirteenth century.[2] Thus supported by claims to patriotism and religious fervor, the monastic knights in Europe have been held in high regard from their own time to the present, while Japan's monk-commanders have been subject to much criticism or to complete disregard.

Another important contrast can be noted in the relative importance of religious rhetoric. Christian rhetoric strongly informed the mission of crusaders and monastic knights, though political and diplomatic motivations certainly came into play as well. But the Japanese monk-commanders do not appear to have resorted to religious ideas at all to justify their activities, even though state ideologies contained the clear notion of mutual dependence between the imperial court and Buddhism. Courtier diaries include frequent references to that co-dependence, and in view of the European example, the lack of express religious justification for monastic violence is a noteworthy difference. The clergies at various monasteries did invoke divine justice whenever they protested or fought to defend their interests, but these claims seem less like calls to holy war and more like war cries invoking the Taira or Minamoto name to challenge central authority, or invocations of the imperial house as justification for local warlords advancing their own interests. The character of its usage suggests that religious rhetoric, to the extent that it *was* used, was no different from other ideologies employed to condone violence, and that such ideologies rarely, if ever, provided the sole motive to fight.

The *sōhei* is a problematic phenomenon not only because of its negative connotations, but also because of its long history and its development as an image and stereotype. Because the image selectively engages a number of elements that can be found in documentary, literary, and artistic sources, it is especially challenging to deconstruct. Other images of monastic warriors that seem closer to what we know from contemporary sources were also prevalent, but they were gradually eliminated in favor of one that clearly distinguished religious warriors from secular ones. In conjunction with this standardization, the view of monastic forces became increasingly negative—with the exception of Benkei, whose transformation into a loyal retainer rescued a positive strand of earlier *sōhei* representations. It was, in short, the Japanese cultural and political contexts that dictated how monastic forces were represented from the late Muromachi age. The *sōhei* stereotype, which clearly marked armed monks by their cowls and *naginata*, had its origins in artistic sources critical of the monastic centers from the late Kamakura age, and it eventually became a general trope for the negative impact temples with military power had on the state. Estate warriors fighting for the temples were not as yet held in disapproval, and they provide a sharp contrast to the hooded and *naginata*-slinging clerics who, by the fourteenth century, were already being depicted as disruptive figures.

By the late sixteenth century, when powerful warlords rose to the fore in national politics, temples such as Enryakuji, as well as Negoroji and the followers of the Jōdo Shinshū sect, were seen as the main obstacles to a more stable and centered society under the new regime. It is hardly surprising that cultural production of the time would reflect negative views of these religious institutions, nor should it baffle us that these images were reinforced substantially during the Hideyoshi invasions of Korea, when monastic armies presented formidable opposition. The term *sōhei* likely came to Japan in this context and soon merged with the monk-warrior stereotype that had become common in cultural sources. It is especially noteworthy, that these early "*sōhei*" representations focused on the monastic forces of the pre-1400 era, not on the military exploits of the temples and religious movements of the sixteenth century. In the eyes of sixteenth-century observers, there appears to have been a distinction between the forces of established monastic centers and the armed resistance associated with the populist sects, indicating that in later years *sōhei* did not simply refer to the problem of monks or clerics who fought, but rather involved a critical judgment about who should or should not fight in the name of their temples.

In the Tokugawa age the *sōhei* image, now matched by a term that reflected its various connotations, was fully taken up by the dominant warrior class and the artists it patronized. That this image served the Tokugawa authorities well is beyond any doubt. The prestige of Buddhist temples seriously eroded as they were reduced to keepers of population registers, funerary sites, and tourist attractions. And in this light, the tenacity of the *sōhei* image—its survival, and even reinforcement from the Meiji era into the present—is somewhat surprising. While political circumstances and the modern separation of politics and religion may provide a partial explanation, this persistence is nevertheless baffling, given the commitment of Japanese historians to the study of original sources. In the end, one can only conclude that the *sōhei* image had become so ingrained by the twentieth century in popular and academic settings that even when scholars recognized contradictions between the construct and the historical sources, they could not disengage themselves from it.

Benkei represents a third strand that, despite its different trajectory, now seems to have merged with that of the *sōhei*. His religious associations notwithstanding, early accounts of Benkei portray him as a full-fledged warrior, not unlike Jōmyō Myōshu in the *Heike monogatari*—a figure consumed by selfish ambition until he pledged loyalty to Minamoto no Yoshitsune. His supposed involvement in attempting to save his master's life as they fled the forces of Yoshitsune's older brother transformed him into a legend larger than life. Early accounts of Benkei show him to be more in the realm of warriors than monks, but he was gradually transformed into a *sōhei* type, except that he, because of his devotion to a warrior hero, was also seen as a model of loyalty. The overwhelming popularity of Benkei and the anti-authoritarianism associated with the *sōhei* appear to have brought these two figures closer than ever in today's cultural production. Benkei and the *sōhei* are now intimately linked in their appearance and reception, and the figure resulting from their merger has traveled successfully far beyond the borders of academe.

By deconstructing the *sōhei* image and looking for clues to the characteristics, role, and meaning of the monastic forces, this study has highlighted the importance of historical context, but it has also pointed to the dangers of uncritically allowing later images and notions to exert undue influence on our interpretations of the past. It further suggests that the category of religious violence provides little if any help in understanding the role of religion and monastic warriors in Japanese history. Instead, a careful examination of the political, military, and ideological contexts in which such violence occurred is far more illuminating and relevant than consideration of religious violence alone. Monastic warriors acted no differently than their secular counterparts, nor do they appear to have been motivated by a religious rhetoric qualitatively different from other ideologies condoning violence in the Heian and Kamakura eras. In fact, the absence of religious rhetoric is itself of great interest, in view of our current assumptions about holy wars and crusaders. It suggests that other factors played at least as important a role as religious commitment for those fighting in the name of the Buddha.

Cultural and political contexts affect and guide historians as they did the artists and commentators of generations past. While the monastic forces provide a fascinating glimpse into Japan's past, the emergence and evolution of the images surrounding them may be more instructive. These developments demonstrate that images do not innocently come to us from the past—they are selected, shaped, or even invented to fit conditions in the societies for which they are created. That artifice might remain undetected and its product a perfect forgery, unless the viewer, whether a young student, amateur historian, or academic, first understands an image's origins, historical basis, and the conditions of the time it purports to portray—or, perhaps more importantly, what those conditions were *not*.

NOTES

Chapter One:
Discourses on Religious Violence and Armed Clerics

1 James Wellman, introduction to conference on "Religion, Conflict, and Violence: Exploring Patterns Past and Present East & West," May 13–14, 2004, University of Washington, http://depts.washington.edu/eacenter/spring_0304.shtml (accessed on September 2, 2004).

2 Marx, *Critique,* 131.

3 Perhaps ironically, in my *The Gates of Power: Monks, Courtiers, and Warriors in Premodern Japan,* I defend the temples' right to demonstrate in this way, albeit in an earlier age.

4 In most cases, temples raised the admission fees more than the actual tax, which drew severe criticism from the media.

5 Nishi, "Sōhei," 256–262; Okuno, "Sōhei no ran," 308–328. The quote can be found in Okuno, 308.

6 In the West, George Sansom, whose *magnum opus* is still used as a textbook by some scholars, is the most glaring critic of Japan's premodern monasteries (*A History of Japan to 1334,* 223ff).

7 Despite his expertise and life-long interest in the warrior class, Jeffrey P. Mass never paid much attention to temples and monks in conjunction with his research on the Minamoto family. See for example, his "The Kamakura Bakufu," in *The Cambridge History of Japan: Volume 3, Medieval Japan.* The two most influential Western works on the warrior class in premodern Japan—William Wayne Farris' *Heavenly Warriors: The Evolution of Japan's Military, 500–1300* and Karl Friday's *Samurai, Warfare and the State in Early Medieval Japan*— do not address monastic warriors directly, although Farris does mention a few violent incidents (pp. 261–263).

8 See Adolphson, *Gates of Power*, 167–168.

9 Weinstein, "Aristocratic Buddhism," 490–494.

10 I make this claim knowing that this situation is slated to change with a new generation of scholars showing an increasing interest in not only the standard edition of the *Heike monogatari* and its battle descriptions, but also in less-known versions and works, including the underused *Genpei seisuiki*, a more expansive account of the same events. Only Kenneth Butler has attempted an in-depth treatment of the Jōmyō passage, but his analysis is limited to the oral composition and the emerging literary tropes of the *Heike monogatari* ("The *Heike monogatari* and Theories of Oral Epic Literature," "The *Heike monogatari* and the Japanese Warrior Ethic").

11 The correct reading of the monk's name, written with the characters 浄妙明秀, is uncertain. Helen Craig McCullough (*The Tale of the Heike*, p. 153), uses Jōmyō Meishū, but following Buddhist conventions, it is more likely Jōmyō Myōshu. See also *Heike monogatari*, vol. 1, 347. To further complicate matters, the *Genpei seisuiki* has a different fourth character (浄妙明春), which would make the reading Jōmyō Myōshun (*Genpei seisuiki*, pp. 355–356).

12 McCullough, *Tale of the Heike*, 153. This quote is also noted in Hurst, *Armed Martial Arts of Japan*, 34–35.

13 Neil McMullin first brought the bias against religious institutions to my attention in his "Historical and Historiographical Issues in the Study of Pre-Modern Japanese Religions," 26, 30.

14 The *naginata* consists of a staff, four to five feet long, to which a curved blade of up to three feet is attached. I have followed Friday's usage of the term glaive instead of the more traditional halberd, since the latter has a straight blade and is primarily used to stab with, while the glaive can be used to cut, swing or thrust (Friday, *Samurai, Warfare and the State,* 86).

15 Since stereotypical images representing monk-warriors appeared long before the term *sōhei* appear in Japanese sources, I will on occasion refer to such representations as "*sōhei* images."

16 Shigeno, *Kohon kokushigan*, 130–131, 146–147, 180.

17 See for example, Takatsu, *Shinpen honbō shōshi*, 95–99; Matsushima, *Teikoku shiyō*, 100–101; Ueda, *Nihon rekishi gatan*, 66.

18 Sakaino, "Sōhei no bakko," 84–89. For a useful survey of early studies on the *sōhei*, see Kinugawa, "Sōhei kenkyū shi," 1–9.

19 *Koji ruien: Heijibu 1*, 283–311. The *Koji ruien* was first published between 1896 and 1914, so the actual compilation probably predates Sakaino's work.

20 Takasu, *Kokumin no Nihon shi*, 372–374.

21 Takeoka, "Heian chō no jiin to sōhei," 73–78. I have reservations regarding the usage of the terms "middle ages" and "medieval" in Japan, primarily because it is a vague and Eurocentric term, whose central characteristics vary too much between scholars. For a critical overview, see Keirstead, "Inventing Medieval Japan," 25–46.

22 Ōya, "Sōhei ron," 519–528; Ōshima, "Sōhei no hassei ki," 23.

23 Ōya, "Sōhei ron," 528.

24 Tsuji, "Sōhei no kigen," 18–19. Tsuji further expanded this chapter in his "Sōhei no gen'yū," 765–824.

25 Tsuji, "Sōhei no gen'yū," 773.

26 Tsuji, "Sōhei no gen'yū," 774.

27 Tsuji, "Sōhei no gen'yū," 783–785.

28 Hioki Shōichi, *Nihon sōhei kenkyū*, 27–31.

29 Hioki, *Nihon sōhei kenkyū*, 30, 90–92.

30 Katsuno, *Sōhei*, 1, 10–17.

31 Katsuno, *Sōhei*, 3.

32 Murayama with Kageyama, *Hieizan*, 86.

33 Hirabayasahi, *Ryōgen*, 99–102.

34 Hiraoka, "Sōhei ni tsuite," 549–550.

35 Hiraoka, "Sōhei ni tsuite," 579–580.

36 Ōshima, "Sōhei no hassei ki," 42–43, 52.

37 Hirata, "Sōhei ron," 150, 176–177; Ōshima, "Sōhei no hassei ki," 28.

38 Hirata, *Sōhei to bushi*, 1.

39 Hirata, *Sōhei to bushi*, 175ff.

40 Hirata, "Sōhei ron," 163–178; Hirata, *Sōhei to bushi*, 175, 243.

41 Tamamuro, "Heian chōmatsu jiin," 52, 55, 67, 76–78; Kinugawa, "Sōhei kenkyū shi," 3–4.

42 Hosokawa, "Sōhei to jiryō shōen," 134–140; Kinugawa, "Sōhei kenkyū shi," 3–5.

43 Ōshima, "Sōhei no hassei ki," 22, 52.

44 Hirata, *Sōhei to bushi*, 294.

45 Kuroda, "Chūsei jisha seiryoku," 249; Kuroda, *Jisha seiryoku*, 32, 34.

46 Takeoka, *Ōchō bunka*, 25–27; Hirata, "Sōhei ron," 150, 176–177; Hirata, *Sōhei to bushi*, 175ff.

47 Hirata, "Nanto hokurei no akusō," 261. Hirata was influenced by Kuroiwa Katsumi, who had earlier pointed out that the term *sōhei* did not appear in premodern sources, but that it did refer to the *akusō*.

48 Mikawa, *Shirakawa hōō*, 154.

49 Kinugawa, "Sōhei kenkyū shi," 1.

50 Watanabe, *Sōhei seisuiki*, 2–8; Takeuchi, *Nihon no rekishi 6: Bushi no tōjō*, contains a chapter entitled "Hōō to sōhei" (294–315).

51 Tsunoda, "Shōmu tennō haka," 341.

52 Hiraoka, "Sōhei ni tsuite," 551.

53 Seita, *Chūsei jiin*, 35–43.

54 Watanabe, *Sōhei seisuiki*, 195–196.

55 Hioki Eigō (b. 1935), *Sōhei no rekishi*, 1. It appears that this work is a privately funded publication.

56 Rénondeau, "Histoire des Moines Guerriers," 159–345. The essay is followed by

a commentary post-script by Paul Demiéville, "Le Bouddhisme et la Guerre," 347–385.

57 Sansom, *A History of Japan to 1334*, 221–223, 269–273.

58 McMullin, *Buddhism and the State*, 21–22, 42–44, 292.

59 Perkins, *Masukagami*, 232.

60 McCullough, *Tale of the Heike*; Wilson, *Hōgen Monogatari*. Like Perkins, Wilson confuses "clergy" with "soldier-monks" (see Wilson, *Hōgen Monogatari*, 27, 32), and McCullough consistently uses *sōhei* for the term *akusō* (evil monks).

61 van Horn, "Sacred Warriors" paper given at the Central States Anthropological Society Annual Meetings, April 2001. The paper is available online at http://www.mindspring.com/~semartialarts/sw.html (accessed on December 5, 2004).

62 Shin, "An Analysis of *Sōhei*."

63 Hirata, "Nanto hokurei no akusō," 269–270, 288.

64 Tsuji, "Sōhei no gen'yū," 765, 792–794. See also Hioki Shōichi, *Nihon sōhei kenkyū*, iii.

65 Katsuno, *Sōhei*, 5–8, 17ff, 113.

66 Watanabe, *Sōhei seisuiki*, 208; Kageyama, "Sōhei gōso no rekishi," 104–115.

67 Hirata, *Sōhei to bushi*, 1, 120–153. Watanabe and many others follow the same pattern of reading into terms in literary and historical sources what is not there. Thus, for example, in volume 4 of the *Genpei seisuiki*, where the burning of the Daigokuden is treated, it states "People saw in their dreams how *sarudomo* came down from Enryakuji with fire in their pine sticks and set fires throughout Kyoto." Watanabe interprets these *sarudomo* as *sōhei* (pp. 210–211), even though there is no indication that it refers to such figures. Indeed, as is well known, the monkeys on Mt. Hiei are known as holy animals and protectors of Hiesha, and here very clearly stand as a metaphor for "shrine servants" *(jinnin)*.

68 Sansom, *A History of Japan to 1334*, 270–273.

69 Seita, *Chūsei jiin*, 42–43.

70 Gomi, *Bushi no jidai, Nihon no rekishi*, 60–61.

71 Mikawa, *Shirakawa hōō*, 158; Kinugawa, "Gōso kō," *Shirin* 85:5, 608, 613–614.

72 Ōshima, "Sōhei no hassei ki," 33–34.

73 Watanabe, *Sōhei seisuiki*, 75–76.

74 Hirata, *Sōhei to bushi*, 59ff.

75 Hirata, *Sōhei to bushi*, 3ff. In point of fact, Hirata spends only about 1/3 of his entire monograph on armed monastics. His energy is rather devoted to the development of monasteries and their clergies from the pre-Nara to the Kamakura age.

76 Hirata, *Sōhei to bushi*, 39–53.

Chapter Two:
The Contexts of Monastic Violence and Warfare

1 *Taishō shinshū daizōkyō,* vol. 24, 1005c. I have benefited from Nasu Eishō's translation as cited in Groner, *Ryōgen and Mt. Hiei,* 359. See also Hirata, *Sōhei to bushi,* 69–70, 156.

2 *Wei shu,* 3033–3034. Watanabe cites this record in his *Sōhei seisuiki* (pp. 2–3), but he fails to note the potential bias in the *Wei shu,* while also getting the year wrong (pp. 2–3). It is also noteworthy that the same citation is included in the *Kansai hikki,* the first work in Japan to use the term *sōhei* (see chapter 5). I am deeply indebted to Jeffrey Moser, a graduate student in Chinese History in the Department of East Asian Languages and Civilizations at Harvard for his invaluable help with the *Wei shu.*

3 Shahar, "Epigraphy, Buddhist Hagiography, and Fighting Monks," 15–21.

4 *Ryō no gige,* "Sōni ryō," article 1, in *Shintei zōho kokushi taikei,* vol. 22, 81; Katsuno, *Sōhei,* 6; Hirata, *Sōhei to bushi,* 16–19; Hioki Eigō, *Sōhei no rekishi,* 51–52. The *Sōni ryō* was most likely included in the Taihō Code of 683, but only survives as part of the 718 Yōrō Code.

5 Aston, *Nihongi,* 152–153. See also *Nihon shoki,* part two, in *Shintei zōho kokushi taikei,* 164–165.

6 *Shoku Nihongi,* Tenpyō jingo 2 (766) 9/6.

7 For arguments for the Nara age as the beginning of armed religious forces, see Tsuji and Watanabe.

8 Kuroda noted, for example, that the violence of the seventh through the ninth centuries was not a question of monks armed to do battle, but a result of individuals resorting to violence to solve disputes (*Jisha seiryoku,* 28). Today's scholars by and large follow this interpretation, focusing on the mid- to late-Heian age. See the survey in the introduction, and, for example, Kinugawa, "Chūsei zenki no kenmon jiin," 5, 21, or Kinugawa, "Sōhei kenkyū shi."

9 "Onsekizan daisōzu (Myōsen) den," in *Shintei zōho kokushi taikei,* vol. 31, 75–76; Sonoda, "Heian bukkyō," 63.

10 *Nihon sandai jitsuroku,* in vol. 4 of *Shintei zōho kokushi taikei,* 352.

11 *Ruijū kokushi,* in *Shintei zōho kokushi taikei,* vol. 6, 320–321.

12 *Fusō ryakki,* Kanpyō 6 (893) 9/5.

13 *Shōyūki,* Kannin 3 (1019) 6/29.

14 Mikael Adolphson, Edward Kamens & Stacie Matsumoto, *Heian Japan, Centers and Peripheries* (forthcoming).

15 *Iken jūnikajō,* in *Gunsho Ruijū,* vol. 17, *Zatsubu,* 127; *Dai Nihon Shiryō [hereafter DNS]* 1:4, Engi 14 (914) 4/28.

16 *Honchō monzui,* in *Shintei zōho kokushi taikei,* 29:2, 41–53; Abe, *Heian zenki seiji shi,* 165.

17 *Chōya gunsai,* in *DNS* 1:6, Shōhei 5 (935) 6/31.

18 *Nihon kiryaku,* Tentoku 3 (959) 3/13; *DNS* 1:10, 539.

19 *Nihon kiryaku,* Anna 1 (968) 7/15. One *tan* equaled 0.279 acres.

20 *Nihon sandai jitsuroku,* Jōgan 17 (875) 5/10; *Nihon kiryaku, Teishin kō ki shō,*
    in *DNS* 1:7. Tengyō 3 (940) 1/25.

21 For a comprehensive study of Ryōgen and his times, see Groner's *Ryōgen and
    Mt. Hiei.*

22 *Jie daisōjō den,* in *Gunsho ruijū,* vol. 4, 15; *DNS* 1:6, 146; Hirata, "Nanto hoku-
    rei no akusō," 263, 266. The *Jie daisōjō den* was completed in 1031.

23 *Tōjō* (刀杖) is commonly translated as "swords and halberds." This is, how-
    ever, problematic, since the *naginata* (glaive) was not used in Japan until the
    late Heian period, perhaps as late as the mid-twelfth century (Friday, *Samu-
    rai, Warfare and the State,* 86). *Tōjō* literally means "swords and staffs," and I
    am not aware of any cases where the term is used to specifically denote swords
    and halberds. Moreover, the character for staff, *tsue,* appears by itself in the
    aforementioned *Jie daisōjō den,* clearly referring to staffs or canes. In a Bud-
    dhist context, *tōjō* appears in both the Kannon and Lotus sūtras as a reference
    to weapons in general, which is supported by representations of Buddhist stat-
    ues with armor from the Nara and Heian ages, which show the Four Guard-
    ian Kings with swords and spears, but no glaives. In Ryōgen's stipulations, the
    usage may indicate weapons in general, but staffs could also be used in fights
    and they were a common companion of monks, as indicated in the document
    pertaining to the rowdy monks Ryōgen encountered in Nara. For these rea-
    sons, I have chosen to retain the original meaning of the compound.

24 *DNS* 1:13, Tenroku 1 (970) 7/16; Groner's work (xii, 358–359).

25 Katsuno, *Sōhei,* 149–152.

26 *DNS* 1:13, 213–214; Watanabe Eshin, "'Jie daishi kishō jūnikajō' ni tsuite," 10–
    11; Groner, *Ryōgen and Mt. Hiei,* 359–360.

27 *DNS* 1:13, 213–214.

28 Ryōgen's close relationship with Fujiwara no Morosuke, whose son became
    the monk's disciple and later succeeded him as Tendai head abbot, is well doc-
    umented. See, McMullin, "The Enryaku-ji and the Gion-Shrine Temple Com-
    plex," 161–184, and Groner's work, which pays much attention to this matter.

29 *Konjaku monogatari shū, Shin Nihon koten bungaku taikei* 37:5, 492–495;
    Abe, *Heian zenki seiji shi,* 283–284; McMullin, "The Enryaku-ji and the Gion-
    Shrine Temple Complex," 161–163.

30 McMullin, "The Enryaku-ji and the Gion-Shrine Temple Complex," 163.

31 For an English language account of the creation of branches, see Adolphson,
    "Institutional Diversity and Religious Integration," in *Heian Japan, Centers
    and Peripheries* (forthcoming).

32 See Hirata, "Nanto hokurei no akusō," 264. The source that first puts the
    blame on Ryōgen is the *Sange yōki senryaku* (supposedly completed on Ōei 6
    [1399] 2/21), which contains a section entitled "Shuto bumon no koto" (Re-
    garding the militarization of the clergy). See *Sange yōki senryaku,* in *Zoku gun-
    sho ruijū,* 27:2, 427. While Tsuji and Katsuno deny Ryōgen's role as an initiator

of armed monastic forces, Watanabe, for example, relying on the fictional account in the *Konjaku monogatari* squarely blames Ryōgen (Watanabe Eshin, "'Jie daishi kishō jūnikajō' ni tsuite," 14–18).

33   *Tendai zasuki*, 54–56; *Fusō ryakki*, Tengen 4 (981) twelfth month; Adolphson, *Gates of Power*, 64; Groner, *Ryōgen and Mt. Hiei*, 218–221.

34   *Fusō ryakki*, Tengen 5 (982) 1/10; Groner, *Ryōgen and Mt. Hiei*, 221–222.

35   *Chōya gunsai*, in *Shintei zōho kokushi taikei*, vol. 1, 414.

36   *Shōyūki*, Eiso 1 (989) 10/1, 29; Kinugawa, "Chūsei zenki no kenmon jiin, 12." The term *seihei* probably refers to professional elite warriors trained with certain weapons, in contrast to commoners, who might just have armed themselves.

37   *Tendai zasuki*, 46–48; Groner, *Ryōgen and Mt. Hiei*, 231–232; Hirata, "Nanto hokurei no akusō," 267; McMullin, "Sanmon-Jimon Schism," 98–99.

38   Groner, *Ryōgen and Mt. Hiei*, 222–229.

39   Kuroda Toshio made this point in his *Jisha seiryoku*, 33.

40   *Shōyūki*, Chōwa 2 (1013) 4/8; *DNS* 2:7, 782–783.

41   *Sakeiki*, Chōgen 8 (1035) 4/4; Hirata, "Nanto hokurei no akusō," 267.

42   From Ryōgen's times, the Enryakuji clergy became known as *sanzen bō*, or the "three thousand monks."

43   Hirata, "Nanto hokurei no akusō," 266–267; *Fusō ryakki*, Chōryaku 3 (1039) 2/18; *Tendai zasuki*, 54–56; *Hyakurenshō*, Chōryaku 3/2/17–19 (p. 20).

44   *Suisaki*, Eihō 1/8/18; *Fusō ryakki*, Eihō 1/4/15. For a perceptive analysis of this incident's impact on court politics, see Mikawa, "Jisha mondai," 100–102.

45   *Suisaki*, Eihō 1/8/1, 18, 20, 9/14, 16, 17, 20, 10/4; *Hyakurenshō*, Eihō 1/6/9, 17, 9/14, 15; *Fusō ryakki*, 322–324; *Tendai zasuki*, 64–65; *Tamefusa kyō ki*, Eihō 1/10/1, in *Shishū* 10 (1979): 102.

46   *Sochiki*, Shōryaku 5 (1081) 3/9; *Suisaki*, same date; *Kōfukuji ryaku nendaiki*, Eihō 1/3; *Hyakurenshō*, Eihō 1/3/6.

47   *Tōnomine engi*, 4–5.

48   See, for example, the works by Katsuno and Hioki Eigō.

49   *Denryaku, Chōshūki, Eikyū gannenki*, Eikyū 1 (1113) int. 3/20, 21, 22, all in *DNS* 3:14, 137–140.

50   *Denryaku*, Eikyū 1/int. 3/29, 4/1; *Chūyūki*, Eikyū 1/4/1; *Tendai zasuki*, 77–78; *DNS* 3:14, 145–147.

51   *Chūyūki*, Eikyū 1/4/30, 5/4; *Kōfukuji ryaku nendaiki*, Eikyū 1/4/29; *Hyakurenshō*, same date (p. 49); *DNS* 3:14, 179–180, 182–183, 185.

52   *Shinkō Kōya shunjū hennen shūroku* (hereafter cited as *Kōya shunjū*), 99; Miyasaka, *Kōyasan shi*, 24–27, 33; *Wakayama-ken no rekishi*, 744; Kuroda, *Jisha seiryoku*, 87. As Atsuta Kō has pointed out ("Negoro sōhei no genryū," 20), the events surrounding Kakuban's leaving Mt. Kōya are only described in a later source, the *Kōya shunjū*, which is strongly favorable to the Kongōbuji faction. Thus, some caution must be urged as to the reliability of its account.

53 *Kōya shunjū*, 112.

54 *Kōya shunjū*, 115; Atsuta, "Negoro sōhei no genryū," 23–24.

55 *DNS* 5:14, Ninji 3 (1242) 7/13; *Kōya shunjū*, 154; *DNS* 5:15, Kangen 1 (1243) 1/25, 7/13, 11/18; *DNS* 5:16, Kangen 1/1/25.

56 *Go-Nijō Moromichi ki, Fusō ryakki, Hyakurenshō*, Kanji 7 (1093) 8; *Denryaku, Chūyūki, Sōgo bunin*, Chōji 1 (1104) 8/8.

57 *Ichidai yōki, Kōfukuji bettō shidai*, Einin 1 (1293) 11/17; *Sanemi kyō ki, Entairyaku, Moromori ki*, Einin 3 (1295) 11/26. For a year full of conflicts between cloisters both within Enryakuji and Kōfukuji, see Kanji 2 (1248) in *DNS* 5:26, 337–338, 344–352, and *DNS* 5:27, 350–355.

58 *Hyakurenshō, Azuma kagami*, in *DNS* 5:11, Katei 3 (1237) 8/5.

59 *Hyakurenshō*, Jishō 1 (1177) 10/7.

60 *Sankaiki*, Angen 1/8/24.

61 *Genpei seisuiki*, 200–204, Jishō 2 (1178) 8/6, 9/20; *Akihiro ō ki, Hyakurenshō*, Jishō 2/10/4; *Gyokuyō*, Jishō 2/10/4, 11/5. The edict was issued on 1178/7/18.

62 *Gyokuyō*, Jishō 3 (1179) 6/5, 10, 7/25, 9/11, 10/3, 11/2; *Sankaiki*, Jishō 3/10/3, 25, 11/2; *Hyakurenshō*, Jishō 3/10/3, 11/2, 5, 7.

63 *Meigetsuki*, Kennin 1 (1203) 10/15, Gankyū 1 (1204) 1/21; *Tendai zasuki*, 136–139; *Meigetsuki, Sanchōki, Hyakurenshō, Nakasuke ō ki*, Ken'ei 1 (1206) 9/25.

64 See Adolphson, *Gates of Power*, 196–198.

65 *Bun'ei gannen Nakatomi sukemasa ki*, Bun'ei 1 (1264) 8/19, 9/2; *Kōfukuji ryaku nendaiki*, Katei 1 (1235), Shōka 2 (1258) 7/2, 8/2 (p. 160, 162). For a detailed treatment of this incident, see Adolphson, *Gates of Power*, 223–226.

66 *Bun'ei gannen Nakatomi sukemasa ki*, Bun'ei 1/9/1–3, Bun'ei 2 (1265) 6/28, 7/22; *Kōfukuji bettō shidai*, 34; *Geki nikki*, Bun'ei 1/9/22.

67 *Denryaku, Chūyūki, Hyakurenshō*, Tennin 1 (1108) 9/10; *Gyokuyō, Kikki, Hyakurenshō, Tōnomine ryakki*, Jōan 3 (1173) 5, 6, 10; *Minkeiki, Meigetsuki, Hyakurenshō, Tendai zasuki, Moromori ki*, Antei 1 (1227) 8/8, Antei 2 (1228), 4–5.

68 *Kanchūki, Zokushi gushō*, Kōan 7 (1284) 8/28; *Zokushi gushō*, Shōwa 1 (1312) 6/9.

69 *Azuma kagami*, Katei 1 (1235) 5/23, 7/24; Katei 1/7/24; *Hyakurenshō*, Katei 1/6/3, int. 6/19–21, 23, 27, 28.

70 *Azuma kagami*, Katei 2 (1236) 2/28, 3/21, 7/24, 8/20, 10/2, 5, 6; *Hyakurenshō*, Katei 2/1/1, 5, 2/19, 21, 7/28. For more details, see Adolphson, *Gates of Power*, 218–222.

71 *Chūyūki*, Kahō 1 (1094) 3/6; *DNS* 3:3, same date; Endō, *Kuramadera*, 94; Hashikawa, *Kuramadera shi*, 23.

72 *Gyokuyō*, Angen 1 (1175) 8/23; *Sankaiki*, Angen 1/8/24; *Hyakurenshō*, same date.

73 *Honchō seiki*, Kyūan 1 (1145) 7/18, Kyūan 2 (1146) 4/25; *Taiki*, Kyūan 1 (1145) 7/12, 9/13; *Kōfukuji ryaku nendaiki*, Kyūan 1 (p. 118).

74 *DNS* 4:9, Jōgen 2 (1208) 2/3.

75 *DNS* 4:14, Jōkyū 1 (1219) 1/14.

76 *DNS* 5:2, Jōō 2 (1223) 6/26.

77 *DNS* 5:2, Karoku 1 (1224) fifth month.

78 Adolphson, *Gates of Power,* 176–178; Tonomura, *Community and Commerce,* 29.

79 Adolphson, *Gates of Power,* 390; Tonomura, *Community and Commerce,* 29–30, 217; *DNS* 5:10, Katei 1 (1235) 7/23, 26, 29.

80 *Chūyūki,* Eikyū 2 (1114) 6/ 30, 7/16; Hioki Eigō, *Sōhei no rekishi,* 111–112.

81 *Taiki,* Ninpei 1/2/23; Hioki Eigō, *Sōhei no rekishi,* 320.

82 *Heihanki,* Hōgen 1 (1156) int. 9/18.

83 Adolphson, *Gates of Power,* 157–166.

84 *Gyokuyō, Sankaiki, Meigetsuki,* Jishō 4 (1180) 3/18, 25.

85 *Heike monogatari,* 163–164; *Gyokuyō,* Jishō 4 (1180) 12/29.

86 *Kikki,* Jūei 2 (1183) 7/27; Hirata, "Nanto hokurei no akusō," 290.

87 There are abundant references to temple followers joining Yoshinaka, although the numbers mentioned are naturally inflated. See for example the *Sankō Genpei seisuiki,* vol. 2, 498ff.

88 *Genpei seisuiki,* 701; Hirata, "Nanto hokurei no akusō," 291–292.

89 *Sankō Genpei seisuiki,* vol. 2, 535–554; *Genpei seisuiki,* 732–740; Hirata, "Nanto hokurei no akusō," 290–291.

90 *Azuma kagami,* Kenkyū 1 (1190) 5/3 (p. 384); *DNS* 4:4, Kenkyū 5 (1194) 11/13 (pp. 717–723); Hirata, "Nanto hokurei no akusō," 293–294. Oddly enough, the *Azuma kagami* also indicates that Kakumyō was prohibited from leaving Hakonesan the following year (*DNS* 4:5, Kenkyū 6 [1195] 10/13). We cannot know why Kakumyō earned the trust of Yoritomo and Masako, only to be ordered into house arrest a year later, but it is possible that this inconsistency is due to the later nature of the source.

91 *Gyokuyō,* Jishō 4 (1180) 9/3, 10/2, Yōwa 1 (1181) 9/6, *Azuma kagami,* Jishō 5 (1185) 1/21; *Koji ruien,* see "sōhei," 195–196.

92 *The Tale of Heike,* 372; *Azuma kagami,* Genryaku 2 (1185) 2/21.

93 *DNS* 4:1, Bunji 2 (1186) 2/3, 6/11; *DNS* 4:2, Bunji 3 (1187) 9/20.

94 *Azuma Kagami,* Bunji 5 (1189) 2/22.

95 *Senji* (imperial edict) cited in *Gyokuei,* in *DNS* 4:11, Kenryaku 2 (1212) 3/22, 710–724; relevant clause on 719–720; *Hyakurenshō,* Kenryaku 2 (1212) 3/22.

96 *Tendai zasuki,* 152; *Kenji sannen nikki,* Kenji 3 (1215) 7/8, 23, 12/16, 25, 27.

97 *DNS* 4:13, Kenpō 2 (1215) 9/10.

98 *Jōkyū ikusa monogatari,* 41, 80–81; *Koji ruien,* see sōhei entry, 291.

99 *Kōya shunjū,* Antei 2 (1228) 11/28, 147; *Meigetsuki,* Kanki 2 (1230) 4, in *DNS* 5:5, 718.

100 It is feasible that the term *sansō buyū* refers more generally to "martial mountain monks," but given the activities of Enryakuji's armed clerics at the time, it is more likely a reference to the latter.

101 *Samurai dokoro sata hen,* in *Gunsho ruijū,* vol. 8, 412–413; See also *Chūsei hōsei shiryō shū* 1, 92–93.

102 *Tsuikahō* 200, Ninji 2 (1242) 3/3, in *Chūsei hōsei shiryō shū* 1, 139; *Tsuikahō* 102, En'ō 1 (1239), 4/13, in *Chūsei hōsei shiryō shū* 1, 108.

103 *Tsuikahō* 200, Ninji 2 (1242) 3/3, in *Chūsei hōsei shiryō shū* 1, 139.

104 *Tendai zasuki,* Bun'ei 2 (1265) 4/13.

105 *Chōya gunsai,* 41–44 (Tenshō 1 [1131] 2/13).

106 *Kamakura ibun* 7, document 4716, *Kaijūsanji gakushūra renshō kishōmon an,* Bunryaku 1 (1234) 12/27, 165–166.

107 *Kōyasan monjo,* vol. 8, document 1763, *Kōyasan shoshū hyōjō okibumi an,* Shōō 2 (1289) 7/6, 75–76; Seita, *Chūsei jiin,* 122–123.

108 For a collaborative work on the transitional nature of the fourteenth century, see Mass, *The Origins of Medieval Japan.*

109 For a useful survey of Yoshimitsu's political exploits, see Hall, "The Muromachi Bakufu," 191–193. See also Imatani, *Muromachi no ōken,* and Imatani and Yamamura, "Not for a Lack of Will or Wile."

110 Adolphson, *The Gates of Power,* 327–333.

111 Adolphson, *The Gates of Power,* 307–315, 319–321.

112 Kuroda Toshio, "Chūsei jisha seiryoku ron," 282–283.

113 Kuroda Toshio, "Chūsei jisha seiryoku ron," 283; Shimosaka, "Sanmon shisetsu," 67–114.

114 *Keiran jūyōshū engi,* 506; Hirata, *Sōhei to bushi,* 241.

115 Conlan, *State of War,* 5.

116 Watanabe, *Sōhei seisuiki,* 152–153.

117 See Adolphson, *The Gates of Power,* 327–345.

118 It is worth noting that recent scholarship suggests the warrior class is not as easily defined as has long been assumed. As in the case of temple warriors, many armed men had other occupations as their main trades, but resorted to using weapons as the situation called for it.

119 See for example, Yi Changhŭi, "Imjin waeran chung ŭisŭnggun ŭi hwaltong e taehayŏ—Sŏsan taesa wa Samyŏngdang ŭl chungsim ŭro" [A Righteous Monk Army during the Hideyoshi Invasion: Examination of Sŏsan taesa and Samyŏngdang]; Nukii Masayuki, "Imjin waeran kwa sŭng ŭibyŏngjang Samyŏng taesa" [The Hideyoshi Invasion and the Righteous Monk Soldier, Samyŏng]; Yang Ŭnyong, "Imjin waeran kwa honam ŭi pulgyo ŭisŭnggun" [The Hideyoshi Invasion and the Monk Army in the Southwest Regions] *Han'guk chonggyo,* 19 (1994): 1–34; Yang Ŭnyong, "Chŏngyu chaeran ŭi sŏkchugwan chŏnt'u wa hwaŏmsa ŭisŭnggun" [The Sŏkchugwan Battle during the Second Hideyoshi Invasion of 1597 and the Righteous Monk Army in the Hwaŏm Temple]. *Kasan hakbo* 4 (1995): 172–189. I am indebted to Jungwon Kim, a graduate student at Harvard, for collecting and summarizing these works for me.

Chapter Three:
The Fighting Servants of the Buddha

1 For an in depth treatment of the Tadatsune disturbance in the early eleventh century, see Karl Friday, "Lordship Interdicted: Taira no Tadatsune and the Limited Horizons of Warrior Ambition," in Adolphson, et al., *Heian Japan, Centers and Peripheries.*

2 Kuroda, *Jisha seiryoku,* 32.

3 *Chūyūki,* Ten'ei 4 (1113) 4/1, 6, 16, 18, 19, 21.

4 *DNS* 3:2, Kanji 6 (1092) 5/20; Kanji 6/9/28.

5 *Meigetsuki,* Kangi 1 (1229) 9/12.

6 Seita, *Chūsei jiin,* 35; Kageyama, *Hieizan,* 103.

7 *Kenro seiyo,* in *Gunsho ruijū,* vol. 17, 793; Seita, *Chūsei jiin,* 35; Kageyama, *Hieizan,* 103. The *Kenro seiyo* is believed to have been written by a certain Ono Akitsugu around the year 1574 in an attempt to chronicle some of the traditions of Enryakuji. Its later authorship casts some doubt on its accuracy for earlier ages, but many of its details can be confirmed in contemporary sources, as shown in this chapter.

8 *Gyokuyō,* Jōan 3 (1173) 7/21.

9 *Heian ibun* 7, Jōan 4 (1174) 1/18, 2833–2834.

10 *Gyokuyō,* Jishō 4 (1180) 5/26, 27.

11 For an instructive example of this view, see Atsuta, who states that "*akusō* was virtually synonymous with *sōhei* during the Heian period" (Atsuta, "Negoro sōhei," 24). See also Hirata's "Nanto hokurei no akusō"; and McCullough, who consistently uses "soldier-monks" for *akusō,* in *Tale of the Heike,* 149, 164, 196, 274.

12 *Taiki,* Kōji 1 (1142) 8/3.

13 *Genpei seisuiki,* 110–111; McCullough, *The Tale of Heike,* 61.

14 *Chūyūki,* Chōji 1 (1104) 10/30.

15 The electronic search, performed on 8/15/04, includes full-text databases of the *Nihon kokiroku, Dai Nihon shiryō, Dai Nihon komonjo,* and *Heian ibun* series.

16 *Heian ibun* 6, document 2919, *Iga no kuni zaichō kanjinra gesu,* Hōgen 3 (1158) 4, 2395; Arai, *Chūsei akutō,* 122.

17 *Iga no kuni Kuroda no shō shiryō,* vol. 1, document 252, *Kansenji an,* Ten'yō 2 (1145) 1/17, 252–253; Arai, *Chūsei akutō,* 130.

18 Thompson, *Customs in Common,* 188.

19 *Heian ibun* 6, document 2471, *Onjōji sō Chōjun ra shinjiki,* Kōji 1/5/8, 2073–2074; *Honchō seiki,* Kōji 1 (1142) 3/17; Arai, *Chūsei akutō,* 89. For more about the idea of justified violence and protests by the entire clergy, see Adolphson, *Gates of Power,* 271–272.

20 *Kamakura ibun* 33, document 25668, *Hyōgo seki kassen akugyō tomogara Kyōmyō shinjō,* Shōwa 4 (1315) eleventh month, 247–248; Koizumi, *Akutō,* 81–85.

21 *Hyōgo ken shi: shiryō hen, chūsei* 5, *Tōdaiji shutora mōshijō an,* 539–540.

22 *Heihanki,* Nin'an 3 (1168) 7/18; Arai, *Chūsei akutō,* 75–77.

23 *Heian ibun* 2, document 303, *Tendai zasu Ryōgen kishō,* Tenroku 1 (970) 10/16, 431–440; Arai, *Chūsei akutō,* 78.

24 *Kōya shunjū,* Hōen 6 (1140) 12/7–8, 97; Atsuta, "Negoro sōhei," 19–20.

25 Hosokawa, "Sōhei to jiryō shōen," 135–136, citing the *Kokan zassan,* unpublished compilation at the Historiographical Institute, volume 1.

26 Arai, *Chūsei akutō,* 78.

27 *Kōfukuji kishiki,* unpublished document, 1.

28 See Tomikura, *Heike monogatari zenchūshaku,* vol. 1, 351, 354–355, and 613–614 (where the quote can be found).

29 Hirata, *Sōhei to bushi,* 175–176.

30 *Tōnomine ryakki,* 444–445; *Kōfukuji kishiki,* 3; Izumiya, *Kōfukuji,* 82–85.

31 *Genpei seisuiki,* 207. By serving the Buddha directly, monastic workers were in other words neglecting their more mundane duties. For a slightly shorter version of this quote, see McCullough, *The Tale of Heike,* 86.

32 *Gyokuyō,* Jishō 3 (1179) 11/2; *Sankaiki,* same date; *Hyakurenshō,* Jishō 3/11/2, 5, 7; see also Adolphson, *Gates of Power,* 158–161.

33 *Tōdaiji monjo,* vol. 5, document 91, *Tōdaiji chūmon dōshu mōshijō,* 201–202.

34 *Tōdaiji monjō,* vol. 12, document 311, *Kuroda no shō shōkanra ukebumi,* Jōan 5 (1175) 5/23, 18–20; *Tōdaiji monjō,* vol. 16, document 784, *Yoda hō jitō Mitsutomo chinjō an,* Shōwa 5 (1316) fifth month, 189–194; *Hyōgo ken shi: shiryō hen, chūsei* 5, *Tōdaiji Hokke dōshu shūgi kiroku,* Shōwa 1 (1312) 9/14, 45.

35 *Tōdaiji monjō,* vol. 5, document 145, *Tōdaiji hokkedō zento mōshijō,* Tokuji 3 (1308) intercalary eighth month, 435–437.

36 *Koji ruien, Heiji bu* 1, 283.

37 There are a number of instructive examples in contemporary documents and diaries, but to note just one, some fifteen *hosshiwara* of Hiesha, Gion and Kiyomizudera were apparently rowdy and violent enough in the sixth month of 1114 that orders were issued to have them arrested. It seems, however, that they ran away, thus escaping punishment. (*Chūyūki,* Eikyū 2 [1114] 6/22, 27, 30, 7/2.)

38 See for example, *Tendai zasuki,* 196, and *Genpei seisuiki,* 80, 114.

39 The Japanese reads: *Kamogawa no mizu, sugoroku no sai, yama hosshi, sorezore chin ga kokoro ni shitagawanu mono.* See *Genpei seisuiki,* 83; *Heike monogatari,* 93; McCullough, *The Tale of the Heike,* 50.

40 *Shunki,* Chōkyū 1 (1040) 4/29.

41 *Gyokuyō,* Jishō 4 (1180) 12/1.

42 *Koryŏ sa,* Hyŏnjong (1014) eleventh month, Sukchong 9 (1104) twelfth month; Yi Sŭnghan, "Koryŏ Sukchong," 18–19.

43 *DNS* 3:8, Kajō 1 (1106) 9/9.

44 *Suisaki,* Eihō 1/8/1, 9/14; *Fusō ryakki,* Eihō 1/4/15, 28.

45 *Eikyūki,* Eikyū 1/4/14 in *DNS* 3:14, 163–164.

46 *Chūyūki,* Eikyū 1/4/30. Another important source confirms the presence of secular warriors in this confrontation:

> On the twenty-fifth day of last [the fifth] month, when the Kōfukuji clergy came to the capital, several members of the government troops dispatched by the noble council to stop them sustained injuries inflicted by the temple's secular warriors *[zokuhei].* These were the deeds of residents of Yamato Province and Kinpusenji's estates, and the imperial police captain was ordered to arrest those fellows promptly. (*Eikyū gannen ki,* Eikyū 1/6/4)

47 *Tendai zasuki,* 99; *Hyakurenshō,* Eiman 1 (1165) 8/9, 10/26, 10/28, 79; *Akihiro ō ki,* in volume 5 of *Shiga-ken shi,* 69–70; *Akihiro ō ki,* unpublished, Eiman 1/8/12, 13, 30; *San'e jōichiki,* Eiman 1/10/16, 320. The quote can be found in the *San'e jōichiki.*

48 *Gyokuyō,* Jishō 4 (1180) 12/12.

49 *Gyokuyō,* Jūei 2 (1183) int. 10/29.

50 *Daigoji zōjiki,* 458–459; Tsuji, "Sōhei no gen'yu," 791–792; Hirata, *Sōhei to bushi,* 181.

51 *Kamakura ibun* 37, document 29069, *Saishōkōin shōen mokuroku an,* Shōchū 2 (1325), third month, 309–313.

52 *Heian ibun* 4, document 1646, *Kansenji* of Chōji 2 (1105) 7/14, 1505; document 1663, *Horikawa tennō senji an* (a copy of an imperial edict from Emperor Horikawa), Kajō 1 (1106) 8/14, 1520; document 1681, *Horikawa tennō senji,* Kajō 2 (1107) 12/28, 1532–1533; *DNS* 3:9, 737–738.

53 *Genpei seisuiki,* 1144–1145; Hirata, *Sōhei to bushi,* 178–179.

54 *Jōkyūki,* 23.

55 *Jōkyū heiranki,* 653; *Jōkyū ikusa monogatari,* 41, 81; Hioki Eigō, *Sōhei no rekishi,* 106–107.

56 Nagashima, *Nara ken no rekishi,* 81; Arai, *Chūsei akutō,* 73–75.

57 *Honchō zoku monzui,* 29; Hirata, *Sōhei to bushi,* 183.

58 *Heian ibun* 4, document 1793, *Toba tennō senmei an,* Ten'ei 4 (1113) 4/15, 1617–1618.

59 *Heihanki,* Ninpei 2 (1152) 6/7, 9; *Honchō seiki,* Ninpei 2/6/11 (quote). For other examples of commoners' use of the temple and shrine immunities, see Hirata, *Sōhei to bushi,* 192–204.

60 *Heian ibun* 5, document 1993, *Shirakawa hōkō ontsugebumi,* Hōan 4 (1123) 7/1, 1728–1729; *Tendai zasuki,* 80; Hirata, *Sōhei to bushi,* 198–199.

61 *Chūyūki,* Hōan 1 (1120) 4/28; *Hyakurenshō,* Hōan 1/4/29.

62 *Hanazono tennō shinki,* Shōwa 3 (1314) 5/1.

63 *Shin'yo gubu shoshō jinnin shihai jō an,* Genkō 1 (1321) 5/18, in *Tōdaiji tōtō Yakushiji'in monjo,* facsimile at the Historiographical Institute; Hiraoka, "Sōhei ni tsuite," 576–577.

64 *Kōfukuji kishiki,* 3; Hioki Eigō, *Sōhei no rekishi,* 77.

65 McCullough, *Tale of the Heike*, 153–154.
66 *Genpei seisuiki*, 579; McCullough, *Tale of the Heike*, 194–195.
67 *DNS* 4:11, Kenryaku 2 (1212) 3/14, pp. 700–712 (quote on p. 711); Nakazawa, *Chūsei no buryoku*, 5–6.
68 *Wakamiya saireiki*, 442; Nakazawa, *Chūsei no buryoku*, 7. Warriors were in fact frequent participants at various shrine festivals in processions as well as in competitions. See, for example, *Kasuga Wakamiya saireizu* and *Tōdaiji Hachiman tegai e ki*, 287.
69 Nakazawa, *Chūsei no buryoku*, 170–171.
70 Friday, *Samurai, Warfare and the State*, 122–123.
71 *Tendai zasuki*, Nin'an 2 (1167), 100; *Sankaiki*, Jishō 3 (1179) 10/3; *Ōei shosha Engyōbon Heike monogatari*, 194–195 ("Sanmon no gakushō to dōshu to kassen no koto: fu sanmon metsubō no koto"); *Genpei seisuiki*, 200; Nakazawa, *Chūsei no buryoku*, 13–14, 164–165.
72 *Azuma kagami*, Jishō 4 (1180) 5/23, 27; Nakazawa, *Chūsei no buryoku*, 165.
73 McCullough, *Tale of the Heike*, 194–195; Nakazawa, *Chūsei no buryoku*, 14.
74 The *Aki no yo no nagamonogatari* belongs to the genre of *otogi zōshi*, which might best be described as short illustrated stories. It emerged first in the middle of the Muromachi period and was popular well into the Edo era. The *Aki no yo no nagamonogatari* tells the story of an Enryakuji monk who falls in love with a young page from Onjōji.
75 *Heike monogatari*, vol. 2, 79; McCullough, *Tale of the Heike*, 194; Nakazawa, *Chūsei no buryoku*, 184–185.
76 *DNS* 4:7, Kennin 3 (1203) 8/7; Nakazawa, *Chūsei no buryoku*, 165.
77 *Azuma kagami*, Kennin 3 (1203) 9/17; *Meigetsuki*, Kennin 3/8/4; Nakazawa, *Chūsei no buryoku*, 165.
78 *Hōnen shōnin eden*, vol. 2, 66–67; Nakazawa, *Chūsei no buryoku*, 182–183.
79 *Meigetsuki*, Kenpō 1 (1213) 7/25, 8/3; Nakazawa, *Chūsei no buryoku*, 166.
80 *Azuma kagami*, Kenpō 1/8/14; Nakazawa, *Chūsei no buryoku*, 166.
81 *DNS* 4:13, Kenpō 3 (1215) 3/16.
82 *DNS* 5:8, Tenpuku 1 (1233) 2/20.
83 *Gyokuyō, Azuma kagami*, Bunji 1 (1185) 3/10, 6/22, 23; *Kikki*, Bunji 1/6/23.
84 *Taiki*, Kōji 1 (1142) 3/16; Nakazawa, *Chūsei no buryoku*, 11.
85 *Kokon chōmonjū*, in *Nihon koten bungaku taikei*, vol. 84, 59; Nakazawa, *Chūsei no buryoku*, 11.
86 Ōshima, "Sōhei no hassei ki," 22.
87 Hirata, *Sōhei to bushi*, 165ff.
88 *Sochiki*, Eihō 1 (1081) 6/9.

Chapter Four:
The Teeth and Claws of the Buddha

1 Mass, *Warrior Government*. See also his "The Kamakura Bakufu," 49. For a more recent and detailed study of the crucial links between provincial warriors and the capital elites, see Friday, *Samurai, Warfare and the State*.

2 *Sonpi bunmyaku*, vol. 1, 313; *Kokushi bunin*, vol. 4, 349–351; Tsunoda, "Jōjin sōzu no yakuwari," 471–472. Although lacking in its analysis of Jōjin's military activities, Tsunoda's chapter is helpful for its comprehensive treatment of the monk's social background and political connections. Hirata's "Nanto hokurei" also offers helpful information about Jōjin.

3 From what we can tell from the genealogical records, Jōjin was one of his father's main heirs, possibly even his oldest son. His choice to become a monk thus appears somewhat puzzling. Perhaps he saw more promise in becoming a ranking monk in one of Japan's most powerful temples than in continuing to battle against them as a local warrior-manager.

4 *Go-Nijō Moromichi ki*, Kanji 7 (1093) 12/8, Eichō 2 (1096) 2/15; *Sōgō bunin*, 170; Tsunoda, "Jōjin sōzu no yakuwari," 473; Hirata, "Nanto hokurei," 272. The Godan-no-hō was a ceremony dedicated to Godai Myōō, in which celebrants prayed for the pacification of rebellions and against disasters and greed in the realm.

5 *Go-Nijō Moromichi ki*, Eichō 1 (1096) 2/12, 15; *Shunki*, Eishō 7 (1052) 7/12.

6 The details regarding the confrontations of 1100 can be found in the diary of Fujiwara no Munetada more than a year later. "A letter arrived from the Tendai head abbot's residence reading as follows: 'What caused the battle that took place at Saitō? Jōjin brought warriors, and attacked Zōnin's dwelling. But the clergy mobilized and confronted them in a battle. During this time, the mountain was closed, and the situation was thus very troubling.'" See *Denryaku*, Kōwa 3 (1101) 12/3; *DNS* 3:6, same date.

7 *Honchō seiki*, Kōwa 5 (1103) 7/13; *Hyakurenshō*, same date; Tsunoda, "Jōjin sōzu no yakuwari," 475–476.

8 *Chūyūki*, Chōji 1 (1104) 6/15, 21; *Sōgō bunin*, Chōji 1 (p. 171). The significance of the addition of the Tōtō clergy should not be underestimated. In particular, it appears that the head administrator of that section's Sanmai'in, Kankei, was quite skilled in leading the clergy in armed confrontations (Tsunoda, "Jōjin sōzu no yakuwari," 476).

9 *Chūyūki*, Chōji 1 (1104) 6/24; *Denryaku*, Chōji 1/6/24–27.

10 *Chūyūki*, Chōji 1 (1104) 6/24.

11 *DNS* 3:3, Kahō 2 (1095) 10/24.

12 *Chūyūki*, Chōji 1/6/22–24, 29, 8/13; *Denryaku*, Chōji 1/7; *Sōgō bunin*, 171.

13 *Chūyūki*, Chōji 1/10/14, 21, 26, twelfth month.

14 *Chūyūki*, Chōji 1/10/26.

15 *Chūyūki*, Chōji 1 (1104) 10/7, 29; Chōji 2 (1105) 10/29.

16 *Tendai zasuki,* 72–73; *Chūyūki,* Chōji 2 (1105) 10/30; *DNS* 3:8, 272; Muraya-
     ma, *Hieizan shi,* 167. This incident is described in more detail in my *Gates of
     Power,* 113–115.

17 *Chūyūki,* Chōji 2 (1105) 10/30.

18 *Chūyūki,* Kajō 1 (1106) 9/30.

19 The idea of "representative justice" in Heian Japan meant not only that elites
     were expected to punish or hand over criminals in their service, but also that
     substitutes could be sent to exile or detained in lieu of a favored retainer.

20 *Chūyūki,* Eikyū 2 (1114) 2/30; *DNS* 3:9, same date.

21 *Chūyūki,* Kajō 2 (1107) 12/30, Tennin 1 (1108) 1/9; *DNS,* 3:9, 744; *Sonpi bun-
     myaku,* vol. 1, 269; *Sōgō bunin,* Kajō 2/12/28; Tsunoda, "Jōjin sōzu no yaku-
     wari," 481. Interestingly, Kankei was a distant relative of Jōjin, as was Muneta-
     da, who was consistently critical of Jōjin's behavior in his diary.

22 *Chūyūki,* Eikyū 2 (1114) 2/20.

23 *Chūyūki,* Gen'ei (1118) 2/15.

24 *Sonpi bunmyaku,* vol. 3, 162; *Kōfukuji bettō sangō keizu,* 27.

25 See Varley, *Warriors of Japan,* 24. The term *sōga* (literally "claws and teeth")
     was well known in Japan during the Heian age from one of the Chinese clas-
     sics, the *Book of Odes* (see Ezra Pound, *The Classic Anthology,* 99), and it ap-
     pears in the *Honchō monzui,* a collection of poems and stories from the ninth
     through the eleventh centuries. In one case, the term specifically refers to the
     imperial police, the *kebiishi* (*Honchō monzui,* 51). I am indebted to Marjan
     Boogert for bringing these sources and citations to my attention during a
     graduate seminar at Harvard in 1999.

26 *Sonpi bunmyaku,* vol. 3, 162; *Kōfukuji bettō sangō keizu,* 27; Tsunoda, "Shōmu
     tennō haka," 339–340. If we go further back in the genealogy, we also find
     that Minamoto no Yorichika (Shinjitsu's great, great, great grandfather) was
     a governor of Yamato Province, but he was exiled because of an appeal from
     Kōfukuji. Yorichika's son, Yorifusa, suffered a similar fate as an Enryakuji
     protest resulted in his deposition as governor and subsequent exile (Hirata,
     "Nanto hokurei," 282).

27 *Kōfukuji bettō sangō keizu,* 27; Tsunoda, "Shōmu tennō haka," 349; Hirata,
     "Nanto hokurei," 283. For more on the beginning of the *insei* age, see Hurst,
     Insei.

28 *Chōshūki, Chūyūki,* Daiji 4 (1129) 11/11; *Kōfukuji bettō shidai,* 13–14.

29 *Chōshūki,* Daiji 4/11/21; *Chūyūki,* Daiji 4/11/12; Tsunoda, "Shōmu tennō
     haka," 342; Uwayokote, "Insei ki no Genji," 174.

30 *Chōshūki,* Daiji 4/11/24, 28, 30; *Chūyūki,* Daiji 4/11/25, 29; *Kōfukuji bettō shi-
     dai,* 13–14; Tsunoda, "Shōmu tennō haka," 341–342.

31 *Chōshūki,* Daiji 4/11/18.

32 *Chōshūki,* Daiji 4/11/18; *Kōfukuji bettō shidai,* 15.

33 *Kōfukuji bettō shidai,* 15.

34 *Taiki,* Hōen 2 (1137) 11/7; *Kōfukuji bettō sangō keizu,* 27; *Kōfukuji bettō shidai,* 15; *Kōfukuji ryaku nendaiki,* 147; *Sonpi bunmyaku,* vol. 1, 162; Motoki, *Insei ki,* 259–260.

35 *Kōfukuji bettō shidai,* 16.

36 *Kōfukuji bettō shidai,* 16–17; *Nanto daishu jūrakuki,* 325–327; Tsunoda, "Shōmu tennō haka," 343–344.

37 *Nanto daishu jūrakuki,* 326; *Hyakurenshō,* Hōen 5 (1139) 11/16, 12/2; *Kōfukuji bettō shidai,* 16–17.

38 *Taiki,* Hōji 1 (1142) 8/3; Tsunoda, "Shōmu tennō haka," 344–345; Hirata, "Nanto hokurei," 285; Uwayokote, "Insei ki no Genji," 167–168, 174–175; Motoki, *Insei ki,* 221–222.

39 *Taiki,* Kyūan 1 (1145) 7/12, 26, 9/13; *Kōfukuji ryaku nendaiki,* 148; *Honchō seiki,* Kyūan 1/7/18.

40 *Kōfukuji sangō bunin,* in *Zoku gunsho ruijū,* 4:2, 706–707; *Kōfukuji bettō sangō keizu,* 27; *Kōfukuji bettō shidai,* 18.

41 *Honchō seiki,* Kyūan 5 (1149) 10/30, 11/25.

42 Tsunoda, "Shōmu tennō haka," 350–351.

43 *Heihanki,* Hōgen 1 (1156) 7/11; *Taiki,* Kyūju 2 (1155) 11/10; *Hōgen monogatari,* in *Nihon koten bungaku taikei,* vol. 31, 85, 125. The *Heihanki* mentions lower numbers for the combating forces, with Taira no Kiyomori heading some three hundred mounted warriors and Tametomo of the Tadazane faction some two hundred. No numbers are noted for Shinjitsu's forces.

44 *Heihanki,* Hōgen 1 (1156) 7/11; *Hōgen monogatari,* 126; Hosokawa, "Sōhei to jiryō shōen," 133.

45 Hirata, "Nanto hokurei," 287; Tsunoda, "Shōmu tennō haka," 348.

46 Tsunoda, "Shōmu tennō haka," 348.

47 *Heihanki,* Hōgen 3 (1158) 7/17; *Hōryūji bettō ki,* in *Zoku gunsho ruijū,* 4:2, 799.

48 *Heian ibun* 5, document 2112, *Tōdaiji kumonjo kanjō,* Daiji 2 (1127) 11/20, 1818–1820; Hisano, "Kakunin kō," 3–4.

49 Hisano, "Kakunin kō," 11–12, 14.

50 *Heian ibun* 6, document 2676, *Kansenji,* Kyūan 5 (1149) 9/12, 2256–2257; document 2919, *Iga no kuni zaichō kanjinra ge,* Hōgen 3 (1158), fourth month, 2393–2396; Hisano, "Kakunin kō," 17.

51 *Heian ibun* 6, document 2919, *Iga no kuni zaichō kanjinra gesu,* Hōgen 3 (1158), 4, 2395; Arai, *Chūsei akutō,* 122.

52 *Heian ibun* 6, document 2947–2948, *Sō Nōe chinjō an,* Hōgen 3/9/11, 2427–2430; Hisano, "Kakunin kō," 18–22.

53 *Heian ibun* 6, documents 2973, 2985, 2987; Hisano, "Kakunin kō," 26–30.

54 *Heian ibun* 7, document 3221, *Kansenji,* Ōhō 2 (1162) 5/22, 2569.

55 *Heian ibun* 7, document 3154, *Shoshin hosshi Ken'yo chinjō an,* Ōhō 1 (1161) 6/9, 2532–2533.

56 *Heian ibun* 7, document 3520, *Kangakuin mandokoro kudashibumi*, Kaō 1
    (1169) 11/19, 2745–2749; document 3547, *Kōfukuji saikondō shutō ge an*, Kaō 2
    (1170), intercalary fourth month, 2761–2765; *Heian ibun* 9, document 4871,
    Sō Kinsai satsumon an, Kaō 2/int. 4/15, 3775–3776; Izumiya, *Kōfukuji*, 84; Hi-
    sano, "Kakunin kō," 31–32.

57 *Kamakura ibun* 3, document 1206, *Tōdaiji sangōra mōshijō an*, Kennin 1 (1201),
    fourth month; *Kugyō bunin* in *Nihon shi sōran*, vol. 2, *kodai, chūsei* 1, 88; *Mei-
    getsuki*, Kennin 2 (1202) 1/23; Hisano, "Kakunin kō," 35–36.

58 Atsuta, "Negoro sōhei," 20–21; *Negoro yōsho: Kakuban kiso shiryō shūsei*, docu-
    ment 93, *Minamoto no Tameyoshi keijō an*, Hōen 6 (1140) 11/26, 120.

59 *Heian ibun* 9, document 4858, *Kii no kuni Daidenpōin sōto ge an*, Nin'an 3
    (1168) 3/3, 3770–3771.

60 *Heihanki*, Nin'an 3 (1168) 5/3; *Gumaiki*, unpublished facsimile at the Histo-
    riographical Institute, University of Tokyo, Nin'an 3/5/3.

61 *Kokawadera engi*, in *Kokawa chō shi*, vol. 3, 183–184.

62 *Heian ibun* 9, document 4859, *Go-Shirakawa jōkō inzen*, Nin'an 3/5/3, 2771;
    Heihanki, Nin'an 3/5/3.

63 *Heian ibun* 9, document 4860, *Kii no kuni Daidenbōin sōto ge an*, Nin'an
    3/8/2, 3771.

64 *Heian ibun* 9, document 4861, *Go-Shirakawa jōkō inzen an*, Nin'an 3/8/9,
    3771–3772.

65 For more details, see Adolphson, *Gates of Power*, 67–74.

66 *Nanto daishu jūrakuki*, 326; *Hyakurenshō*, Hōen 5 (1139) 11/16, 12/2; *Kōfukuji
    bettō shidai*, 16–17.

67 *Hyakurenshō*, Chōkan 1 (1163) 7/25, 77–78; *Kōfukuji bettō shidai*, 19; *Kōfukuji
    ryaku nendaiki*, 150.

68 *Kōfukuji bettō shidai*, 18–19.

69 *Sankaiki*, Nin'an 2 (1167) 4/19, 23, 5/7, 15; *Gyokuyō*, Nin'an 2/4/18, 19; *Hei-
    hanki*, Nin'an 2/5/15; *Kōfukuji bettō shidai*, 19; *Kōfukuji ryaku nendaiki*, 151.

70 Takahashi, "Sonshō hōshinnō," 1; Kawagishi, "Seireikai shugo no bushi," 151,
    153.

71 For a more in depth treatment of the origins and battles over the abbotship of
    Shitennōji, see Adolphson, *Gates of Power*, 208–216.

72 *DNS* 5:5, Kanki 1 (1229), tenth month, 317–318; *Minkeiki*, Kanki 1/10/25;
    Kawagishi, "Seireikai shugo no bushi," 152.

73 *DNS* 5:6, Kanki 3 (1231) 9/3, 767–770; *Meigetsuki*, Kanki 3 (1231) 9/3;
    Hyakurenshō, Kanki 3/10/20.

74 *DNS* 5:8, 672. The white robes were apparently not appropriate for such bat-
    tles, but it is unclear whether they became a hindrance to movement or the au-
    thor here indicates a certain category of monks.

75 See the entries in the *Meigetsuki* and the *Minkeiki*, as well as a number of let-
    ters sent by Sonshō to the court included in *DNS* 5:8, 672–680. The com-

plete collection of Sonshō's letters has been published in "Sonshō hōshinnō shōsoku shū honshō hokke kyō shihai," in *Mukō shi shi: shiryō hen*, 374–412.

76 *Meigetsuki*, Tenpuku 1 (1233) 2/20; *DNS* 5:8, Tenpuku 1/20/20, 670–680. Quote on p. 670.

77 *Meigetsuki*, Tenpuku 1/4/1; *DNS* 5:8, 671–680.

78 *DNS* 5:9, Bunryaku 1 (1234) 2/19; Takahashi, "Sonshō hōshinnō," 3–4. One of the Rokuhara *tandai* at this point was Hōjō Shigetoki, who became a well-known shogunal regent. For more on Shigetoki, see Carl Steenstrup's *Hōjō Shigetoki*.

79 *DNS* 5:9, Bunryaku 1 (1234) 5/8; Takahashi, "Sonshō hōshinnō," 4–5.

80 *DNS* 5:10, Katei 1 (1235) int. 6/26, 7/8, 23, 29, 12/12, Katei 2 (1236) 1/8; *Tendai zasuki*, 197–205.

81 For more details on the events leading up to Go-Daigo's policies until his exile, see Adolphson, *Gates of Power*, 291–295, and Goble, *Kenmu*, chapters 1–3.

82 Hioki Shōichi, *Nihon sōhei kenkyū*, 180–182, 186; McCullough, *Taiheiki*, 30–31; *Tendai zasuki*, 329–330, 331–332; Mori, *Kōjitachi no Nanbokuchō*, 12–16. Moriyoshi used the name Ōtō no miya (The Prince of the Big Pagoda), not his Buddhist name, when signing documents during this time. This "big pagoda" is believed to refer to the one in Hosshōji in the eastern part of Kyoto, where Moriyoshi resided (Mori, 17–18). Mori's study offers a detailed account of Moriyoshi's life and exploits, but is simultaneously weak in its treatment of the monastic forces, which are all bundled together as *sōhei* (see for example pp. 10, 19, 31, 34).

83 *Ōtō no miya shutsujin zu* (private collection), depicted in Mori, 33–34 and McCullough, *Taiheiki*, opposite p. 31; *Masu kagami*, 312.

84 *Tendai zasuki*, 329–335; Collcutt, *Five Mountains*, 95.

85 Goble, *Kenmu*, 121; *Tendai zasuki*, 332–333; McCullough, *Taiheiki*, 31, 58–62; Mori, *Kōjitachi no Nanbokuchō*, 28–29.

86 Goble, *Kenmu*, 121–122; *Tendai zasuki*, 333–334; McCullough, *Taiheiki*, 31, 63–64.

87 Goble, *Kenmu*, 124–125; McCullough, *Taiheiki*, 101, 105–106; *Tendai zasuki*, 335; Tsuji, *Nihon bukkyō shi: chūsei 3*, 67; Mori, *Kōjitachi no Nanbokuchō*, 35–36.

88 Goble, *Kenmu*, 127–128; *Wakayama-ken shi: Chūsei*, 286; McCullough, *Taiheiki*, 176–177, 192–200; Mori, *Kōjitachi no Nanbokuchō*, 36–37.

89 Goble, *Kenmu*, 132–135; McCullough, *Taiheiki*, 205–221, 237–240, 250–259, 320–321; Mori, *Kōjitachi no Nanbokuchō*, 38–39.

90 Perkins, *Clear View Mirror*, 219–220; McCullough, *Taiheiki*, 341–345; Mori, *Kōjitachi no Nanbokuchō*, 44–48. The details surrounding Moriyoshi's appointment as shogun are unclear, but Mori convincingly argues that the prince began using the title soon after the bakufu headquarters in Rokuhara fell on 1333/5/7, even before he had entered the capital (pp. 45–46).

91 Mori, *Kōjitachi no Nanbokuchō*, 48–49.

92 McCullough, *Taiheiki*, 379–380; Mori, *Kōjitachi no Nanbokuchō*, 57–59.

93 McCullough, *Taiheiki*, 381–384; Mori, *Kōjitachi no Nanbokuchō*, 59–64.

94 *Taiheiki*, vol. 2, 123–126; Mori, *Kōjitachi no Nanbokuchō*, 66–67.

95 Adolphson, *Gates of Power*, 299–303; *Tendai zasuki*, 341; Goble, *Kenmu*, 252–256; Nagashima, *Nara-ken no rekishi*, 90; Atsuta, "Chūsei kōki no shōen," 428.

96 *Tendai zasuki*, 342–343; Goble, *Kenmu*, 259.

97 The lack of class consciousness among warriors prior to the Kamakura age is noted in Friday, *Samurai, Warfare and the State*, 10.

Chapter Five:
Constructed Traditions

1   Several later accounts offer a number of variations on these themes. See, for example, Helen McCullough, *Yoshitsune*, 39–43, 121–127.

2   Hirata, *Sōhei to bushi*, 112–113; Katsuno, *Sōhei*, iii–vi; Hioki Eigō, *Sōhei no rekishi*, 51, 59, 89, 93, 121, 131, 137; *Nihon rekishi daijiten*, entry for *sōhei*.

3   Hirata, *Sōhei to bushi*, especially 175–178.

4   See, for example, Seita, *Chūsei jiin*, 29–31; Hirata, *Sōhei to bushi*, 112–113.

5   Adolphson, *Gates of Power*, 251–252; *Tengu sōshi, Zegaibō e, Shinshū Nihon emakimono zenshū*, vol. 27, color plate 2; *Tsuchigumo sōshi, Tengu sōshi, Ōeyama ekotoba, Zoku Nihon no emaki*, vol. 26, 20–21.

6   Adolphson, *Gates of Power*, 253–254; *Hōnen shōnin eden*, in *Zoku Nihon emaki taisei*, vol. 2, 114–115, 120–122.

7   Adolphson, *Gates of Power*, 254–255.

8   Wakabayashi, "The Dharma for Sovereigns and Warriors," 37–38, 54–59.

9   *Emakimono ni yoru Nihon jōmin seikatsu ebiki*, vol. 3, 143; Kuroda, *Sugata to shigusa*, 31.

10 *Emakimono ni yoru Nihon jōmin seikatsu ebiki*, vol. 4, 146; *Kasuga gongen kenki e*, in *Zoku Nihon emaki taisei*, vol. 14, 8–10; Kuroda Hideo, *Sugata to shigusa*, 31.

11 *Emakimono ni yoru Nihon no jōmin seikatsu ebiki*, vol. 5, 118; *Bokie*, in *Nihon emakimono zenshū*, vol. 20, 12–13; Kuroda Hideo, *Sugata to shigusa*, 31; *Emakimono sōran*, 277–280.

12 Kuroda, *Sugata to shigusa*, 33–45.

13 Gomi, *Emaki wo yomuaruku*, 61–62; *Emakimono sōran*, 50–53. See also Arai, *Chūsei akutō*, 101.

14 *Kitano Tenjin engi*, in *Zoku Nihon no emaki*, vol. 15, scroll 2, section 10.

15 *Chūyūki*, Daiji 5 (1130) 5/17; Arai, *Chūsei akutō*, 114–115, n. 54.

16 *Nanto sōzoku shikifuku ki*, in *Dai Nihon bukkyō zensho*, vol. 73, *Fukugū sosho*, 549.

17 *DNS* 5:3, Karoku 1 (1235), 3–7; Hiraoka, "Sōhei ni tsuite," 570.

18 *Ruijū seyō shō*, in *DNS* 5:20, 549. Hiraoka, "Sōhei ni tsuite," quotes this document on p. 569, but as suggested by his flawed punctuation, he did not interpret it correctly.

19 *Nihon byōbu e shūsei*, vol. 12, 92–93.

20 There are several versions of the scrolls dedicated to Ippen. The version con-
sulted here devotes the first four scrolls to Ippen, but the last six focus on
Shinkyō, his disciple and successor. The scrolls are believed to have been compiled by a monk named Sōshun around 1303. See Imai, "Emakimono no naka
no Ippen," 146.

21 *Meigetsuki*, Kenpō 1 (1213) 7/25; *Azuma kagami*, Kenpō 1/8/14.

22 *DNS* 5:8, 672.

23 *Tengu sōshi*, 45.

24 *Ishiyamadera engi*, 24–25.

25 *Ishiyamadera engi*, 16. The scene with the young page and the monk seems
to support Kuroda Hideo's contention that figures with long hair and bright
robes were in fact boys.

26 *Ishiyamadera engi*, 54.

27 *Kitano Tenjin engi*, *Nihon emakimono zenshū*, vol. 8, 34.

28 *Yugyō shōnin engi e*, *Nihon emakimono zenshū*, vol. 23, plates 12 and 13. An
English explanation of the plates can be found on pages 12 and 13.

29 Several studies have dealt with this scroll, and Japanese scholars continue to
debate regarding their interpretation and creational contexts. See, for example, Uchida, "Kasuga Gongen kenki e," 164–175.

30 *Kasuga gongen kenki e*, *Zoku Nihon no emaki*, vol. 13, 49, 74.

31 *Kasuga gongen kenki e*, 12–13.

32 Friday, *Samurai, Warfare and the State*, 86–87. See also Kondō, *Chūsei-teki
bugu*, 85.

33 *Heian ibun* 4, document 1793, *Toba tennō senmei an*, *Iwashimizu monjo*, Ten'ei
4 (1113) 4/15, 1617–1618.

34 *DNS* 4:11, Kenryaku 2 (1212) 3/14.

35 McCullough, *Heike monogatari*, 153–154.

36 Conlan, *State of War*, 176–177.

37 *Kiyomizudera engi*, *Shinnyodō engi*, 38–39.

38 *Emakimono sōran*, 102–104.

39 "Benkei on the Bridge," in Waley, *The Nō Plays of Japan*, 83.

40 McCullough, *Yoshitsune*, 122–123. Benkei brings his *naginata* when he faces
Yoshitsune a second time (p. 124).

41 Benkei's appearance seems to vary between different theater forms but the
naginata is unmistakably used.

42 *Zōhin senshū*, 29.

43 For two authoritative treatments of Japanese sword schools, see Hurst, *Armed
Martial Arts*, especially, 27–52, and Friday, *Legacies of the Sword*.

44 Friday, *Legacies of the Sword*, (pp. 30, 32–33) and Hurst, *Armed Martial Arts*, (pp. 44, 50) both note In'ei in their studies.

45 Hōzōin Sōjutsu Preservation Society, http://www4.kcn.ne.jp/~hozoin/hozonkai.htm.

46 For more on these screens, see Adolphson, *Gates of Power*, 274–279.

47 *Rennyo shōnin eden*, in *Rennyo shōnin eden no kenkyū*, 3, color plate insert.

48 Tsang, "The Development of Ikkō ikki," 7, 275.

49 *Kansai hikki*, in *Nihon zuihitsu taisei*, vol. 17, 229.

50 *Koryŏ sa*, vol. 1, Kojong, fourth year, fifth month (22:11b), 443; King Kongmin, eighth year, twelfth month (39:21a), 784.

51 Yi Changhŭi, "Imjin waeran chung ŭisŭnggun ŭi hwaltong e taehayŭ," 221–222.

52 *Dai Nihon shi*, vol. 13, 457; Kuroda, *Jisha seiryoku*, 32; Hirata, "Sōhei ron," 163.

53 For a comprehensive treatment of the persecution of Buddhism in the early years of the Meiji period, see Ketelaar, *Of Heretics and Martyrs*.

54 For an English language account of the early years of the Historiographical Institute, see Mehl, *History and the State*. For the compilation of the *Dai Nihon shiryō*, see in particular 148–154.

55 See *DNS* 3:2, Kanji 7 (1093) 8/18; *DNS* 4:15, Jōkyū 3 (1221) 5/14. The less detailed *Shiryō sōran* also contains some ten references to *sōhei* in its headings (*Shiryō sōran* 3:3, 529; 5:5 778; 6:7, 63; 7:8, 218–219; 8:8, 700, 703, 705).

56 For representative selection, see Takatsu, *Shinpen honbō shōshi*, 95–99; Matsushima, *Teikoku shiyō*, 100–101; Ueda, *Nihon rekishi gatan*, 66.

57 Nishi, "Sōhei, koto shinzei hōkisu," 256–262; Okuno, "Sōhei no ran imada owarazu," 308–328.

58 Ishinomori, *Manga Nihon no rekishi*, vol. 13, 22–29.

59 I am indebted to Timur Mukhminov, a Harvard graduate, for bringing Maeda's work and the exhibit to my attention.

60 Turnbull, *Japanese Warrior Monks*, inside cover, 33–34. Turnbull's only pre-1600 image is the 1113 battle scene from the Kasuga scrolls, which shows monastic warriors looking all but indistinguishable from the secular warriors. He notes that "only one monk, on the extreme left, is dressed in a headcowl" (p. 44), but there is in fact no such figure in the part of the scroll reproduced. To top things off, the image was published in reverse.

61 See, for example, McCullough, *Yoshitsune*, 109.

62 *Kii minpō*, September 28 and October 3, 2005.

63 *Ishikawa kenritsu rekishi hakubutsukan*. Ishikawa-ken History Museum. http://www.pref.ishikawa.jp/muse/rekihaku/rekitai/rekitai.html. Accessed May 18, 2006.

64 *Shi: The Way of the Warrior. Book One, Revised Edition*, 7.

65 Although no new episodes have been created in the last decade or so, the series is still thriving through republications and special editions. A movie also

appears to be in the making. See Crusade Fine Arts, http://www.crusade-finearts.com.

66 Shin Jin Kan International and the Sohei Society, http://www.sohei.com/home.html, and http://www.sohei.com/sohei.html. Accessed on 5/24/06.

67 See McCullough, *Tale of the Heike*, 310–312.

68 There are, to my knowledge, no pre-1600 textual accounts of mounted warriors using the *naginata*, and visual sources of the same age consistently depict the weapon in the hands of footsoldiers.

69 NHK *Taiga dorama: Yoshitsune* (2005), episode 1. An even more egregious job is done on the famous battle at the Gojō Bridge, shown in episode 5, in which Yoshitsune balances on then jumps off Benkei's *naginata*, influenced, it seems, by films such as *Crouching Tiger, Hidden Dragon*.

Chapter Six:
Sōhei, Benkei, and Monastic Warriors

1 Tsang, "The Development of Ikkō ikki," 14, 270–271.

2 Seward, *The Monks of War*, 64. The Albigensian wars and persecution were the topic of Emmanuel LeRoi Ladurie's *Montaillou: Cathars and Catholics in a French Village, 1294–1324*.

REFERENCES

Primary Sources

Sources only included in the *Dai Nihon shiryō [DNS]* series are not cited as individual entries. Chinese characters (漢字) are provided for titles of primary sources and for authors of secondary sources to assist the reader wishing to pursue the topics further.

Aki no yo no nagamonogatari 秋の世の長物語。The Metropolitan Museum of Art, New York.

Akihiro ō ki 顕広王記。Unpublished. Kunaichō shoryōbu, Tokyo.

———. In *Shiga-ken shi*, vol. 5. Compiled by Shiga-ken. Tokyo: Sanshūsha, 1928.

———. *Zoku shiryō taisei*, vol. 21. Kyoto, Rinsen shoten, 1967.

Azuma kagami 吾妻鏡。*Shintei zōho kokushi taikei*, vols. 32–33. Tokyo: Yoshikawa kōbunkan, 1936.

Bokie 慕帰絵。In *Nihon emakimono zenshū*, vol. 20, *Zenshin shōnin e, Bokie*. Tokyo: Kadokawa shoten, 1966.

Bun'ei gannen Nakatomi Sukemasa ki 文永元年中臣資匡記。Included in *Kasuga-sha kiroku*, vol. 1, 377–415. Compiled by Miyagawa Tadamaro. Nara: Kasuga taisha, 1955.

Chōshūki 長秋記。*Zōho shiryō taisei*, vols. 16–17. Kyoto: Rinsen shoten, 1965.

Chōya gunsai 朝野群載。*Shintei zōho kokushi Taikei*, vol. 1. Tokyo: Yoshikawa kōbunkan, 1965. [Tokyo: Kondō kappansho, 1901.]

Chūsei hōsei shiryō shū 中世法制史料集。16th edition. 3 vols. Edited by Satō Shin'ichi and Ikeuchi Yoshisuke. Tokyo: Iwanami shoten, 2002.

Chūyūki 中右記。*Zōho shiryō taisei*, vols. 9–14. Kyoto: Rinsen shoten, 1965.

Crusade Fine Arts. William Tucci. http://www.crusadefinearts.com. Accessed on May 17, 2006.

Dai Nihon shi 大日本史。17 vols. Tokyo: Dai Nihon yūbenkai, 1929.

Dai Nihon shiryō 大日本史料。*[DNS]*. 6 series. Edited by Shiryō hensanjo. Tokyo: Tōkyō daigaku, 1903.

Daidenbōin hongan hijiri goden 大伝法院本願聖御伝。In *Zoku shiseki shūran*, vol. 1, 411–468. Tokyo: Kondō shuppanbu, 1917–1930.

Daigo zōjiki 醍醐雑事記。Tokyo: Daigoji, 1973.

Daisenji engi 大山寺縁起。Unpublished facsimile at the Historiographical Institute, University of Tokyo.

Denryaku 殿暦。*Dai Nihon kokiroku*, 4:1–4. Tokyo: Iwanami shoten, 1956.

DNS. See *Dai Nihon shiryō*.

Eikyū gannen ki 永久元年記。In *Gunsho ruijū*, vol. 18, *Zatsubu*, 455–471. Tokyo: Keizai zasshisha, 1893–1894.

Engyōbon Heike monogatari 延慶本平家物語。*Daitōkyū kinen bunkō zō*. Printed facsimile. Tokyo: Koten kenkyūkai, 1964.

Entairyaku 園太暦。7 vols. *Shiryō sanshū: Kokiroku hen*. Tokyo: Zoku gunsho ruijū kanseikai, 1970–1986.

Fusō ryakki 扶桑略記。*Shintei zōho kokushi taikei*, vol. 12. Tokyo: Yoshikawa kōbunkan, 1965.

Geki nikki 外記日記。*Zoku shiseki shūran*, vol. 1. Tokyo: Kondo shuppansha, 1930.

Genpei seisuiki 源平盛衰記。Tokyo: Kokubun bunkō kankōkai, 1927.

Go-Nijō Moromichi ki 後二条師通記。*Dai Nihon kokiroku*, 5:1–3. Tokyo: Iwanami shoten, 1956.

Gogumaiki 後愚昧記。*Dai Nihon kokiroku* 17:1–4. Tokyo: Iwanami shoten, 1980–1982.

Gumaiki 愚昧記。Unpublished facsimile at the Historiographical Institute, University of Tokyo.

Gyokuyō 玉葉。3 vols. Tokyo: Tokyo kappan kabushiki gaisha, 1906. Reprint, Tokyo: Meicho kankōkai, 1993.

Hanazono tennō shinki 花園天皇宸記。(*Hanazono in shinki* 花園院宸記). 3 vols. *Shiryō sanshū*. Tokyo: Zoku gunsho ruijū kanseikai, 1986.

———. *Zōho shiryō taisei*, vols. 2–3. Kyoto: Rinsen shoten, 1965.

Heian ibun 平安遺文。13 vols. Edited by Takeuchi Rizō. Tokyo: Tōkyōdō shuppan, 1963–1974.

Heihanki (Hyōhanki) 兵範記。*Zōho shiryō taisei*, vols. 18–22. Kyoto: Rinsen shoten, 1965.

Heike monogatari 平家物語。3 vols. Edited by Mizuhara Hajime. Tokyo: Shinchōsha, 1979.

Heike monogatari: Engyōbon. See *Engyōbon Heike monogatari*.

Hōgen monogatari 保元物語。*Nihon koten bungaku taikei*, vol. 31. Tokyo: Iwanami shoten, 1961.

Honchō monzui 本朝文粋。*Shintei zōho kokushi taikei*, 29:2. Tokyo: Yoshikawa kōbunkan, 1965.

Honchō seiki 本朝世紀。*Shintei zōho kokushi taikei,* vol. 9. Tokyo: Yoshikawa kōbunkan, 1935.

Honchō zoku monzui 本朝續文粋。*Shintei zōho kokushi taikei,* 29:2. Tokyo: Yoshikawa kōbunkan, 1965.

Hōnen shōnin eden 法然上人絵伝。*Zoku Nihon no emaki,* vols. 1–3. Tokyo: Chūō kōronsha, 1991.

———. *Zoku Nihon emaki taisei,* vol. 2. Tokyo: Chūō kōronsha, 1981.

Hōryūji bettō ki 法隆寺別当記。In *Zoku gunsho ruijū,* 4:2, 789–835. Tokyo: Zoku gunsho ruijū kanseikai, 1958.

Hōzōin Sōjutsu Preservation Society. "Nara hōzōinryū sōjutsu hōzankai." http://www4.kcn.ne.jp/~hozoin/hozonkai.htm. Accessed May 15, 2006.

Hyakurenshō 百練抄。*Shintei zōho kokushi taikei,* vol. 11. Tokyo: Yoshikawa kōbunkan, 1965.

Hyōgo ken shi: shiryō hen, chūsei 5 兵庫県史、史料編、中世 5。Edited by Hyōgo ken shi henshū senmon iinkai. Hyōgo ken: Hyōgo ken shi henshū senmon iinkai, 1992.

Ichidai yōki 一代要記。*Kaitei sekishū shūran,* vol. 1. Tokyo: Kondō kappansho, 1900.

Iga no kuni Kuroda no shō shiryō 伊賀国黒田荘史料。Edited by Takeuchi Rizō. Tokyo: Yoshikawa kōbunkan, 1974.

Iken jūnikajō 意見十二箇条。In *Gunsho ruijū,* vol. 17, *Zatsubu,* 115–128. Tokyo: keizai zasshisha, 1893–1894.

———. *Honchō monzui. Shintei zōho kokushi taikei,* 29:2, 41–53. Tokyo: Yoshikawa kōbunkan, 1965.

Ishikawa kenritsu rekishi hakubutsukan [Ishikawa-ken History Museum]. http://www.pref.ishikawa.jp/muse/rekihaku/rekitai/rekitai.html. Accessed April 18, 2005.

Ishiyamadera engi 石山寺縁起。*Nihon no emaki,* vol. 16. Compiled by Komatsu Shigemi. Tokyo: Chūō kōronsha, 1988.

Jie daisōjō den 慈恵大僧正伝。In *Gunsho ruijū,* vol. 4. Tokyo: Keizai zasshisha, 1898.

Jōkyū heiranki 承久兵乱記。In *Kaitei shiseki shūran,* vol. 12, 593–681. Tokyo: Kondō kappanjo, 1902.

Jōkyū ikusa monogatari 承久軍物語。In *Kokushi sōsho: Jōkyūki.* Tokyo: Kokushi kenkyūkai, 1921.

Jōkyūki 承久記。In *Kokushi sōsho: Jōkyūki.* Tokyo: Kokushi kenkyūkai, 1921.

Kamakura ibun 鎌倉遺文。42 vols. Compiled by Takeuchi Rizō. Tokyo: Tōkyōdō shuppan, 1971–1992.

Kanchūki 勘仲記。*Shiryō taisei,* vols. 26–27. Tokyo: Naigai shoseki kabushiki gaisha, 1931–1944.

———. *Zōho shiryō taisei,* vols. 34–36. Kyoto: Rinsen shoten, 1965.

Kansai hikki 閑際筆記。In *Nihon zuihitsu taisei,* vol. 17. Tokyo: Yoshikawa kōbunkan, 1975.

Kasuga gongen kenki e 春日権現験記絵。*Zoku Nihon no emaki,* vol. 13. Tokyo: Chūō kōronsha, 1993.

———. *Zoku Nihon emaki taisei,* vols. 14–15. Tokyo: Chūō kōronsha, 1982.

Kasuga Wakamiya saireizu 春日若宮祭礼図。*Shintō taikei: Jinja hen,* vol. 13, *Kasuga,* 389–436. Tokyo: Shintō taikei hensankai, 1978–1992.

Keiran jūyōshū engi 溪嵐拾葉集縁起。*Shinshū Taishō daizōkyō,* vol. 76, 503–507. Tokyo: Taishō issaikyō kankōkai, 1931.

Kenji sannen ki 建治三年記。In *Gunsho ruijū,* vol. 18, 390–399. Tokyo: Naigai shoseki, 1930.

Kenro seiyo 蹇驢嘶余。In *Gunsho ruijū,* vol. 17, 793–804. Tokyo: Keizai zasshisha, 1902.

Kikki 吉記。*Zōho shiryō taisei,* vols. 29–30. Kyoto: Rinsen shoten, 1965.

Kitano Tenjin engi 北野天神縁起。*Nihon emaki taisei,* vol. 21. Tokyo: Chūō kōronsha, 1978.

———. *Nihon emakimono zenshū,* vol. 8. Tokyo: Kadokawa shoten, 1959.

———. *Zoku Nihon no emaki,* vol. 15. Tokyo: Chūō kōronsha, 1991.

Kiyomizudera engi, Shinnyodō engi 清水寺縁起、真如堂縁起。In *Zoku zoku Nihon emaki taisei: denki, engi hen,* vol. 5. Edited by Komatsu Shigemi. Tokyo: Chūō kōronsha, 1994.

Kōfukuji bettō sangō keizu 興福寺別当三綱系図。Unpublished facsimile at the Historiographical Institute, University of Tokyo.

Kōfukuji bettō shidai 興福寺別当次第。In *Dai Nihon bukkyō zensho: Kōfukuji sōsho,* part 2, 1–59. Tokyo: Bussho kankōkai, 1917.

Kōfukuji kishiki 興福寺軌式。Facsimile of unpublished document, the Historiographical Institute, University of Tokyo.

Kōfukuji ryaku nendaiki 興福寺略年代記。In *Zoku gunsho ruijū,* 29:2, 107–205. Tokyo: Yoshikawa kōbunkan, 1965.

Kōfukuji sangō bunin 興福寺三綱補任。In *Zoku gunsho ruijū,* 4:2, 701–788. Tokyo: Zoku gunsho ruijū kanseikai, 1958.

Kokawadera engi shū 粉河寺縁起集。In *Kokawa chō shi,* vol. 3, 155–230. Tokyo: Kokawa chō shi hensan, 1988.

Kokon chōmonjū 古今著聞集。*Nihon koten bungaku taikei,* vol. 84. Tokyo: Iwanami shoten, 1966.

Kokushi bunin 国司補任。5 vols. Edited by Miyazaki Yasumitsu. Tokyo: Zoku gunsho ruijū kanseikai, 1990.

Konjaku monogatari shū 今昔物語集。*Shin Nihon koten bungaku taikei,* 37:1–5. Tokyo: Iwanami shoten, 1996.

Koryŏ sa [History of the Koryŏ Dynasty]. 3 vols. Soŭl tŭkpyŏl-si: Asea muhwasa, 1972.

Kōya shunjū. See *Shinkō Kōya shunjū hennen shūroku.*

Kōyasan monjo 高野山文書。8 vols. *Dai Nihon komonjo: Iewake 1.* Tokyo: Tokyo daigaku shiryō hensanjo, 1903–1907.

Kugyō bunin 公卿補任。*Nihon shi sōran,* vol. 2, *Kodai, chūsei* 1. Tokyo: Tōkyō inshōkan, 1984.

Masu kagami 増鏡。*Nihon koten zensho,* vol. 54. Edited by Oka Kazuo. Tokyo: Asahi shinbunsha, 1969.

Meigetsuki 明月記。3 vols. Tokyo: Kokusho kankōkai, 1911–1912.

Minkeiki 民経記。7 vols. Tokyo: Iwanami shoten, 1975–1995.

Moromori ki 師守記。11 vols. *Shiryō sanshū.* Tokyo: Zoku gunsho ruijū kanseikai, 1968.

Nakasuke ō ki 仲資王記。Unpublished. Kunaichō shoryōbu, Tokyo.

———. In *Zoku shiryō taisei.* Kyoto: Rinsen shoten, 1965.

Nanto daishu jūrakuki 南都大衆入洛記。*Zoku gunsho ruijū,* 29:2, 325–329. Tokyo: Zoku gunsho ruijū kanseikai, 1959.

Nanto sōzoku shikifuku ki 南都僧俗式服記。In *Dai Nihon bukkyō zensho,* vol. 73, *Fukugū sosho,* 547–571. Tokyo: Bussho kankōkai, 1927.

Negoro yōsho 根来要書。In *Kakuban kiso shiryō shūsei.* Tokyo: Kōrakudō, 1994.

Nihon byōbu e shūsei 日本屏風絵集成。Vol. 12, *Fuzokuga, kōbu fuzoku.* Tokyo: Kōdansha, 1980.

Nihon kiryaku 日本記略。3 vols. *Shintei zōho kokushi taikei.* Tokyo: Yoshikawa kōbunkan, 1980.

Nihon sandai jitsuroku 日本三代実録。*Shintei zōho kokushi taikei,* vol. 4. Tokyo: Yoshikawa kōbunkan, 1981.

Nihon shoki 日本書紀。Tokyo: Yoshikawa kōbunkan, 1984.

NHK *Taiga dorama: Yoshitsune.* Nippon hōsō kyōkai, 2005.

Ōei shosha Engyōbon Heike monogatari 応永書写延慶本平家物語。Edited by Yoshizawa Yoshinori. Tokyo: Hakuteisha, 1961.

Onsekizan daisōzu (Myōsen) den 音石山大僧都（明詮）伝。*Shintei zōho kokushi taikei,* vol. 31, 75–77. Tokyo: Yoshikawa kōbunkan, 1930.

Rennyo shōnin eden 蓮如上人絵伝。*Rennyo shōnin eden no kenkyū.* Kyoto: Shinshū Ōtani-ha shūmusho shuppanbu, 1994.

Ruijū kokushi 類聚国史。*Shintei zōho kokushi taikei,* vols. 5–6. Tokyo: Kokushi taikei kankōkai, 1933.

Ruijū seyō shō 類聚世要抄。Unpublished document.

Ryō no gige 令義解。*Shintei zōho kokushi taikei,* vol. 22. Tokyo: Yoshikawa kōbunkan, 1939.

Sakeiki 左経記。*Zōho shiryō taisei,* vol. 6. Kyoto: Rinsen shoten, 1965.

Samurai dokoro sata hen 侍所沙汰篇。In *Gunsho ruijū,* vol. 8, 407–417. Tokyo: Naigai shoseki kabushiki gaisha, 1940.

Sanchōki 三長記。*Shiryō taisei* 25. *Heikoki, Sanchōki.* Tokyo: Naigai shoseki, 1936.

San'e jōichiki 三会定一記。*Dai Nihon bukkyō zensho: Kōfukuji sōsho,* part 1, 289–432. Tokyo: Ushio shobō, 1931.

Sanemi kyō ki 実躬卿記。Unpublished. Tokyo daigaku shiryō hensanjo, Tokyo.

———. *Dai Nihon kokiroku,* vols. 20–21. Tokyo: Iwanami shoten, 1991–1994.

Sange yōki senryaku 山家要記浅略。In *Zoku gunsho ruijū,* 27:2. Tokyo: Zoku gun-
  sho ruijū kanseikai, 1926.
Sankaiki 山塊記。*Shiryō taisei,* vols. 19–21. Tokyo: Naigai shoseki kabushiki gai-
  sha, 1936.
Sankō Genpei seisuiki 参考源平盛衰記。3 vols. Kyoto: Rinsen shoten, 1982.
Shi: The Way of the Warrior. William Tucci. Book One, Revised Edition. Crusade
  Comics, 1995.
Shinkō Kōya shunjū hennen shūroku 新校高野春秋編年集録。Compiled by Hi-
  nonishi Shinjō. Tokyo: Daimonsha, 1982.
Shiryō sōran 史料綜覧。22 vols. Tokyo: Insatsukyoku chōyōkai, 1923.
Shoku Nihongi 続日本紀。*Shintei zōho kokushi Taikei.* Tokyo: Yoshikawa kōbunkan,
  1982.
Shōyūki 小右記。*Shiryō taisei,* vols. 1–3. Tokyo: Naigai shoseki, 1936.
Shunki 春記。*Zōho shiryō taisei.* Kyoto: Rinsen shoten, 1965.
Sochiki 帥記。In *Zōho shiryō taisei,* vol. 5. Kyoto: Rinsen shoten, 1965.
Sōgō bunin 僧綱補任。In *Dai Nihon bukkyō zensho: Kōfukuji sōsho,* vol. 1, 61–288.
  Tokyo: Bussho kankōkai, 1915.
"Sonshō hōshinnō shōsoku shū Honshō hokke kyō shihai" 尊性法親王消息集
  (飜摺法華経紙背)。In *Mukō shi shi: shiryō hen,* 374–412. Kyoto: Mukō shi
  shi hensan kakariinkai, 1985.
Sonpi bunmyaku 尊卑文脈。5 vols. Tokyo: Yoshikawa kōbunkan, 1962.
Suisaki 水左記。*Zōho shiryō taisei,* vol. 8. Kyoto: Rinsen shoten, 1965.
Taiheiki 太平記。*Shinpen Nihon koten bungaku zenshū,* vols. 54–57. Tokyo:
  Shōgakkan, 1994.
Taiki 台記。*Zōho shiryō taisei,* vols. 23–25. Kyoto: Rinsen shoten, 1965.
Taishō shinshū daizōkyō 大正新修大蔵経。Tokyo: Taishō issaikyō kankōkai, 1926.
Tamefusa kyō ki 為房卿記。In *Shishū* 10 (1979): 67–130.
Tendai zasuki 天台座主記。Compiled by Shibuya Gaiji. Tokyo: Daiichi shobō,
  1973.
Tengu sōshi, Zegaibō e 天狗草紙。是外貌会。*Shinshū Nihon emakimono zenshū,* vol.
  27. Tokyo: Kadokawa shoten, 1978.
Tōdaiji Hachiman tegai e ki 東大寺八幡手蓋会記。*Zoku gunsho ruijū,* 3:1, 255–
  324. Tokyo: Zoku gunsho ruijū kanseikai, 1938.
Tōdaiji monjo 東大寺文書。*Dai Nihon komonjo: Iewake 18.* 15 vols. Tokyo: Tōkyō
  daigaku, shiryō hensanjo, 1944–1992.
Tōdaiji tōtō Yakushi'in monjo 東大寺塔頭薬師寺院文書。Unpublished facsimile at
  the Shiryōhensanjo, University of Tokyo.
Tōdaiji zoku yōroku 東大寺続要録。In *Zokuzoku gunsho ruijū,* vol. 11, *Shūkyōbu,*
  1–194. Tokyo: Kokusho kankōkai, 1907.
Tōnomine engi 多武峰縁起。In *Dai Nihon bukkyō zensho: Jishi sōsho,* vol. 2, 4–5.
  Tokyo: Bussho kankōkai, 1980.
Tōnomine ryakki 多武峰略記。In *Dai Nihon bukkyō zensho: Jishi sōsho,* vol. 2.
  Tokyo: Bussho kankōkai, 1913.

———. *Gunsho ruijū*, vol. 15, *Shake bu*, 438–468. Tokyo: Keizai zasshisha, 1901.

Tsuchigumo sōshi, Tengu sōshi, Ōeyama ekotoba 土蜘蛛草紙、天狗草紙、大江山絵詞。*Zoku Nihon no emaki*, vol. 26. Tokyo: Chūō kōronsha, 1993.

Wakamiya saireiki 若宮祭礼記。In *Shintō taikei: Jinja hen*, vol. 13, *Kasuga*, 437–454. Tokyo: Shintō taikei hensankai, 1985.

Wei shu 魏書。Beijing: Zhonghua shuju, 1974.

Yugyō shōnin engi e 遊行上人縁起絵。*Nihon emakimono zenshū*, vol. 23. Tokyo: Kadokawa shoten, 1968.

Zōhin senshū 蔵品選集。Edited by Kanagawa kenritsu rekishi hakubutsukan. Yokohama: Kanagawa ken bunkazai Kyōkai, 1995.

Zokushi gushō 続史愚抄。*Shintei zōho kokushi taikei*, vol. 13. Tokyo: Yoshikawa kōbunkan, 1929.

Secondary Sources

Abe Takeshi 阿部猛。*Heian zenki seiji shi no kenkyū*. Tokyo: Takashina shoten, 1990.

Adolphson, Mikael. *The Gates of Power: Monks, Courtiers, and Warriors in Premodern Japan*. Honolulu: University of Hawai'i Press, 2000.

———. "Institutional Diversity and Religious Integration: The Establishment of Temple Networks in the Heian Age." In *Heian Japan, Centers and Peripheries*, edited by Adolphson, Kamens, and Matsumoto, forthcoming.

———, with Edward Kamens and Stacie Matsumoto, eds. *Heian Japan, Centers and Peripheries*. Honolulu: University of Hawai'i Press, forthcoming.

Arai Takashige 新井孝重。*Chūsei akutō no kenkyū*. Tokyo: Yoshikawa kōbunkan, 1990.

Aston, W. G. *Nihongi: Chronicles of Japan from the Earliest Times to A.D. 697*. Rutland, Vermont and Tokyo: Charles E. Tuttle, 1972.

Atsuta Kō 熱田公。"Chūsei kōki no shōen to sonraku." In *Wakayama-ken shi: chūsei*, 425–487.

———. "Negoro sōhei no genryū." *Wakayama-ken shi kenkyū* 7 (1980): 14–27.

Butler, Kenneth Dean, Jr. "The Birth of an Epic: A Textual Study of the *Heike monogatari*." Ph.D. diss., Harvard University, 1964.

———. "The *Heike monogatari* and the Japanese Warrior Ethic." *Harvard Journal of Asiatic Studies* 29 (1969): 93–108.

———. "The *Heike monogatari* and Theories of Oral Epic Literature." *Bulletin of the Faculty of Letters* [Seikei University], vol. 2 (1966): 37–54.

Collcutt, Martin. *Five Mountains: The Rinzai Zen Monastic Institution in Medieval Japan*. Cambridge, MA: Harvard University Press, 1981.

Conlan, Thomas D. *State of War: The Violent Order of Fourteenth Century Japan*. Ann Arbor, MI: University of Michigan, Center for Japanese Studies, 2003.

Demiéville, Paul. "Le Bouddhisme et la Guerre." *Mélanges Publiés par L'Institut des Hautes Études Chinoises* (1957): 347–385.

Emakimono ni yoru Nihon jōmin seikatsu ebiki 絵巻物による日本常民生活絵引。5 vols. Tokyo: Kanagawa daigaku Nihon jōmin bunka kenkyūjo, 1964–1968.

Emakimono sōran 絵巻物総覧。Compiled by Umezu Jirō. Tokyo: Kadokawa shoten, 1995.

Endō Shūsaku 遠藤周作。*Kuramadera*. Kyoto: Tankōsha, 1978.

Farris, William Wayne. *Heavenly Warriors: The Evolution of Japan's Military, 500–1300*. Cambridge: Harvard University Press, 1992.

Friday, Karl. *Legacies of the Sword: The Kashima-Shinryū and Samurai Martial Culture*. Honolulu: University of Hawai'i Press, 1998.

———. "Lordship Interdicted: Taira no Tadatsune and the Limited Horizons of Warrior Ambition," in Adolphson, Kamens and Matsumoto, eds., *Heian Japan, Centers and Peripheries*, forthcoming, University of Hawai'i Press.

———. *Samurai, Warfare and the State in Early Medieval Japan*. New York and London: Routledge, 2004.

Fukuda Toyohiko 福田豊彦。"Ōchō gunji kikō to nairan." *Iwanami kōza Nihon rekishi* 4: *Kodai*, 81–120. Tokyo: Iwanami shoten, 1976.

Goble Andrew. *Kenmu: Go-Daigo's Revolution*. Cambridge, MA: Harvard University Press, 1996.

Gomi Fumihiko 五味文彦。*Bushi no jidai, Nihon no rekishi*, vol. 4. Tokyo: Iwanami shoten, 2000.

———. *Emaki wo yomuaruku Kasuga kenki e to chūsei*. Kyoto: Tankōsha, 1998.

Groner, Paul. *Ryōgen and Mt. Hiei*. Honolulu: University of Hawai'i Press, 2002.

Hall, John Whitney. "The Muromachi Bakufu." In *The Cambridge History of Japan: Volume 3, Medieval Japan*, edited by Yamamura Kozo, 175–230. Cambridge: Cambridge University Press, 1990.

Hashikawa Tadashi 橋川正。*Kuramadera shi*. Kyoto: Kuramayama kaihi jimukyoku shuppanbu, 1926.

Hioki Eigō 日置英剛。*Sōhei no rekishi: Hō to yoroi wo matotta arahosshitachi*. Tokyo: Ebisu kōshō shuppan, 2003.

Hioki Shōichi 日置昌一。*Nihon sōhei kenkyū*. Tokyo: Heibonsha, 1934. Reprinted Tokyo: Kokusho kankōkai, 1942.

Hirabayashi Moritoku 平林盛得。*Ryōgen*. Tokyo, Yoshikawa kōbunkan, 1976.

Hiraoka Jōkai 平岡定海。*Nihon jiin shi no kenkyū*. Tokyo: Yoshikawa kōbunkan, 1981.

———, ed. *Ronshū Nihon bukkyō shi*, vol. 3, *Heian jidai*; vol. 4, *Kamakura jidai*. Tokyo: Yūzankaku shuppan, 1986–1988.

———. "Sōhei ni tsuite." In *Nihon shakai keizai shi kenkyū zokuhen*, edited by Hogetsu Keigo sensei kanreki kinenkai, 547–581. Tokyo: Yoshikawa kōbunkan, 1967.

Hirata Toshiharu 平田俊春。"Nanto hokurei no akusō." In *Ronshū Nihon bukkyō shi*, vol. 3, *Heian jidai*, edited by Hiraoka Jōkai, 261–295. Tokyo: Yūzankaku shuppansha, 1986.

———. "Sōhei ron." In Hirata Toshiharu, *Heian jidai no kenkyū,* 145–178. Tokyo: Yamaichi shobō, 1943.

———. *Sōhei to bushi.* Tokyo: Nihon kyōbunsha, 1965.

Hisano Nobuyoshi 久野修義。"Kakunin kō: Heian makki no Tōdaiji akusō." *Nihon shi kenkyū* 219 (November 1980): 1–34.

Hori Daiji 堀大慈。"Sōhei no seikatsu." In *Shinshū Ōtsu-shi shi,* vol. 1, *Kodai,* 465–492. Compiled by Ōtsu shiyakusho. Ōtsu: Nihon shashin insatsu kabushiki gaisha, 1978.

Hosokawa Kameichi 細川亀市。"Sōhei to jiryō shōen." *Shūkyō kenkyū* 8.5 (1931): 127–140.

Hurst III, G. Cameron. *Armed Martial Arts of Japan: Swordsmanship and Archery.* New Haven: Yale University Press, 1998.

———. *Insei: Abdicated Sovereigns in the Politics of Late Heian Japan, 1086–1185.* New York: Columbia University Press, 1976.

Imai Masaharu 今井雅晴。"Emakimono no naka no Ippen: Ippen hijiri e ni miru Ippen no yugyō." In *Nihon no meisō: Yugyō no sutehijiri Ippen.* Tokyo: Yoshikawa kōbunkan, 2004.

Imatani Akira 今谷明。*Muromachi no ōken: Ashikaga Yoshimitsu no ōken sandatsu keikaku.* Tokyo: Chūō kōronsha, 1990.

———. *Sengoku ki no Muromachi bakufu.* Tokyo: Kadokawa shoten, 1975.

Imatani Akira and Kōzo Yamamura. "Not for a Lack of Will or Wile: Yoshimitsu's Failure to Supplant the Imperial Lineage." In *Journal of Japanese Studies* 18.1 (1992): 45–78.

Ishinomori Shōtarō 石ノ森章太郎。*Manga Nihon no rekishi,* vol. 13, *Insei to bushi to sōhei.* Tokyo: Chūō kōronsha, 1997–1999.

Izumiya Yasuo 泉谷康夫。*Kōfukuji.* Tokyo: Yoshikawa kōbunkan, 1997.

Kageyama Haruki 影山春樹。*Hieizan.* Tokyo: Kadokawa shoten, 1975.

———. "Sōhei gōso no rekishi." In Kageyama Haruki, *Hieizan,* 104–115. Tokyo: Kadokawa shoten, 1975.

Katsuno Ryūshin 勝野隆信。*Sōhei.* Tokyo: Shibundō, 1966.

Kawagishi Kōkyō 川岸宏教。"Seireikai shugo no bushi: Sonshō hōshinnō bettō jidai no Shitennōji ni tsuite." In *Bukkyō shisō ronshū,* 149–162. Tokyo: Heirakuji shoten, 1976.

Keirstead, Thomas. "Inventing Medieval Japan: The History and Politics of National Identity." *The Medieval History Journal* 1.1 (1998): 25–46.

Ketelaar, James. *Of Heretics and Martyrs in Meiji Japan: Buddhism and Its Persecution.* Princeton: Princeton University Press, 1990.

Kinugawa Satoshi 衣川仁。"Chūsei zenki no kenmon jiin to buryoku." *Nenpō chūsei shi kenkyū* 25 (2000): 1–28.

———. "Gōso kō." *Shirin* 85.5 (September 2002): 603–636.

———. "Sōhei kenkyū shi to sono kadai." *Atarashii rekishigaku no tame ni* 227 (1997): 1–9.

Koizumi Yoshiaki 小泉宜右。*Akutō.* Tokyo: Kyōikusha, 1981.

Koji ruien: Heijibu 1 古事類苑、兵事部一。Tokyo: Koji ruien kankōkai, 1934. Reprinted, Tokyo: Naigai shoseki, 1935.

Kondō Yoshikazu 近藤好和。*Chūsei-teki bugu no seiritsu to bushi.* Tokyo: Yoshikawa kōbunkan, 2000.

Kuroda Hideo 黒田日出男。*Sugata to shigusa no chūsei shi: Ezu to emaki no fūkei kara.* Tokyo: Heibonsha, 1986.

Kuroda Toshio 黒田俊雄。"Chūsei jisha seiryoku ron." In *Iwanami kōza, Nihon rekishi,* edited by Asao Naohiro et al., vol. 6, *chūsei* 2, 245–295. Tokyo: Iwanami shoten, 1975.

———. *Jisha seiryoku: mō hitotsu chūsei no shakai.* Tokyo: Iwanami shoten, 1980.

———. *Nihon chūsei no kokka to shūkyō.* Tokyo: Iwanami shoten, 1976.

Ladurie, Emmanuel LeRoi. *Montaillou: Cathars and Catholics in a French Village, 1294–1324.* London: Scolar, 1978.

Marx, Karl. *Critique of Hegel's "Philosophy of Right."* Translated by Joseph O'Malley and Annette Jolin. Cambridge: Cambridge University Press, 1970.

Mass, Jeffrey P. "The Kamakura Bakufu." In *The Cambridge History of Japan: Volume 3, Medieval Japan,* edited by Yamamura Kozo, 46–88. Cambridge: Cambridge University Press, 1990.

———, ed. *The Origins of Medieval Japan: Courtiers, Clerics, Warriors, and Peasants in the Fourteenth Century.* Stanford: Stanford University Press, 1997.

Matsushima Gō 松島剛。*Teikoku shiyō.* Tokyo: Shun'yōdō, 1899.

McCullough, Helen Craig, trans. *The Taiheiki: A Chronicle of Medieval Japan.* 3rd ed. Rutland, VT and Tokyo: Tuttle, 1985.

———. *The Tale of the Heike.* Stanford: Stanford University Press, 1988.

———, trans. *Yoshitsune: A Fifteenth Century Chronicle.* Stanford: Stanford University Press, 1966.

McMullin, Neil. *Buddhism and the State in Sixteenth-Century Japan.* Princeton University Press: Princeton, 1984.

———. "The Enryaku-ji and the Gion-Shrine Temple Complex in the Mid-Heian Period." *Japanese Journal of Religious Studies* 14.2–3 (1987): 161–184.

———. "Historical and Historiographical Issues in the Study of Pre-Modern Japanese Religions." *Japanese Journal of Religious Studies* 16.1 (1989): 3–40.

———. "The Sanmon-Jimon Schism in the Tendai School of Buddhism: A Preliminary Analysis." *Journal of International Associations of Buddhist Studies* 7.1 (1984): 83–105.

Mehl, Margaret. *History and the State in Nineteenth-Century Japan.* New York: St. Martin's Press, 1998.

Mikawa Kei 美川圭。"Jisha mondai kara miru insei no seiritsu." In *Kodai, chūsei no seiji to bunka,* edited by Uwayokote Masataka. Kyoto: Shibunkaku shuppan, 1994.

———. *Shirakawa hōō: chūsei wo hiraita teiō.* Tokyo: Nihon hōsō shuppan kyōkai, 2003.

Miyasaka Yūshō 宮坂宥勝。*Kōyasan shi.* Tokyo: Kōyasan bunka kenkyūkai, 1962.

Mori Shigeaki 森茂暁。*Kōjitachi no Nanbokuchō: Godaigo tennō no mibun.* Tokyo: Chūō kōronsha, 1988.

Motoki Yasuo 本木泰雄。*Insei ki seiji shi kenkyū.* Kyoto: Shibunkaku shuppan, 1996.

Murayama, Shūichi 村山修一。*Hieizan shi: Tatakai to inori no seichi.* Tokyo: Tōkyō bijutsu, 1994.

———, and Kageyama Haruki. *Hieizan: sono shūkyō to rekishi.* Tokyo: Nihon hōsō shuppankai, 1970.

Nagashima Fukutarō 永島福太郎。"Nanto no sōhei to Heike no yakiuchi." Nagashima Fukutarō, *Nihon rekishi sōsho,* vol. 3, *Nara,* 130–141. Tokyo: Yoshikawa kōbunkan, 1963.

———. *Nara-ken no rekishi.* Tokyo: Yamakawa shuppansha, 1980.

Nakazawa Katsuaki 中沢克昭。*Chūsei no buryoku to jōgaku.* Tokyo: Yoshikawa kōbunkan, 1999.

Nihon rekishi daijiten 日本歴史大事典。Tokyo: Kawade shobō shinsha, 1973.

Nishi Nobito 西野人。"Sōhei, koto shinzei hōkisu." *Chūō kōron* 100.5 (1985): 256–262.

Nukii Masayuki. 貫井正之。"Imjin waeran kwa sŭngŭibyŏngjang Samyŏng taesa" [The Hideyoshi Invasion and the Righteous Monk Soldier, Samyŏng]. In *Samyŏngdang Yujŏng.* Compiled by Samyŏngdang kinyŏm saŏphae. Seoul: Chisik sanŏpsa, 2000.

Okuno Tetsuji 奥野哲士。"Sōhei no ran imada owarazu." *Chūō kōron* 101.10 (1986): 308–328.

Ōshima Yukio 大島幸雄。"Sōhei no hassei ki ni kan suru isshiki ron." In *Nihon kodai shigaku ronshū,* 19–54. Tokyo: Komazawa Daigaku gakuin shigakkkai kodai shi bukai, 1979.

Ōya Tokujō 大屋徳城。"Sōhei ron." In Ōya Tokujō, *Nihon bukkyō shi no kenkyū,* vol. 2, 509–583. Kyoto: Hōzōkan, 1929.

Perkins, George W. *Masukagami. The Clear Mirror: A Chronicle of the Japanese Court During the Kamakura Period (1185–1333).* Stanford: Stanford University Press, 1986.

Pound, Ezra. *The Classic Anthology Defined by Confucius.* Cambridge, MA: Harvard University Press, 1954.

Rénondeau, G. "Histoire des Moines Guerriers du Japon." *Mélanges Publiés par L'Institut des Hautes Études Chinoises* (1957): 159–345.

Sakaino Tetsu 境野哲 (Sakaino Kōyō 境野黄洋)。"Sōhei no bakko." In Sakaino Tetsu, *Nihon bukkyō shiyō,* 82–90. Tokyo: Kōmeisha, 1901.

Sansom, George. *A History of Japan to 1334.* Stanford: Stanford University Press, 1958.

Seita Yoshihide 清田義英。*Chūsei jiin hoshi no kenkyū.* Tokyo: Keibundō, 1995.

Seward, Desmond. *The Monks of War: The Military Religious Orders.* London: Penguin Books, 1995.

Shahar, Meir. "Epigraphy, Buddhist Hagiography, and Fighting Monks: The Case of the Shaolin Monastery." *Asia Major,* third series, 13.2 (2000): 15–36.

Shigeno Yasutsugu 重野安繹。*Kohon kokushigan.* Tokyo: Tokyo teikoku daigaku, 1890.

Shimosaka Mamoru 下坂守。"Sanmon shisetsu seido no seiritsu to tenkai." *Shirin* 58.1 (1975): 67–114.

Shin, Jennifer. "An Analysis of *Sōhei,* Japan's Militant Buddhist Monks." Masters thesis, University of California, Berkeley, 2004.

Shin Jin Kan International and the Sohei Society. http://www.sohei.com/home .html, and http://www.sohei.com/sohei.html. Accessed on May 24, 2006.

Sonoda Kōyū 園田香融。"Heian bukkyō." In *Shūkyō shi,* edited by Kawasaki Tsuneyuki, 47–86. Tokyo: Taikei Nihon shi sōsho, 1964.

Steenstrup, Carl. *Hōjō Shigetoki, 1198–1261, and his role in the history of political and ethical ideas in Japan.* London: Curzon Press, 1979.

Takahashi Shin'ichirō 高橋慎一朗。"Sonshō hōshinnō to jisha funsō." *Haruka naru chūsei* 19 (May 2001): 1–8.

Takasu Baikei 高須梅渓 (Takasu Yoshijirō 高須芦次郎)。*Kokumin no Nihon shi,* vol. 3, *Heian jidai.* Tokyo: Waseda daigaku shuppanbu, 1922.

Takatsu Kuwasaburō 高津鍬三郎。*Shinpen honbō shōshi.* Tokyo: Konkōdō, 1897.

Takeoka Katsuya 竹岡勝也。"Heian chō no jiin to sōhei." In *Rekishi chiri Nihon heisei shi,* 73–96. Tokyo: Nihon rekishi chiri gakkai hen, 1926.

———. *Ōchō bunka no sanshō.* Tokyo: Kadokawa shoten, 1971.

Takeuchi Rizō 竹内理三。"Hōō to sōhei." In *Nihon no rekishi 6: Bushi no tōjō,* 294–315. Tokyo: Chūō kōronsha, 1980.

Tamamuro Taijō 圭室諦成。"Heian chōmatsu jiin no shakai no shakaiteki kōsatsu." *Shigaku zasshi* 43.1 (1931): 45–82.

Thompson, E. P. *Customs in Common: Studies in Traditional Popular Culture.* New York: The New Press, 1993.

Tomikura Tokujirō 富倉徳次郎。Heike monogatari *zenchūshaku.* 4 vols. Tokyo: Kadokawa shoten, 1966–1968.

Tonomura, Hitomi. *Community and Commerce in Late Medieval Japan: The Corporate Villages of Tokuchin-ho.* Stanford: Stanford University Press, 1992.

Tsang, Carol Richmond. "The Development of Ikkō ikki, 1500–1570." Ph.D. diss., Harvard University, 1995.

Tsuji Zennosuke 辻善之助。*Nihon bukkyō shi: Chūsei.* 3 vols. Tokyo: Iwanami shobō, 1947.

———. *Nihon bukkyō shi: Jōsei hen.* Tokyo: Iwanami shoten, 1944.

———. "Sōhei no gen'ryū." In *Nihon bukkyō shi: Jōsei hen,* 765–824. Tokyo: Iwanami shoten, 1944.

———. "Sōhei no kigen." In *Nihon bukkyō shi no kenkyū: Zokuhen,* 16–38. Tokyo: Konkōdō shoseki, 1931.

Tsunoda Bun'ei 角田文英。"Jōjin sōzu no yakuwari: Sōhei dan soshikisha toshite no." In Tsunoda Bun'ei, *Ōchō no eizō: Heian jidai shi no kenkyū,* 471–487. Tokyo: Tōkyōdō shuppan, 1970.

———. "Shōmu tennō haka to Kōfukuji sō Shinjitsu." In Tsunoda Bun'ei, *Ōchō no meian: Heian jidai shi no kenkyū,* vol. 2, 337–355. Tokyo: Tōkyōdō shuppan, 1977.

Turnbull, Stephen. *Japanese Warrior Monks, AD 949–1603.* Oxford: Osprey Press, 2003.

Uchida Reiko 内田玲子。"*Kasuga Gongen kenki e* kan 19 kentō." *Setsuwa bungaku kenkyū* 38 (2003.6): 164–175.

Ueda Kazutoshi 上田万年。*Nihon rekishi gatan.* Tokyo: Bun'ōkaku, 1910.

Uwayokote Masataka 上横手雅敬。"Insei ki no Genji." In *Gokenin sei no kenkyū,* 153–192. Tokyo: Yoshikawa kōbunkan, Gokenin sei kenkyū kai, 1981.

van Horn, Wayne. "Sacred Warriors: A Comparative Analysis of the Medieval Religious Military Orders of Europe and Japan." Unpublished paper given at the Central States Anthropological Society Annual Meetings, April 2001. http://www.mindspring.com/~semartialarts/sw.html. Accessed December 5, 2004.

Varley, H. Paul. *Warriors of Japan as Portrayed in the War Tales.* Honolulu: University of Hawai'i Press, 1994.

Wakabayashi, Haruko. "The Dharma for Sovereigns and Warriors: Onjō-ji's Claim for Legitimacy in *Tengu sōshi," Japanese Journal of Religious Studies* 20.1–2 (2002): 33–66.

Wakayama-ken no rekishi 和歌山県の歴史。Tokyo: Yamakawa shuppansha, 1970.

Wakayama-ken shi: Chūsei 和歌山県史:中世。Compiled by Wakayama ken shi hensan iinkai. Osaka: Dai Nihon insatsu kabushiki gaisha, 1994.

Waley, Arthur. *The Nō Plays of Japan.* New York: Grove Press, 1957.

Watanabe Eshin 渡辺恵進。"Jie daishi kishō jūnikajō' ni tsuite." In *Ganzan jie daishi no kenkyū,* edited by Watanabe Eshin, 1–16. Ōtsu: Dōbōsha shuppan, 1984.

Watanabe Morimichi 渡辺盛道。*Sōhei seisuiki.* Tokyo: Sanseidō, 1984.

Weinstein, Stanley. "Aristocratic Buddhism." In *The Cambridge History of Japan: Volume 2, Heian Japan,* edited by Donald Shively and William McCullough, 449–516. Cambridge: Cambridge University Press, 1999.

Wellman James. Introduction to conference on "Religion, Conflict and Violence: Exploring Patterns Past and Present East & West," May 13–14, 2004, University of Washington. http://depts.washington.edu/eacenter/spring_0304.shtml. Accessed on September 2, 2004.

Wilson, William R. *Hōgen Monogatari: The Tale of the Disorder in Hōgen.* Tokyo: Sophia University, 1971.

Yamamura, Kozo, ed. *The Cambridge History of Japan: Volume 3, Medieval Japan.* Cambridge: Cambridge University Press, 1990.

Yang Ŭnyong. "Chŏngyu chaeran ŭi sŏkchugwan chŏnt'u wa hwaŏmsa ŭisŭnggun" [The Sŏkchugwan Battle during the Second Hideyoshi Invasion of 1597 and the Righteous Monk Army in the Hwaŏm Temple]. *Kasan hakbo* 4 (1995): 172–189.

———. "Imjin waeran kwa honam ŭi bulgyo ŭisŭnggun" [The Hideyoshi Invasion and the Monk Army in the Southwest Regions]. *Han'guk chonggyo* 19 (1994): 1–34.

———, ed. *Imjin waeran kwa pulgyo ŭisŭnggun* [The Hideyoshi Invasion and the Righteous Monk Army]. Seoul: Kyŏngsŏwŏn, 1992.

Yi Chaech'ang. "Koryŏ sidae sŭnggun dŭl uiri hoguk hwaltong" [The Activities of Monk Armies in the Defense of the Fatherland during the Koryŏ Dynasty]. In *Imjin waeran kwa pulgyo ŭisŭnggun,* edited by Yang Ŭnyong, 125–138. Seoul: Kyŏngsŏwŏn, 1992.

Yi Changhŭi. "Imjin waeran chung ŭisŭnggun ŭi hwaltong e taehayŏ: Sŏsan taesa wa Samyŏngdang ŭl chungsim ŭro" [A Righteous Monk Army during the Hideyoshi Invasion: Examination of Sŏsan taesa and Samyŏngdang]. Compiled by Samyŏngdang kinyŏm saŏphae. Seoul: Chisik sanŏpsa, 2000.

Yi Sŭnghan. "Koryŏ Sukchong dae hangmagun chojik ŭi chŏngch'i' gŏk baegyŏng" [Political background of the organization of *hangmagun* during the Sukchong's reign in Koryŏ]. *Yŏksa hakbo* 137 (1993): 1–32.

INDEX

ABOUT THE AUTHOR

Mikael Adolphson received his doctorate in Japanese history from Stanford University. He is the author of *The Gates of Power: Monks, Courtiers, and Warriors in Premodern Japan* (2000) and coeditor (with Edward Kamens and Stacie Matsumoto) of *Heian Japan, Centers and Peripheries* (2007). He is currently associate professor of Japanese history in the Department of East Asian Languages and Civilizations, Harvard University.